The 100 Greatest Swimmers in History

ROWMAN & LITTLEFIELD SWIMMING SERIES

Series Editor: John Lohn

The Rowman & Littlefield Swimming Series looks at competitive swimming from a number of perspectives, providing readers with the historical context of the events, athletes, and developments that have shaped the sport.

They Ruled the Pool: The 100 Greatest Swimmers in History, by John Lohn, 2013.
Duels in the Pool: Swimming's Greatest Rivalries, by Matthew De George, 2013.
Pooling Talent: Swimming's Greatest Teams, by Matthew De George, 2014.
The Most Memorable Moments in Olympic Swimming, by John Lohn, 2014.
The 100 Greatest Swimmers in History, updated edition, by John Lohn, 2018.

The 100 Greatest Swimmers in History

Updated Edition

John Lohn

ROWMAN & LITTLEFIELD
Lanham • Boulder • New York • London

Published by Rowman & Littlefield
An imprint of The Rowman & Littlefield Publishing Group, Inc.
4501 Forbes Boulevard, Suite 200, Lanham, Maryland 20706
www.rowman.com

Unit A, Whitacre Mews, 26-34 Stannary Street, London SE11 4AB

British Library Cataloguing in Publication Information Available

Library of Congress Cataloging-in-Publication Data

Names: Lohn, John, 1976- author.
Title: The 100 greatest swimmers in history / John Lohn.
Other titles: They ruled the pool | One hundred greatest swimmers in history
Description: Updated edition. | Lanham, Maryland : Rowman & Littlefield,
   [2018] | Includes bibliographical references and index.
Identifiers: LCCN 2018003984 (print) | LCCN 2018010947 (ebook) | ISBN
   9781538113837 (electronic) | ISBN 9781538113820 (cloth : alk. paper)
Subjects: LCSH: Swimmers—United States—Biography.
Classification: LCC GV837.9 (ebook) | LCC GV837.9 .L64 2018 (print) | DDC
   797.2/10922 [B] —dc23
LC record available at https://lccn.loc.gov/2018003984

♾™ The paper used in this publication meets the minimum requirements of American National Standard for Information Sciences—Permanence of Paper for Printed Library Materials, ANSI/NISO Z39.48-1992.

Printed in the United States of America

Contents

Acknowledgments

This book is dedicated to my family, whose support through the years has provided strength and made this endeavor possible. To my wife, Dana: You have been a constant source of encouragement since the day we met, and every day we're together is a blessing. Our twin daughters, Taylor and Tiernan, and youngest daughter, Tenley, light up the world with their smiles and have added so much joy to my life. To my parents: Not a day goes by when your guidance through the years goes unnoticed or unappreciated. Finally, a sincere thank-you goes to Peter H. Bick, a friend I met through the swimming world and a talented photographer, who generously contributed the images contained in this book.

Introduction

THE PURPOSE

Put a bunch of fans in a room, and it is inevitable that an argument will break out—sooner rather than later—over who was the best in a particular sport. Baseball debates will include Babe Ruth and Willie Mays. Football battles will feature Jim Brown and Joe Montana. Basketball arguments will pit Wilt Chamberlain against Michael Jordan. And those are just the well-known names, and just a few sports.

A profile of swimming does not rival that of the aforementioned sports. However, that does not mean there is no room for healthy debate between fans. Like any sport, there are enough knowledgeable and passionate fans willing to look across the sport's landscape—both present and past—and determine a pecking order for the athletes who have made the pool their athletic milieu.

So goes the purpose of this book. *The 100 Greatest Swimmers in History* (previously *They Ruled the Pool*) seemed like an appropriate title for an endeavor that aims to rank the top-100 swimmers in history. Selecting the title, though, was the easiest part of the process. The difficult task was comparing and ranking hundreds of athletes across various eras, events, and countries. It required the dissection of accomplishments and record performances, discussions with those who possess expertise in the sport, and a good deal of revision, especially with the production of this second edition.

This book was the end result, and while it does not represent an undisputed ranking of the top-100 swimmers the world has seen, the list was thoroughly compiled and reflects what has been achieved in more than 100 years of competitive action. And, if nothing else, this book can serve as a launching point for one of those debates that might not be settled but that is part of the fabric of sports.

THE PROCESS

So what was the process for selecting the 100 greatest swimmers in history? It was based on a considerable amount of research and relied on numerous conversations—past and present—with those who regularly cover the sport, as well as coaches who have a feel for the history of swimming.

The first step of the process was to create a pool (pardon the pun) of swimmers from which to choose. By analyzing accomplishments at the international level, I identified approximately 200 individuals as candidates for inclusion. From that point forward, I whittled the list down.

The first athletes selected were those with the greatest individual Olympic success, a group including the likes of Michael Phelps, Mark Spitz, Katie Ledecky, Dawn Fraser, and Krisztina Egerszegi. While Phelps and Spitz delivered the finest Olympic performances in history during their respective eras, Fraser and Egerszegi were the first two swimmers to win an Olympic title in the same event at three consecutive Olympiads, and Ledecky has been nothing short of dazzling since emerging as a world-class performer in 2012.

I continued to select athletes based on several factors, from Olympic medals to world-record performances to medals won at the World Championships. In some cases, where athletes competed in the same era, I assessed head-to-head competition. Versatility, too, played a role, with swimmers covering a variety of strokes receiving additional consideration.

Ultimately, I pared the list down to the 100 names included in the book, but a final step was required. They needed to be ranked from 1 to 100. Accomplishing this task required a repeat of the initial process—weighing Olympic performances, world records, and World Championship results. However, in this ranking stage, I placed a greater emphasis on comparing athletes from similar eras. Once that order was established, I completed a cross-era analysis.

There will be disagreements on the final order, which is a normal reaction when it comes to a book of this nature. What cannot be argued is the exhaustive nature of the selection process, a multipart ordeal that measured a number of factors.

A NEW EDITION

Like any other sport, swimming is constantly evolving, with new names emerging on the worldwide scene and established athletes adding additional achievements to their portfolios. So, in the five years that elapsed since the first edition of this endeavor, plenty transpired to necessitate changes in the rankings.

A handful of athletes bolstered their resumes, leading to leaps up the ranking hierarchy. Meanwhile, six athletes ultimately accomplished enough over the past four years to warrant inclusion in the top 100. But with their emergence and entry came a dilemma: Who gets bumped? For each new addition, a deletion was required, and this was no simple task. After all, it's not easy to remove someone with credentials that identify him/her as an Olympic medalist and all-time great.

In the end, Katie Ledecky, Sun Yang, Katinka Hosszu, Anthony Ervin, Adam Peaty, and Sarah Sjostrom made their way into the top 100. In turn, Ulrike Richter, Tom Jager, Nobutaka Taguchi, Ulrike Tauber, Ute Geweniger, and Satoko Tanaka moved into the under-consideration category. Of those knocked out of the top 100, Richter, Tauber, and Geweniger were the easiest decisions, due to their involvement with East Germany's systematic doping program of the 1970s and 1980s. There is no question their performances were artificially aided, thus lessening their impact when measured against athletes with clean histories.

The biggest change to the rankings from the initial edition to this version of the book is the inclusion of Ledecky as the top female swimmer in history, and ranked third in the overall list. When *They Ruled the Pool* was first published, Ledecky was not far removed from capturing the gold medal in the 800-meter freestyle as a 15-year-old at the 2012 Olympic Games in London. Still, there was no way to predict the success that followed—dominance of the freestyle events from 200 through 1500 meters, a large collection of world titles, and a performance at the 2016 Olympic Games in Rio de Janeiro that brought a trio of individual gold medals in a history-making week.

Still, where did Ledecky belong? There was no doubt she deserved a spot in the top-10, but did she belong ahead of the first edition's top female, American Tracy Caulkins? Did she deserve to rate ahead of Hungarian Krisztina Egerszegi? Ultimately, the answer was yes to both questions, the primary reasons being her consistency and the fact that she has created a chasm between herself and her rivals.

THE TOP TWO . . . THEN?

If there was one aspect of this project that qualified as easy, it was the identification of the individuals for the number 1 and number 2 positions on the list. As difficult as it was to determine who was slotted 13th and who was slotted 14th, figuring out the top of the chart took little effort. Michael Phelps and Mark Spitz were slam-dunk choices.

It's fitting, really, for Phelps and Spitz to headline the top-100 list, for as long as the sport is analyzed on a historical basis, the two American men will be linked. It was Spitz who set the standard for excellence in swimming, destroying the record books in the late 1960s and early 1970s and punctuating his career with the greatest Olympic performance of all time—to that point.

At the 1972 Olympics in Munich, Spitz was perfect. He entered seven events and won them all. In itself, that accomplishment was staggering. Spitz, though, took on legendary status when each of his victories—four individual and three relay—was delivered in world-record time. Spitz became an instant icon, and his greatness went unmatched for more than three decades.

Then Phelps came along.

As the teenager from Baltimore set more and more world records and excelled across numerous disciplines, the inevitable comparisons surfaced. Was Phelps the second coming of Spitz? Ultimately, the answer was no—he was more. However, it was a process for Phelps to surpass a man who was once deemed untouchable.

At the 2004 Olympics, Phelps made his first attempt to replicate—and surpass—the Spitzian seven. While he won eight medals, only six were gold, and an epic performance was viewed by some media outlets as a failure. Four years later, at the 2008 Olympics in Beijing, Phelps captured his white whale and officially was anointed the greatest swimmer in history.

In Beijing, through a combination of dominating triumphs and nail-biting wins, Phelps won eight gold medals, five of them individual. He, not Spitz, became the measuring stick for greatness. In addition, he took swimming to mainstream levels rather than the every-fourth-year phenomenon it previously was. This was Phelps's longtime goal.

Up until 2008, an argument could have been made for Spitz as the number 1 swimmer to ever dive into a pool. Phelps put an end to that debate. What cannot be debated, however, is the standing of Phelps and Spitz at the top of this top-100 list. There was no juggling when it came to number 1 or number 2. This was the easy part of the project. The rest? That's another story.

COMPARING ERAS

There was the excellence of Johnny Weissmuller in the 1920s. There was the dominance of Don Schollander in the 1960s. There was the superiority of Roland Matthes in the 1970s. And there was the brilliance of Matt Biondi in the 1980s. How can these men—all legends of the sport—be successfully compared with one another?

This chore was not supposed to be an easy one, but one of the more difficult duties was measuring athletes from different eras against one another. Without a common denominator for comparison, weighing the accomplishments of athletes separated by 50 years or more was far from a perfect science.

While Olympic medals and world-record performances bolstered an athlete's case for inclusion more than anything else, there was the need to look at these areas with an open mind. For one, the Olympic program of earlier years was not nearly as thorough as today's program. Consider this: At the 2016 Olympic Games in Rio de Janeiro, there were 16 events on the schedule for both men and women. More than 50 years earlier, at the 1964 Games, there were 10 events for men and eight for women. Forty years prior to that, the 1924 Olympics featured only six events for men and five for women.

Obviously, then, the opportunity to pile up the Olympic medals has become easier over time. Of course, "easier" is a relative term, for capturing an Olympic medal is anything but a shrug-of-the-shoulders achievement. However, one must wonder how many medals Weissmuller could have won during his heyday if the schedule had been expanded.

Despite the limitations placed on early-era athletes due to the schedule, there were advantages. Compared with what athletes of today face, swimmers from years past did not have nearly as much competition as exists in the current era. For a good portion of the 20th century, the United States and Australia were the primary contenders for gold medals. Although those nations remain superpowers, recent competitions have seen athletes from Zimbabwe, Tunisia, Suriname, and Singapore earn medals in Olympic competition. Simply put, swimming has become a more global sport.

There was once a time when the best American swimmer in a particular event would have been an instant contender for Olympic gold. Those days are gone. Although the top American remains a medal contender in nearly all events, other countries have enhanced their talent pools and are challenging the biggest nations more than ever.

Additionally, swimmers today must more carefully select their schedules. Sure, more events are available. However, with semifinal rounds existing in all events of 200 meters or less, additional racing can wear down the body. This scenario was not an obstacle for past swimmers, such as Mark Spitz en route to his seven gold medals at the 1972 Olympics. Then, swimmers only had to negotiate the preliminary round before advancing to the championship final. Less fatigue on the body kept the athletes fresher and, therefore, able to handle hefty schedules without significant drop-offs in performances.

The creation of the World Championships by FINA, the international governing body for swimming, also affects how different eras are compared. Before the World Championships debuted in 1973, the Olympics served as the primary measuring stick in the sport. And while the Olympics is still the premier event, the World Championships have etched a firm place in the sport's history. It's a delicate process to measure the success of athletes who raced at the World Championships without penalizing those who did not get the opportunity for that additional global competition.

Finally, world-record performances varied in the way they were assessed. In the earlier days of the sport, world records were lowered by greater percentages than what we see in the present, which is usually a hundredth of a second sliced here and there. The best way to look at world records from the early days of swimming is to assess their longevity. Those that endured for several years clearly held greater significance than those with a shorter shelf life.

In no way was measuring different eras easy, and there is a gray area when making comparisons. However, looking at the eras with a number of factors in mind made the process possible and more manageable.

EFFECT OF POLITICS

Politics and sports have been linked for years and will continue to influence one another in the centuries ahead. The relationship, however, has been ugly at times and came into play when constructing the list, which is the focal point of this book. How to handle politics and its impact on the history of swimming is a delicate issue.

Because of World War I and World War II, three versions of the Olympic Games were canceled. The 1916 Games were wiped out by World War I, while the Games of 1940 and 1944 were lost to World War II. As a result, the Olympic aspirations of some athletes were dashed. For those who were fortunate enough to realize their Olympic opportunity, their accomplishments could have been greater.

Beyond the world wars, politics significantly affected the athletic landscape during the first half of the 1980s. In 1980, President Jimmy Carter announced that the United States was boycotting the Olympic Games in Moscow as a protest of the Soviet Union's invasion of Afghanistan. Athletes across many sports, including swimming, saw their hard work and training go unrewarded. Rather than have the chance to measure themselves on the biggest stage and against the best of the best, they could do nothing more than watch the Games unfold on television.

At the peak of their careers, the likes of Rowdy Gaines, Tracy Caulkins, and Mary T. Meagher were bitten by the political bug. While they got the chance to compete at the 1984 Olympics, they were haunted by a missed opportunity. In addition, their exploits at the 1984 Games were also affected. That year, in what was retaliation for the American boycott of 1980, the Soviet Union led a boycott of its own, one that included East Germany and other Eastern Bloc countries.

Both Games featured events that lacked some of the finest swimmers in the world, and questions have remained ever since as to what would have unfolded had the boycotts not taken place. As this book was compiled, assumptions were not made concerning the likely finishing positions of athletes affected by the boycott. However, as the selection process unfolded, the missed opportunities that were experienced by some candidates were taken into account while measuring their actual achievements.

THE DOPING DILEMMA

Before the compilation of the top-100 list started, a difficult—and controversial—decision needed to be made. The question was simple: Should those associated with the systematic doping program instituted by East Germany in the 1970s and 1980s be eligible for consideration? The answer to that query, however, was much more difficult.

When East German sports officials and coaches were running their country's doping program, it was a dark period for the sport. Athletes from other nations who were clean and relying solely on pure talent were at a distinct disadvantage not only racing a rival but also competing against chemical enhancement. A few individuals spoke out, including Shirley Babashoff of the United States, and accused the East Germans of improprieties. Yet without any confirmation of guilt, Babashoff was labeled a sore loser for her statements.

Still, it was hard to chalk up East Germany's success to nothing more than hard work and discipline. The rise of East German swimmers in the 1970s was so meteoric that doubts immediately surfaced. Not only were the country's athletes dominating at the Olympic Games and World Championships, routinely registering gold–silver–bronze finishes, but the world-record book was shredded. Not since the early days of the sport were there such drastic drops in time.

Eventually, the cover over the doping program was removed, and what the world had long suspected was confirmed. With the fall of the Berlin Wall in 1989 and the unification of East Germany and West Germany, documents were released that confirmed the systematic doping program. State Plan 14.25, as it was known, oversaw the administration of steroids to East German athletes, the majority of whom were teenage girls. In many cases, the performance-enhancing drugs were given at the end of workouts in order to facilitate the recovery process.

"In addition to a sophisticated talent identification system and the best professional coaching and training methods in the world at the time, the East German athletes also received the best in medical and, unbeknownst to most swimmers, chemical support," reads a statement at the International Swimming Hall of Fame. "This included regularly administered doses of Oral-Turinabol (OT), an East German–manufactured anabolic steroid. It was the mainstay of State Plan 14.25, the secret policy directing the pharmacological development of sport nationwide. Doctors passed the little pink and blue pills on to coaches, who doled them out in daily rations of the vitamins to their trusting athletes."

The global reaction to the confirmation of the doping program was not surprising. A "told-you-so" sentiment prevailed. However, there were mixed reactions from the athletes who took part in the program, primarily without their knowledge. Some wanted their records stricken from the history books, aware they had received an unfair advantage. Some took the stance that they did not know what was happening and that their hard work should not be penalized for something out of their control. Others went the route of denial, steadfastly claiming that they were clean. Still more wondered what could have been.

"The worst thing is they took away from me the opportunity to ever know if I could have won the gold medals without the steroids," East Germany's Rica Reinisch once stated. "That's the greatest betrayal of all."

Despite the proof of the doping program's existence, the International Olympic Committee (IOC) and FINA have never erased the East German performances from the record book. Nor have any medals been taken away and awarded to the next athlete in line, such as Babashoff, whose career was defined by silver-medal finishes behind East German athletes.

The International Swimming Hall of Fame, which inducted many East German swimmers, made the decision to place a doping disclaimer on those connected to the systematic doping program. However, it did not remove any of the athletes from the Hall of Fame, pointing to the decisions made by the IOC and FINA.

"While we know today that many of the East German athletes who have been honored by the International Swimming Hall of Fame have been identified in documents as having received steroids and hormones, none ever tested positive in tests administered by the International Olympic Committee (IOC) and their accomplishments continue to be recognized by both the IOC and the Federation International de Natation Amateur (FINA)," states the International Swimming Hall of Fame. "As the recognized Hall of Fame of FINA, ISHOF continues to honor the achievements of the athletes of the former German Democratic Republic as both products and victims of a corrupt sports system and as a warning to young athletes about the consequences of using performance enhancing drugs."

Not everyone agrees with the International Swimming Hall of Fame's decision to continue to recognize athletes proven to have used performance-enhancing drugs, even if there is a disclaimer alongside their Hall of Fame entry. And not everyone is going to agree with the decision by this author to include East German athletes in the top-100 list. Yet that is the call that has been made.

As unfair as the East German advantages may have been, the fact remains that the accomplishments of Petra Schneider, Kornelia Ender, and Kristin Otto, among others, took place. History shows these women to have won Olympic and World Championship medals and set world records, and the objective of this book is to honor the top-100 swimmers in history based on their achievements in the pool.

Had the IOC stripped any of the athletes of their titles, the situation would be much different, for the accomplishments would not be officially recognized. That development has not taken place, nor does it appear that it will at any point in the near future. Therefore, the approach here is similar to that of the International Swimming Hall of Fame. The athletes will be recognized for what they achieved but with a description of what aided these accomplishments.

FEEL FREE TO ARGUE

A beautiful aspect of sports is the way they are open to interpretation, and swimming is no different. Finding a consensus on the top-100 performers in the sport's history is unlikely to take place. While this current list lends itself to debate, it must also be viewed as a work in progress. By next year, a few active athletes who are already ranked will have added accolades to their résumés, and, therefore, warrant movement up the ladder. In addition, a few athletes who did not make the first or second rankings will have done enough to deserve inclusion, and this will also require the removal of a current position holder.

What this book does is provide an informed review and analysis of those who have raced in the pool as well as a starting point for a healthy back-and-forth debate.

A Quick Look at the Top 100

- The gender breakdown was close, with 56 male swimmers making the cut as opposed to 44 females. Considering the additional opportunities afforded men through the years, such as extra events and an earlier start in Olympic competition, the slightly higher male count makes sense.
- Only three of the athletes selected do not own an Olympic medal of any color. South Africa's Karen Muir and Jonty Skinner never got the chance to race for an Olympic title because of the International Olympic Committee's ban on South Africa for its apartheid practices. Meanwhile, Australia's Tracey Wickham made the personal choice to bypass the 1980 Olympics, where she would have been among the favorites for gold in the distance-freestyle events.
- Considering that the United States has won 365 more medals than any other country in swimming, it is not surprising that it has the most representation on the top-100 list. The United States leads the way with 48 selections, easily ahead of Australia, which ranks second with 15 selections.
- At the time of publication, eight athletes on the top-100 list remained active, thus providing themselves the chance to bolster their portfolios for further movement up the list in future editions.
- A few coaches stood out for having the most athletes rank in the top 100, led by the legendary James "Doc" Counsilman. The man oversaw the Indiana University dynasty of the 1960s and early 1970s and was the mentor to Mark Spitz, Charles Hickcox, Jim Montgomery, and Gary Hall Sr.
- For a country with a thirtieth of the population of the United States, Hungary deserves to be highlighted. The Eastern European nation has six athletes on the list, including a pair in the top 13, Krisztina Egerszegi and Tamas Darnyi. Egerszegi is one of only three athletes to win an individual event at three con-

secutive Olympiads, performing the feat in the 200 backstroke in 1988, 1992, and 1996.

- Australia has a rich tradition of producing elite performers in the men's distance-freestyle events (400/1500), a fact that is supported by the inclusion of five distance athletes in the top 100. Grant Hackett and Murray Rose check in at 21st and 22nd, with Kieren Perkins (34th), John Konrads (66th), and Andrew Charlton (82nd) also securing recognition.

- Of the 100 athletes selected, three are East German women who were part of the systematic doping program in use by their country during the 1970s and 1980s. Kornelia Ender tops the East Germans at number 16 and is followed by Kristin Otto (number 23) and Petra Schneider (number 56). Ulrike Richter, Ulrike Tauber, and Ute Geweniger made the top 100 in the first edition of the book, but have since been bumped to under-consideration status.

- American Dara Torres boasts the most Olympic appearances in the sport with five, but it is the nature of those appearances that is even more impressive. One of the great sprinters in history, Torres qualified for the Olympics in 1984, 1988, and 1992, then entered retirement. She returned to the sport and qualified for the 2000 Games, then retired again before qualifying for the 2008 Olympics, where she earned the silver medal in the 50 freestyle. So, Torres's five Olympic bids were made over the course of seven Olympiads.

- Dara Torres, though, is not the only five-time Olympian in the top 100. American Michael Phelps and Zimbabwe's Kirsty Coventry were competitors at the 2000, 2004, 2008, 2012, and 2016 Games.

- The story of Anthony Ervin is one that is difficult to comprehend. The co-champion in the 50 freestyle at the 2000 Olympic Games in Sydney, Ervin was viewed as a sprint sensation in the making. However, he drifted away from the sport for nearly a decade, only to make a triumphant return to the 2012 and 2016 Olympiads, the latter producing his second gold medal in the 50 freestyle, 16 years after the first.

1

Michael Phelps

Country: United States
Birth date: June 30, 1985
Events: Multiple
Olympic medals: Twenty-eight
World Championship medals: Thirty-three

There is a basic tenet in sports journalism that suggests "never say never." This tenet, however, does not apply to Michael Phelps, the American who changed what is considered possible in the sport and raised the bar to heights never before seen. At the risk of committing sportswriting blasphemy, there is a good chance that we will never see an athlete like Phelps come along again. Wait, let's go a step further: There's no chance we're going to see another Michael Phelps.

How to write this chapter is tricky. It could go a number of ways. Is it best to run down the achievements of Phelps in chronological fashion? Or is it better to attempt to order his accomplishments by merit? Ultimately, it will be a combination of those approaches, although it does make sense to venture back to the beginning.

Phelps was never an athlete who bloomed late or suddenly surged. He's always been a star, setting national age-group records even before his teenage years, performances that suggested a future like nothing previously produced. As an 11-year-old, Phelps started working with coach Bob Bowman. It was the beginning of a relationship—sometimes heated—that took Phelps from prodigy to all-timer, and it did not take Bowman long to realize that he was working with a special talent. By the time Phelps was 12 years old in 1997, Bowman had a conversation with Phelps's family, preparing them for what was to come.

"I told them that things are going to change, and they'll never be the same," Bowman said. "I wanted everyone to be ready for 2000. Debbie [Phelps's mom] said, 'Oh, no, not Michael, he's too young.' But I told her, 'What are we going to do to stop it? When he's ready to go, he's got to let it go.'"

Indeed, Phelps let it go—and at awe-inspiring levels. Nineteen years after the conversation Bowman had with Phelps's mom, a chat that projected greatness, Phelps left the sport as the undisputed number 1 performer the pool has seen. The record shows Phelps finished with 28 Olympic medals, 10 more than any other athlete in Olympic lore. Twenty-three of those medals were gold, 14 more than anyone else in history. He set 29 individual world records, global marks spread over five events, an illustration of his versatility. He won 33 medals at the World Championships, 26 of them gold. Both of those figures are records.

The true launching point to this excellence was the summer of 2000. While all eyes were focused on other story lines at the 2000 U.S. Olympic Trials in Indianapolis, Phelps soon drew a spotlight that never went away, and only brightened in intensity. Charging down the final lap of the 200 butterfly, the 15-year-old Phelps finished second to Tom Malchow to qualify for the Sydney Olympic Games and became the youngest male swimmer to qualify for the Olympics in 68 years. A month later, he placed fifth in the final of the 200 butterfly at the Olympics, less than a half-second off the podium.

The arc of Phelps's career took off after Sydney. In 2001, he became the youngest man to set a world record, setting a global standard in the 200 butterfly at just 15 years, nine months. That year also brought the first world title of his career, a gold medal in his specialty event. While Phelps became an all-around swimmer, the 200 butterfly will always be his trademark, the discipline that lit a wildfire of success.

By the next year, Phelps was an international star in the individual medley events, too, and by the 2003 World Championships, he was the sport's poster boy. Sure,

Australian Ian Thorpe was still dominating the freestyle events, but no one could match Phelps's range, which produced gold medals—and world records—at the World Championships in the 200 butterfly, 200 individual medley, and 400 individual medley. There was also a silver medal in the 100 butterfly, and the hype for the 2004 Olympics was beginning to rev up. It had been more than 30 years since Mark Spitz won seven gold medals at the 1972 Olympics in Munich, but Phelps seemed capable of matching the feat at the Athens Games.

"I think Michael is capable of winning seven, just like I was capable of winning seven," Spitz said prior to Athens. "But a lot of things had to happen just right for me. And the U.S. relays were unquestionably stronger in 1972, relative to the competition. I hope he does it. It would be great for the sport and great for Michael. And it's already been great press for me that he's trying."

Ultimately, not everything unfolded perfectly for Phelps at the 2004 Olympics. While he won both butterfly events and both individual medley disciplines and was a gold medalist in two relays, that made only six victories. As Spitz suggested, the United States was not invincible in the 400 freestyle relay, where Phelps and his teammates settled for the bronze medal. Another third-place finish was recorded in the 200 freestyle, a newer event for Phelps and where he ran into two of the greats in the sport: Thorpe and Pieter van den Hoogenband of the Netherlands. Still, Phelps became the first person to win eight medals in an Olympiad, and his career was only in its infancy.

As the four-year buildup to the 2008 Olympics in Beijing unfolded, Phelps continued to star. He won six medals, five of which were gold, at the 2005 World Championships and followed two years later with seven gold medals at the World Championships in Melbourne, a showing that Bowman still considers the finest of his protégé's career. It would have been eight gold medals, too, if not for a disqualification by the United States in the preliminaries of the last event, the 400 medley relay. Nonetheless, Phelps was again geared up for a run at Spitz, and this time he got the job done.

At the Beijing Games in 2008, Phelps fascinated the sporting world with an eight-day performance that might be the finest individual effort athletics has ever seen. Turning back all challenges, he won eight gold medals and set seven records to surpass the feats of Spitz. Making the show even more entertaining was his mix of dominating victories and comeback triumphs, notably his win over Serbian Milorad Cavic in the 100 butterfly. Trailing the entire race and his perfect run seemingly set to end, Phelps found a way to get to the wall a hundredth of a second ahead of his rival, thus preserving history. Already a high-profile figure, Phelps was now a legend.

The triumph over Cavic is considered the defining moment of Phelps's career, instinct taking over in the most pressure-filled of circumstances. With just 10 meters to race, Phelps found himself a half-body length behind Cavic, and while the American was surging, there didn't appear to be enough room remaining to complete a comeback win.

But as Phelps approached the wall, and as Cavic glided into the finish, Phelps instinctively took an extra half stroke, a decision that enabled him to hit the touchpad ahead of his challenger by the smallest of margins. It was the seventh victory of the Olympiad for Phelps, set the stage for his record-setting eighth, and added an extra element of flair to a week that didn't need it.

"Everything was accomplished," Phelps said after his Beijing program wrapped up. "I will have the medals forever. Nothing is impossible. With so many people saying it couldn't be done, all it takes is an imagination, and that's something I learned and something that helped me."

Always one to seek out motivation, Phelps took offense to several comments during his Beijing bonanza. He did not appreciate Thorpe's assertion that no one could win eight gold medals at a single Olympiad. Further, he was fueled by Cavic's suggestion that Phelps was beatable in the 100 butterfly and that it would be good for the sport if Phelps was derailed.

As much as Phelps was motivated by the words of his foes, motivation proved to be hard to come by after the Beijing Games. Really, who could blame him? With nothing left to achieve, Phelps frequently skipped practices in the years ahead, opting to relax and play golf, among other endeavors. Yet his talent enabled him to add 13 medals between the 2009 and 2011 World Championships. However, he was passed by Ryan Lochte in 2010 and 2011 as the top guy in the sport, with Lochte beating Phelps in the 200 individual medley and 200 freestyle at the 2011 World Championships.

Believing that the London Games would be his swan song, Phelps wanted to leave the sport on a high note, and a six-medal haul at the 2012 Games, including individual gold medals in the 100 butterfly and 200 individual medley, allowed for that scenario to unfold. There was also a silver medal in the 200 butterfly and relay triumphs in the 800 freestyle relay and 400 medley relay, the latter event closing out Phelps's career in a perfect way. As the most decorated Olympian of all time, Phelps was lauded by his fellow athletes on the final night of the swimming competition and given a special award for his lifetime achievements by FINA, the international governing body of the sport.

"I wanted to change the sport and take it to a new level," Phelps said. "That was a goal of mine. If I can say I've done that, then I can say I've done everything I've wanted to do in my career. This sport has done so much for me, and I'll continue to give back as much as I can."

Although Phelps left London with another six medals, he and Bowman have since admitted that the performance was largely one of smoke and mirrors—and Phelps's unmatched talent. Even ahead of the 2012 Games, Phelps was not fully invested in his craft, unable to wholly focus on the task at hand, with skipped and half-effort practices dotting his preparation. Simply, Phelps relied on his vast skill set to overcome his lack of dedication.

Phelps's journey to greatness was not always easy, and only he is to blame for some of the speed bumps. In 2005, he was charged with DUI after being pulled over in his native Baltimore. Meanwhile, a photograph printed by a British tabloid in 2009 showed Phelps smoking marijuana and generated a brief suspension for the transgression by USA Swimming.

After more than a year away from competition following the 2012 Olympics, Phelps started down the comeback trail in the spring of 2014, racing in USA Swimming Grand Prix action in Mesa, Arizona. This comeback was supposed to be measured, Bowman devising a blueprint for Phelps to smoothly glide toward the 2016 Olympics in Rio de Janeiro. Phelps, however, forced a change in plan.

In September 2014, Phelps was arrested for a second DUI charge. This time, Phelps followed a night of drinking and poker playing at a local casino by speeding and crossing a double yellow line in Baltimore's Fort McHenry Tunnel. When stopped by police, Phelps's blood-alcohol level was nearly twice the legal limit. Phelps eventually received probation for the violation, and the incident served as a major wakeup call.

Immediately after the DUI incident, Phelps retreated to his home, blocking out the world and those close to him. Eventually, family and friends got through the wall and convinced Phelps to enter a rehabilitation center to face his troubles. He ultimately spent 45 days at The Meadows, a rehab center in Wickenburg, Arizona. The stay allowed Phelps to face some of the demons and issues in his life, including alcohol use and the long-strained relationship with his father, Fred.

"I wound up uncovering a lot of things about myself that I probably knew, but I didn't want to approach," he said of his time in rehab. "One of them was that for a long time, I saw myself as the athlete that I was, but not as a human being. I would be in sessions with complete strangers who know exactly who I am, but they don't respect me for things I've done, but instead for who I am as a human being. I found myself feeling happier and happier. And in my group, we formed a family. We all wanted to see each other succeed. It was a new experience for me. It was tough. But it was great."

Phelps emerged from the treatment facility with a renewed outlook on himself and a rekindled fire to excel on the way to the Rio Games, which would be Phelps's second farewell to the sport. A reinvigorated Phelps was fully dedicated to his training and intent on closing his career in the proper way—with 100 percent effort. It was an approach that yielded positive results in the summer of 2015, as Phelps produced three world-leading times at the United States National Championships. With Phelps barred from the World Championships by USA Swimming, due to his DUI charge, the National Championships served as Phelps's only major competitive option, and he used the platform to deliver a statement to those he would see at the next summer's Olympiad.

His deep commitment to training and renewed love for the water were not lost on Phelps, a historian of his sport and able to better gauge his level than any other. At one point during his training and preparation for Rio, Phelps told his longtime agent, Peter Carlisle: "Peter, it's going to be interesting. I've never really given it everything I have."

Having successfully navigated the dangerous waters of the United States Olympic Trials, Phelps arrived in Rio with much hoopla. Already the greatest performer in swimming history, a simple question followed him: What would he do for a finale? The answer was provided on the second night of competition when Phelps, handling the second leg of the United States's 400 freestyle relay, produced a superb split and powered his country to the gold medal. Specifically, it was Phelps's turn that declared a special week was in the offing. Coming off the wall, Phelps produced several dominating underwater dolphin kicks and emerged comfortably ahead of the field. In an instant, it was clear: The legend was in peak form.

In the ensuing days, Phelps made history. He reclaimed his title in the 200 butterfly, the event that started it all, won a fourth consecutive gold in the 200 individual medley, and fueled a pair of triumphant American relays. He also earned a share of the silver medal in the 100 butterfly, an event won by Singapore's Joseph Schooling, who as a youth swimmer viewed Phelps as an idol.

Beyond his performances in the pool, there was something different about the way Phelps savored the week. As opposed to the standoffish demeanor that was previously a trademark, Phelps enjoyed the week in Rio, a loose and nostalgic deportment unable to be missed, especially by those familiar with Phelps from the beginning.

"This was the cherry on top that I wanted. I couldn't be any happier with the end of my career," Phelps said in Rio.

To say Phelps's career was nearly flawless is an understatement. Even in the events that were not his trademarks, such as the backstrokes and 100 freestyle, he ranked

Michael Phelps, with coach, Bob Bowman

among the best in the world. Meanwhile, he attracted considerably more attention than the sport ever experienced before his era started. Olympic coverage by NBC centered around swimming, and membership in United States Swimming has risen, most notably among younger males who were inspired by what they saw from Phelps.

Going forward, as unfair as it might be for the rest of the world, Phelps will be the measuring stick for multievent excellence. It is difficult to foresee anyone matching what he achieved. Additionally, there is no way Phelps will harbor any regrets over his career. As the cliché goes, no stone was left unturned.

"This all started and began with one little dream as a kid, to try to change the sport of swimming and do something no one else has ever done—and it turned out pretty cool," Phelps said.

2

Mark Spitz

Country: United States
Birth date: February 10, 1950
Events: Freestyle and butterfly
Olympic medals: Eleven

For more than 30 years, until the emergence of Michael Phelps, Mark Spitz was the slam-dunk choice as the greatest swimmer in history. A man who excelled in a variety of events and over a variety of distances, Spitz did not just become the poster boy for his sport. Rather, he was an American sports icon, his identity solidified by the seven gold medals he won at the 1972 Olympic Games in Munich, all in world-record time.

Spitz's name first gained attention in the mid-1960s. He was the best high school swimmer in the country and by 1967 had begun to etch himself as the best in the world. Setting his first world records in 1967, Spitz went to the Pan American Games in Winnipeg and left with five gold medals—three in relay duty and individual titles in the 100 and 200 butterfly events. It was a performance that raised great expectations for the 1968 Olympics in Mexico City, including lofty goals by Spitz himself.

Claiming that he could win every event in which he was entered at the 1968 Games, the boastful Spitz was knocked off his pedestal during his first Olympic appearance. While he won four medals, a tremendous haul for most, he failed to capture gold in an individual event. The shortcomings included a major miss in the 200 butterfly, where he finished last in the championship final as the world-record holder. He managed to earn the silver medal in the 100 butterfly, another event in which he was the world-record holder, and was the bronze medalist in the 100 free-style. It was a humbling experience.

"I had a difficult time [at the] 1968 Olympic Games in Mexico City where I was expected to win a lot of gold medals," Spitz said. "And if I just look at my performance of winning two gold, a silver, and a bronze, I mean that is pretty remarkable. But the problem was, is that I didn't win a gold medal in two events I held a world record in. . . . And that was just the reason I basically had this fire in my system to be able to want to actually go for another four years. And I found it kind of difficult to work out and train. But I had a focus, and the focus was to do the best I could."

Spitz followed his disappointment in Mexico City by regaining his status as the number 1 swimmer in the world. Over the next few years, while competing for the powerhouse program at Indiana University, he routinely set world records and again built momentum entering the Olympic Games. By the time the 1972 Games in Munich rolled around, Spitz was surging. This time, he wouldn't come up short.

Kicking off his second Olympiad was the 200 butterfly, the event in which he struggled the most at the previous Olympics. In his second attempt, Spitz easily picked up the gold medal and set a world record. It was a 180-degree shift from 1968 and the perfect way to embark on history. The confidence Spitz gained from that performance carried over to victories in the 100 butterfly, 100 freestyle, and 200 freestyle and as a member of all three triumphant American relays. Each of the wins was recorded in world-record time, and Spitz, known for his mustache, was an instant celebrity. However, he was also drained.

"I was exhausted by the time it came to my last individual event, the 100-meter freestyle," he said. "And I have to say that the last stroke that I took at the Olympic Games, I don't think I could have taken another stroke. I was 100 percent up until the last stroke, and I literally had one drop of gas in my tank at the end of that. So thank goodness it ended."

Having produced the finest Olympic effort of all time, Spitz's image was splashed across numerous magazine covers, and he was in high demand for endorsement deals and speaking engagements. The unprecedented nature of his performance kept Spitz as a marquee name for years down the road, even as he was no longer competitively involved in the sport he dominated. He also skipped ahead of Johnny Weissmuller as the greatest swimmer in history.

Although his legacy as a legend is firmly established, Spitz could have done more had there been greater post-collegiate opportunities afforded during his era. The first edition of the World Championships was held in 1973, and Spitz undoubtedly would have been the star, as he was still improving at the time of his retirement. In addition, he likely could have flourished at the 1976 Olympics in Montreal, where he would have been just 26 years old and, potentially, at the peak of his career. Of course, what Spitz would have done after Munich is nothing more than speculation.

What is known is that Spitz packaged a career that was nothing short of phenomenal. His 11 Olympic medals rank among the most in history, and his nine gold medals place him in a tie for second on the all-time Olympic chart, behind only Phelps. A 1977 inductee into the International Swimming Hall of Fame, Spitz set 26 individual world records during his career, spread over the 100 freestyle, 200 freestyle, 400 freestyle, 100 butterfly, and 200 butterfly. He set seven world marks each in the butterfly events. His career also included 24 national championships and 38 American records.

Spitz was considered the measuring stick for Phelps, especially as Phelps took aim at Spitz's record for the most gold medals at the Olympics. It was a mark he achieved in 2008, thanks to eight gold medals. Regardless of the fact that Spitz was surpassed by Phelps, his greatness has not been tarnished.

"I never swam for glory, only the satisfaction of being recognized as the best in the world," he said.

For more than three decades, there was no debate.

3

Katie Ledecky

Country: United States
Birth date: March 17, 1997
Event: Freestyle
Olympic medals: Six
World Championship medals: Fifteen

When phenoms come along, regardless of sport, the narrative typically goes down in one of two ways. Either the precocious youngster exceeds expectations and attains legendary status, or the prodigy flames out in stunning fashion, the fall usually painful and very public. Count Katie Ledecky in the success-story category.

It has only taken Ledecky half a decade to etch herself as the third-greatest swimmer in history, trailing only a pair of Olympic icons in Michael Phelps and Mark Spitz. That meteoric rise was jump-started in the summer of 2012, when Ledecky first prevailed at the United States Olympic Trials in the 800 freestyle, and followed at the London Games by capturing the gold medal by more than four seconds, ahead of Spain's Mireia Belmonte and defending champion Rebecca Adlington of Great Britain.

The way Ledecky won her first Olympic title provided a glimpse of what was to come over the next several years, as the American bolted to the front of the field and dared her competition to go with her. Ultimately, they could not handle her blistering pace, and Ledecky stood at the pinnacle of her sport as a 15-year-old, the world record just out of her grasp. Ever since, her rivals have been unable to handle the power of Ledecky.

"That's a young lady that just showed resolve," said USA Swimming National Team Director Frank Busch of Ledecky's initial Olympic triumph. "(She seemed to be saying), 'I don't know what I'm doing, but if somebody is going to go with me, I'm going to make you hurt.' Nobody could go with her. This is a young lady just determined to win."

Winning—and by large margins—has been Ledecky's calling card in the ensuing years, huge medal counts and global standards routine for a young woman who first displaced Janet Evans as USA Swimming's distance queen, and then rose to status as the finest female to make the pool her place of work.

Between 2013 and 2015, Ledecky rewrote what was perceived as possible in the distance-freestyle events. After leaving the World Championships in 2013 with gold medals in the 400 freestyle, 800 freestyle, and 1500 freestyle, the longer two events producing world records, Ledecky actually exceeded those accomplishments at the 2015 version of the World Championships, where she set world records in the 400 freestyle, 800 freestyle, and 1500 freestyle, and added a gold medal in the 200 freestyle.

What Ledecky managed at those two editions of the World Championships set her up to be the female centerpiece of the 2016 Olympic Games in Rio de Janeiro, and Ledecky did not disappoint. By winning the 200 freestyle and 400 freestyle, and repeating as the champion of the 800 freestyle, Ledecky became the first swimmer since Debbie Meyer in 1968 to win three freestyle crowns in a single Olympiad. She added another gold medal in the 800 freestyle relay, and claimed a silver medal as a member of Team USA's 400 freestyle relay.

"Sitting in this position now, I still do want more," Ledecky said in Rio. "I want to continue to succeed in this sport. I want to have the great opportunities to compete on this level. It's that same feeling. I just love this atmosphere. I love the Olympics. I love being here. I love forming these bonds with my teammates. I love meeting people from all different countries, and I want to have these opportunities again. I want to win medals to represent my country really well."

The desire to represent the United States admirably continued in the year following the Rio Games, as Ledecky won a third consecutive World Championship in the 400 freestyle, 800 freestyle, and 1500 freestyle, and was the silver medalist in the 200 freestyle. With the addition of two relay medals, Ledecky moved her career total to 14 gold medals at the World Championships, a record for a female athlete.

Still, the medal counts only tell part of Ledecky's story. A more-detailed look at Ledecky's prowess can be found by examining her career-best performances in comparison to what others have been able to manage. Simply, Ledecky has been racing the clock, her foes competing for minor medals behind a woman who has been dominant.

"She's never been afraid of a goal," said her coach from 2013 through 2016, Bruce Gemmell. "She's not afraid of anything. She goes after what she wants."

Through the end of 2017, a glance at Ledecky's ledger reveals how she has raced in another universe. In the 400 freestyle, Ledecky owned the nine-fastest times ever, and 14 of the fastest 15 marks, with her best time of 3:56.46 nearly three seconds clear of history's second-fastest performer, Italian Federica Pellegrini (3:59.15).

In the 800 freestyle, Ledecky owned the 15-fastest efforts of all time, and 18 of the swiftest 20. Her world record of 8:04.79 sits almost 10 seconds faster than Rebecca Adlington's 8:14.10, a time that won her the 2012 Olympic title and makes Adlington the second-fastest swimmer in event history.

As for the 1500 freestyle, which becomes an Olympic event for women at the 2020 Games in Tokyo, Ledecky owned the seven-fastest times ever, her 15:25.48 world record 13-plus seconds faster than anyone else has ever produced.

Will Ledecky eventually hit a wall and begin to drift back to the field? If her desire is any indication, much more can be expected from Ledecky in the years ahead.

"I think Rio showed me what was possible," said Ledecky, who enrolled at Stanford University following the Rio Games. "I just focused on what I wanted to achieve and really focused on those goals I'd set in 2013. Just seeing how I could step-by-step chip away at those and then ultimately achieve those goals, achieve what I wanted to achieve in Rio, it was such a great process, such a great four years. So I want to do everything I can to set myself up in a similar way [for Tokyo]."

4

Tracy Caulkins

Country: United States
Birth date: January 11, 1963
Events: Multiple
Olympic medals: Three
World Championship medals: Eight

Among female swimmers, Tracy Caulkins's versatility had never before been seen and has never been replicated in the years following her retirement. Equally proficient in the freestyle, backstroke, breaststroke, and butterfly, Caulkins remains the only swimmer to hold an American record in each discipline. Consequently, it is not surprising that her talent was best displayed in the individual medley events, where she had the opportunity to combine her skills from each stroke.

Caulkins found stardom quickly, breaking her first American records in 1977 while in her early teens. For the next seven years, she accomplished nearly everything there was to achieve in the sport, from establishing world records to winning world championships to the highlight of her career: claiming three gold medals at the 1984 Olympic Games in Los Angeles.

Although numerous swimmers through the years have excelled in multiple events, no one has matched the range of Caulkins, who was capable of being one of the world's finest performers in every discipline. Even Michael Phelps, the greatest Olympian in history, cannot claim to be an American-record holder in every stroke, the distinction achieved by Caulkins.

Caulkins made her first significant impact on the international scene at the 1978 World Championships in Berlin, Germany. A summer after first proving her worth in American competition, she won five gold medals and a silver medal, including individual victories in the 200 butterfly, 200 individual medley, and 400 individual medley. The effort fueled her selection for the prestigious Sullivan Award, given to the top amateur athlete in the United States. Her performances figured to transfer to the 1980 Olympics in Moscow, but Caulkins never got the chance to compete in those Games because of the American boycott instituted by President Jimmy Carter to protest the Soviet Union's 1979 invasion of Afghanistan.

In Moscow, Caulkins was expected to duel in the 400 individual medley with East Germany's Petra Schneider. Caulkins would have entered the Olympics as the reigning world champion while Schneider entered as the world-record holder, having broken Caulkins's global standard. Of course, the boycott interfered with the anticipated showdown, and Schneider went on to dominate easily, prevailing by more than 10 seconds. As Schneider earned the gold medal, Caulkins was left to wonder about the future of her career.

"I suppose I could be over the hill in 1984," said Caulkins while assessing her Olympic prospects following the announcement of the American boycott of the Moscow Games. "I don't worry about it, but I'm aware it could happen."

While it can be argued that her finest moment in the sport was stolen by political action, Caulkins remained active. She was a 12-time NCAA champion for the University of Florida, and at the 1982 World Championships, she won bronze medals in the 200 and 400 individual medley events. Two years later, after finally receiving her Olympic opportunity, Caulkins won both medley events at the 1984 Games. She added a third gold medal in relay duty for the United States.

Despite her success at the 1984 Olympics, Caulkins was past the peak of her career and record-setting days. Additionally, she did not face the best competition, as the Eastern bloc countries, in retaliation for the U.S. boycott of the 1980 Games, opted to boycott the Los Angeles Games. Nonetheless, the body of her work is what is remembered.

"Tracy has always been, in my opinion, the greatest female swimmer in history," said Olympic champion Rowdy Gaines, a close friend of Caulkins. "But what's more important to me is the fact that she will always be the nicest person I have ever met in the sport. You will never find one person to say a negative thing about her. She is and always will be a first-class human being. And her advice to me before my own Olympic race in 1984 was instrumental in helping me win gold as well."

Caulkins, while in the middle of tackling her full schedule, took the time to sit with Gaines and attempt to build his confidence before his final of the 100 freestyle. Buoyed by his conversation with Caulkins, Gaines went on to win the gold medal. Ironically, Gaines edged Australian Mark Stockwell, whom Caulkins later married.

After the 1984 Olympics, Caulkins retired. She was inducted into the International Swimming Hall of Fame in 1990 and remains the measuring stick for multievent female swimmers. Each time a young swimmer shines in multiple events, Caulkins's name surfaces for comparative reasons. Still, no one has matched her exploits.

During her career, she set 5 world records and 63 American records in addition to winning 48 national titles. Her world-record total likely would have been higher had

Caulkins not competed during an era when East German women were dominant in the sport—and set long-standing world records—because of a systematic doping program overseen by their coaches.

Only a few names are thrown into the hat for discussion as the greatest female swimmer in history, including the likes of American distance aces Katie Ledecky and Janet Evans, Australian Dawn Fraser, and Hungarian Krisztina Egerszegi. Caulkins's name makes the short list.

"Is she the greatest woman swimmer of all time?" asked U.S. Olympic coach Don Gambril at the conclusion of the 1984 Olympic Games. "I think you would have to call her that."

5

Krisztina Egerszegi

Country: Hungary
Birth date: August 16, 1974
Events: Backstroke and individual medley
Olympic medals: Seven
World Championship medals: Three

Krisztina Egerszegi's homeland might be dwarfed in size by the United States and Australia, the world's premier swimming superpowers, but Hungary has a rich tradition in the sport, one that dates to the first modern Olympics in 1896. There is no question that Egerszegi is one of the torchbearers for Hungarian swimming, thanks to her vast achievements during a career that contends for the best produced by a female.

Egerszegi would have been long remembered for her prowess had her first Olympiad been her last, but the backstroke/individual medley specialist did not just excel at a young age. At a time when women swimmers did not have lengthy careers, Egerszegi flourished for three Olympics and left the sport in the same way she entered it on the international stage: on top.

As a 14-year-old at the 1988 Olympics in Seoul, Egerszegi made history in the 200 backstroke by becoming the youngest Olympic swimming champion. That gold medal was complemented by a silver medal in the 100 backstroke. The accomplishments were far from a surprise to her coach, Laszlo Kiss.

"I quickly realized I had found a real pearl, whose sports career had to be nurtured with a lot of responsibility," said Kiss, who started coaching Egerszegi when she was a 12-year-old. "When I first diagnosed Krisztina's technique in the four strokes, I immediately realized that she was an ideal backstroker, with thin thighs, broad shoulders, large palms, loose and flexible shoulders, and an excellent buoyancy on

19

the surface of the water. These characteristics enabled her to become a world-class backstroker."

Egerszegi took the potential that Kiss saw in her and turned it into a career that rates among the finest by a woman. It is widely accepted that Katie Ledecky, Tracy Caulkins, Janet Evans, and Egerszegi are the four best female swimmers in history, all exhibiting overwhelming dominance. Egerszegi's most dominant days were in 1991 and 1992, when she won gold medals in the 100 and 200 backstroke events along with the 400 individual medley at both the European Championships and the Olympic Games.

Her performances at the 1992 Olympics in Barcelona received the greater attention, largely because of the bigger stage and the way Egerszegi defeated her competition. In addition to winning the 100 backstroke by nearly half a second, the Hungarian won the 200 backstroke by more than a two-second margin. The difference in the 200 backstroke was not a surprise, however, as she set a world record in 1991 that ended up enduring for nearly 17 years.

Four years after Barcelona, Egerszegi was again busy collecting medals and making history. When she prevailed in the 200 backstroke in 1996 in Atlanta, she became just the second athlete in Olympic swimming history to win an event in three consecutive Olympiads, joining Australian Dawn Fraser, who was the gold medalist in the 100 freestyle at the 1956, 1960, and 1964 Games. For good measure, Egerszegi's last Olympics included a bronze medal in the 400 individual medley.

Swimming is a sport in which prolonged dominance, especially over three Olympiads, is hard to attain. Not only is maintaining peak physical condition a difficult task, but there is always the emergence of younger talent seeking to knock off the veterans. Egerszegi's portfolio clearly portrays someone who defied the odds. Today, there is only one other member of the club started by Fraser and joined by Egerszegi. At the 2012 Olympics, Michael Phelps became a three-time Olympic champion in the 200 individual medley and 100 butterfly, and he followed in 2016 by winning the 200 medley on a fourth straight occasion.

If her backstroke and medley excellence was not enough, Egerszegi also earned a European Championship in the 200 butterfly, thus extending her range to a place where few have waded. Her overall haul of seven medals in Olympic action was complemented by a sweep of the backstroke events at the 1991 World Championships and 13 medals (9 gold) at the European Championships, 12 of which were garnered in individual competition.

6

Janet Evans

Country: United States
Birth date: August 28, 1971
Events: Distance freestyle and indi-
    vidual medley
Olympic medals: Five
World Championship medals: Five

Arguments can be made for Janet Evans ranking as the greatest female swimmer in history, such was her dominance during her peak time and the longevity of the world records she established. Unlike many of the premier female swimmers, Evans was small in stature but relied on a seemingly endless surge of energy to power past her opponents.

Evans's talent was revealed to the public in 1987 when she packaged a sterling performance at the Pan Pacific Championships and set several world records throughout the year. At the Pan Pacific Championships, Evans captured gold medals in the 400 freestyle and 400 individual medley to go with a silver medal in the 800 freestyle. During the course of the year, she set world records over the 400 freestyle, 800 freestyle, and 1500 freestyle, setting herself up for a banner showing at the 1988 Olympics in Seoul.

While Matt Biondi was the star of the men's competition at the 1988 Games, Evans was the darling of the women's competition. The 17-year-old won gold medals in the 400 freestyle, 800 freestyle, and 400 individual medley, and her world-record time in the 400 freestyle stood as the global standard for nearly 18 years. As for the 400 individual medley, her victory in that event was a testament to her endurance as much as it was her mastery of the four strokes.

"Janet likes to be challenged," said one of her coaches, Bud McAllister. "I know she's always going to work hard. She'll tell me what she can do, and I'll stand there and time her, and she'll be right on it. An athlete like Janet knows her body better than anyone. She asks me to help her set her goals, but she tells me how she feels physically. And she keeps asking for more. She's the best I've ever seen at responding to pressure."

Evans's efforts in the late 1980s were undoubtedly the highlights of her career and included a repeat of her triple-gold showing from Seoul at the 1989 Pan Pacific Championships. At that meet, Evans set the world record in the 800 freestyle, a mark that endured for almost 19 years. Her other world record, in the 1500 freestyle, lasted for 19 years, too. Considering the longevity of those records, Evans was clearly ahead of her time.

Even though Evans was no longer at her peak form in the early 1990s, she remained a major force. At the 1991 World Championships, she prevailed in the 400 freestyle and 800 freestyle and added a silver medal in the 200 freestyle, an event that was a sprint for the distance queen. She carried that momentum into the 1992 Olympics in Barcelona, where she repeated as the champion of the 800 freestyle and settled for the silver medal behind Germany's Dagmar Hase in the 400 freestyle. Two years later, Evans won the last individual medal of her international career, taking gold at the 1994 World Championships in the 800 freestyle, a race that saw American Brooke Bennett win the bronze medal.

As Evans declined, Bennett was a rising star on the distance scene and viewed as the heir apparent to Evans. It was a role that Bennett embraced, and she was not afraid to voice her confidence. On several occasions, Bennett indicated that she felt Evans was intimidated by her presence and the prospect of another American ruling the distance events. Not surprisingly, Evans did not take kindly to her rival's comments.

"Why is there so much attention on her?" she said. "You guys tell me. A lot of people say they see some of me in Brooke. But her times aren't anything that are going to be remembered in five years. Unless she goes faster, 10 seconds faster, then I'd say she reminds me of myself. I'm really not impressed."

Ultimately, Evans lost the battle with Bennett. At the 1996 Olympics in Atlanta, Evans was sixth in the 800 freestyle, a race won by Bennett. Evans also failed to qualify for the final of the 400 freestyle. She made a comeback more than a decade later, but Evans failed to advance beyond the preliminary round at the 2012 U.S. Olympic Trials.

A 45-time national champion and seven-time NCAA champion at Stanford University, Evans was inducted into the International Swimming Hall of Fame in 2001. She finished her career by setting seven world records and was named World Swimmer of the Year by *Swimming World Magazine* in 1987, 1989, and 1990. Most recently, she played an instrumental role on the committee that successfully bid to have Los Angeles named the host of the 2028 Olympic Games.

7

Dawn Fraser

Country: Australia
Birth date: September 4, 1937
Event: Freestyle
Olympic medals: Eight

Any knowledgeable swimming fan will instantly rattle off the name of Dawn Fraser when asked to identify some of the greats of the sport. The Australian was one of the first female megastars, her talent on display for an extended period of time and so impressive that 50 years after her retirement, Fraser can still be argued as the greatest woman freestyler of all time.

While Fraser excelled in several freestyle distances, her ownership of the 100 freestyle was her defining characteristic. For a 15-year period, spanning 1956–1971, Fraser held the world record in the event and broke the global standard on 10 occasions, lowering the mark from 1:04.5 in 1956 to 58.9 in 1964, a record that endured for seven years. In 1962, she became the first woman to break the one-minute barrier. Fraser used a men's event as motivation to continually lower her world record.

"A female freestyle swimmer could swim as fast as a male butterfly swimmer," Fraser said. "If a world record in the men's butterfly was 60 seconds, I was going to make sure I could swim that fast. That's how I kept all my world records down."

Fraser's world records exhibit just a portion of her dominance in the 100 freestyle. After winning the gold medal over countrywoman Lorraine Crapp at the 1956 Olympics in Melbourne, Fraser repeated as champion in the 1960 Games, this time prevailing by 1.6 seconds. What she did in 1964, however, was unprecedented. Fraser again won the 100 freestyle and became the first swimmer—male or female—to win an event at three consecutive Olympiads.

Half a century after becoming the first member of the threepeat club, Fraser's feat has been matched by only two other swimmers despite several attempts across various events. Hungary's Krisztina Egerszegi won the 200 backstroke at the 1988, 1992, and 1996 Olympics, while Michael Phelps was the champion of the 200 individual medley and 100 butterfly at the 2004, 2008, and 2012 Games, with Phelps also winning the 200 medley at the 2016 Olympics.

Under the guidance of coach Harry Gallagher, Fraser also excelled in the 200 and 400 freestyle events, setting four world records in the 200 distance. However, it was not an Olympic event during Fraser's career, preventing her from adding additional medals to her final count of eight. She managed a silver medal in the 400 freestyle at the 1956 Olympics and won four medals in relay competition: a gold and three silver. Much of her success was a combination of a close relationship with her coach and knowing how to balance her training.

"I probably have a different mental approach to swimming than most people," she said. "I actually enjoy training most of the time. When I don't want to train, I don't. If it comes, it comes, and I don't force myself. Nine years ago, when I started swimming seriously, I did absolutely everything my coach, Harry Gallagher, told me to, but then two years ago I began using my own judgment more and more, and we both feel that this arrangement is better. In other words, our relationship is not that of coach and pupil but more like that of brother and sister."

For all her accolades, Fraser's rebellious personality frequently put her at odds with the Australian Swimming Union. In her final Olympiad, she chose to walk in the Opening Ceremony rather than rest up for the start of the swimming competition, which was the advice of the Union. She also chose to wear an older swimsuit for her races instead of the suit that was provided by the Australian team sponsor.

After she was done competing, Fraser got into her deepest trouble. Fraser was arrested by Japanese police for stealing an Olympic flag outside the Emperor's Palace. She was ultimately released and not charged for the incident, but the Australian Swimming Union levied a 10-year ban on Fraser as a penalty for her actions. If Fraser had any designs on competing at the 1968 Games, the ban ended those aspirations.

"They took me to the Marunouchi Police Station, and they were going to charge me," Fraser said of the flag incident. "They got an interpreter who was the lieutenant of the police station, and he couldn't believe it was Dawn Fraser. They decided then because of who I was, Dawn Fraser, they let us off."

8

Johnny Weissmuller

Country: United States
Birth date: June 2, 1904
Death date: January 20, 1984
Event: Freestyle
Olympic medals: Five

Depending on the fan base, Johnny Weissmuller is known for two identities. Some people know Weissmuller as the man who made the Tarzan character famous in the movies. Before his film days, however, Weissmuller established himself as one of the first swimming stars, a winner of five Olympic gold medals in freestyle events.

Weissmuller is renowned in the swimming world as one of the great freestylers in history, his two Olympic titles in the 100-meter freestyle—widely regarded as the premier event in the sport—providing the proof for that distinction. En route to his identity as a freestyle legend, Weissmuller had to defeat fellow American Duke Kahanamoku. He made his first move toward that status by breaking Kahanamoku's world record in the 100 freestyle in 1922, lowering the standard from 1:00.4 all the way to 58.6. He further lowered the world record to 57.4 in early 1924, months before he and Kahanamoku faced off in the Olympics in Paris.

It was at the Olympic Games, though, where Weissmuller firmly surpassed his rival as the greatest freestyler of all time. Although Kahanamoku was the Olympic champion in the 100 freestyle in 1912 and 1920 (the 1916 Games were canceled by World War I), he was no match for Weissmuller at the 1924 Games, losing by more than two seconds. In addition to winning the gold medal in the 100 freestyle, Weissmuller also emerged victorious in the 400 freestyle and as a member of the U.S. 800 freestyle relay. Four years later, at the 1928 Olympics in Amsterdam, Weissmuller repeated his gold medals in the 100 freestyle and in the 800 freestyle relay.

That Weissmuller ever had the chance to represent the United States is a classic chapter of his career.

As the 1924 Olympics in Paris neared, questions surrounding Weissmuller's American citizenship began to surface, and with good reason. Weissmuller was actually born—according to official records—on June 2, 1904, in the small town of Friedorf, part of Romania. Although he moved to the United States with his parents seven months later, he was not an American citizen.

This fact became an issue leading up to the Paris Games because Weissmuller needed official documentation of his citizenship to secure an American passport, which would enable his travel to the Olympics. For this reason, Weissmuller put into motion a major ruse, one that proved to be successful.

His father once insisted that Weissmuller was born in Chicago, but this claim was later changed to Windber, a small town in Pennsylvania. Indeed, a Weismuller was born in this town, but it was Johnny's younger brother Peter. Using this familial connection to his advantage, Weissmuller got hold of baptismal records from St. John Cantius Catholic Church for his brother, Petrus Weissmuller. Inserted between the first and last names and in different ink and penmanship was "John." Weissmuller asserted that this official record was his, and it met the needs to allow his participation in the 1924 Olympics.

"After satisfying Olympic and government officials of his American citizenship, Weissmuller joined the U.S. team and swam in Paris," stated a 1984 *Sports Illustrated* article on the doubts concerning Weissmuller's citizenship. "He became an instant national hero. It seemed nobody now wanted to raise questions about his citizenship. Claiming Windber as his birthplace not only gave Weissmuller the opportunity to produce 'proof' of his American birth, but also provided him with a new hometown, which in later years would welcome him back as its most famous native son."

Weissmuller ran with the deceit for years, even celebrating a day in his honor in Windber in 1950, years after his Olympic exploits. On that day, Weissmuller went as far as to say, "I have always wanted a hometown, and now I have one. This is the biggest thrill I ever had in my life and this includes the events when I won the Olympic titles in 1924 and 1928 and was presented medals by the queen of the Netherlands."

Throughout his life, Weissmuller ensured that his secret was well protected. He never told his family of his true birthplace, including his five wives and only son, Johnny Jr., and he told his biographer that he was born in Windber, Pennsylvania. According to the *Sports Illustrated* article, those in Romania who knew the true story of his birth in their homeland did not want to ruin his success, for they were proud of what he achieved.

After Weissmuller died in 1984, his son learned of the truth when he was interviewed about the topic. After the initial shock, he toasted his father: "To the old man. He sure could keep a secret."

Weissmuller was so ahead of his time that his second world record in the 100 freestyle endured for more than 10 years, holding up until 1934. A 1965 inductee of the International Swimming Hall of Fame, Weissmuller set 51 world records and won 52 national titles during his career, records and championships that were spread over various distances. Had the Olympic program been as expansive as it is today, Weissmuller likely would have won additional gold medals in the 50 and 200 freestyle events. He also competed in water polo in two Olympiads, earning a bronze medal in 1924, and was chosen by the Associated Press in 1950 as the greatest swimmer who ever lived.

For some, Weissmuller is better known for his portrayal of the Tarzan character. Although he was not the first actor to play the Tarzan role, Weissmuller is credited with being the most popular. He portrayed the character 12 times between 1932 and 1948, his swimming success serving as the springboard toward landing the coveted role. Weissmuller was first considered for the role when Cyril Hume, a Hollywood screenwriter working on a film adaptation of *Tarzan the Ape Man*, saw Weissmuller swimming in a hotel pool. Hume immediately knew that he wanted the Olympic champion to play the lead character in the film.

Although Weissmuller is often cited as developing the best known of the Tarzan yells, which are part of Hollywood lore, he never viewed himself as a great actor. Rather, he continued to view himself as a swimmer who happened to transition into a second career.

"How can a guy climb trees, say 'Me, Tarzan, you, Jane,' and make a million?" he once asked. "The public forgives my acting because they know I was an athlete. They know I wasn't make-believe. I started out as a scrawny kid in Chicago, and even that was lucky. It got me to swimming. Then all the good breaks in the world happened and kept on happening."

9

Ian Thorpe

Country: Australia
Birth date: October 13, 1982
Event: Freestyle
Olympic medals: Nine
World Championship medals: Thirteen

Before Michael Phelps arrived on the scene, Australian Ian Thorpe was mentioned in discussion concerning the greatest swimmer of all time. He was not given the title, but Thorpe was considered a contender for that distinction, such was his prowess in the freestyle events. Ultimately, he never reached those heights, having left the sport in his prime. Nonetheless, Thorpe is a lock for a top-10 position.

Thorpe is widely regarded as the best middle-distance swimmer in history but also exhibited enough talent to be a global force in events as short as the 100 freestyle and as long as the 800 freestyle. In addition, he was adept enough at all strokes to once medal in the 200 individual medley at the World Championships.

As a 14-year-old at the 1998 World Championships, Thorpe gave the swimming world a glimpse of what was to come. In becoming the youngest male world champion of an individual event, Thorpe bettered the competition in the 400 freestyle. In less than four minutes, he put his sport on alert that great things were on the way. Thorpe did not disappoint.

Competing in a home Olympics in 2000 in Sydney, Thorpe walked away with five of an eventual nine career Olympic medals, his total shared for the record by an Australian swimmer. His victory in the 400 freestyle was the individual highlight, and his anchor leg of Australia's triumphant 400 freestyle and 800 freestyle relays followed closely behind. In the shorter relay, Thorpe handled the anchor leg and overtook American Gary Hall Jr., enabling Australia to hand the United States its first Olympic defeat in event history.

The next year, at the World Championships in Japan, Thorpe put together one of the finest single-meet performances the sport has seen. Setting world records in the 200 freestyle, 400 freestyle, and 800 freestyle, Thorpe also guided Australia to gold medals in all three relays and became the first person to capture six gold medals at the World Championships.

"If you were going to do a Frankenstein, if you were going to put a swimmer together from scratch, you'd build Ian Thorpe," said Australian coach Brian Sutton.

The 2002 Commonwealth Games featured a repeat of Thorpe's excellence at the World Championships, with one addition. Showing his skill in another event, Thorpe earned a silver medal in the 100 backstroke. At the next year's World Championships, he expanded his portfolio with a sweep of the 200 and 400 freestyle and added a silver medal in the 200 individual medley and a bronze medal in the 100 freestyle.

Unbeknownst to the sport, Thorpe's final exhibition of his daunting talent was the 2004 Olympic Games in Athens, where he won the 200 and 400 freestyle events, took bronze in the 100 freestyle, and earned silver in the 800 freestyle relay. His win in the 200 freestyle, which was deemed the Race of the Century, was his hallmark triumph. Not only did Thorpe topple a burgeoning Michael Phelps, who finished in the bronze-medal position, but he also beat rival Pieter van den Hoogenband for the third straight time at a major international competition, joining the previous two versions of the World Championships. It was van den Hoogenband who denied Thorpe the gold medal in the event at the Sydney Games.

"I told him, 'Now we're even,'" van den Hoogenband said after his Olympic duels with Thorpe were evened at one each.

Although it was no surprise that Thorpe took time away from the sport in 2005, skipping the World Championships in Montreal, few expected Thorpe's hiatus to be prolonged. However, that is exactly what occurred, with the Aussie opting to remain in retirement through the 2007 World Championships and the 2008 Olympic Games in Beijing. As Phelps took down Thorpe's world record in the 200 freestyle, there were no more head-to-head matchups.

A comeback attempt finally made its way onto Thorpe's agenda in 2011, but his push for a third Olympic berth turned out to be a disaster, or, as Thorpe called it, "a nightmare." The man nicknamed the Thorpedo was a nonfactor at the 2012 Australian Olympic Trials, failing to qualify for the London Games in the 100 freestyle and 200 freestyle. Despite the failed comeback, Thorpe was satisfied with his effort.

"I think it's better to attempt something and fail than it is to not even attempt it, so I'm glad that I've been prepared to put myself on the line there," he said.

For his career, Thorpe totaled 9 Olympic medals and 13 World Championship medals, including 11 gold medals. He set six world records in the 200 freestyle, five world records in the 400 freestyle, and two world records in the 800 freestyle.

10

Matt Biondi

Country: United States
Birth date: October 8, 1965
Events: Freestyle and butterfly
Olympic medals: Eleven
World Championship medals: Eleven

The comparisons were inevitable given his schedule and pursuits. Because Matt Biondi shared many of the same events as the iconic Mark Spitz, he was dubbed as the heir apparent to—at the time—the greatest swimmer in history. And because he chased seven gold medals at the 1988 Olympics, a feat that Spitz pulled off at the 1972 Games, Biondi was going to be further measured against *the man* of the previous generation.

Ultimately, Biondi did not replicate the Spitzian performance that stood as the Olympic Holy Grail until Michael Phelps came along. Nonetheless, Biondi put together a career that was phenomenal both for its longevity and for its diversity. Really, it was easy to identify the Californian as one of the top-10 athletes his sport has seen.

Biondi's first Olympic foray was nothing overwhelming, simply an appearance in the victorious U.S. 400 freestyle relay at the 1984 Games in Los Angeles. That experience, however, provided Biondi with a strong sense of the Olympic atmosphere and a feel for how to handle the spotlight. It was an important moment considering how brightly the lights were about to shine on the biggest rising star in the American ranks.

By the time the 1986 World Championships had concluded, Biondi had seven medals in his pocket. He left Madrid with three gold medals, a silver medal, and three bronze medals. While he was the world champion in the 100 freestyle, his individual medals in the 50 freestyle, 200 freestyle, and 100 butterfly added to his mystique and seemingly could be converted to gold at the 1988 Olympics. Not surprisingly, the comparisons to Spitz started in earnest, including those by famed American coaches. Could this be the guy who matches what was believed to be an untouchable accomplishment?

"I don't feel it's a fair comparison," said Biondi's coach Nort Thornton. "But people are going to do it. You can't stop them. It's unfortunate people get compared, but that's human nature. The rules have changed, and people can't swim as many events as they were able to in 1972. There are certain comparisons like the speed they both travel through water, but Matt is definitely not Mark. He is his own swimmer. Someday people will be comparing another young swimmer to Matt. That's the way it works.

"He was born with all the right tools. He has an incredible feel for the water. It's hard to describe. It's the same feel a pianist has for the keys and an artist's brush has for the canvas. He is able to sense the water pressures on his hands. He sets his hands at the right pitch, like a propeller on a boat. He is able to pitch his blades at the right angle. A lot of people don't have that awareness."

Biondi delivered a superb performance in Seoul, capturing five gold medals, a silver medal, and a bronze medal. He was the Olympic champion in the 50 freestyle, in which he set a world record, and the 100 freestyle. The other three gold medals were from relay action. Meanwhile, he was the silver medalist in the 100 butterfly and the bronze medalist in the 200 freestyle.

As sensational as Biondi was over the course of the meet, he was particularly disappointed with his effort in the 100 butterfly, where he was beaten by Suriname's Anthony Nesty. Leading for the majority of the race, Biondi appeared headed for what would have been a sixth gold medal, only to be edged at the wall by Nesty, who prevailed by a hundredth of a second and became the first Olympic champion from his country. Biondi bounced back later that night by anchoring the United States to the gold medal in the 800 freestyle relay.

"I guess today I went from bum to hero in an hour or so," Biondi said. "In the 100 fly, I swam 99 meters like an Olympic champion. . . . I had been winning the race easily the whole way. It's been eating me up. After all, what's a 100th of a second? Could I have won with longer fingernails? A slightly quicker start? Looking at the tape of the race just makes me sick to my stomach."

A multiple NCAA champion at the University of California, Berkeley, Biondi wasn't done after Seoul. He remained one of the premier swimmers in the sport and repeated as world champion in the 100 freestyle in 1991. At those World Championships, he added two gold medals in relay duty and a silver medal in the 50 freestyle. A year later, at the 1992 Olympics, Biondi was part of two winning relays and won a silver medal in the 50 freestyle. However, he finished fifth in the 100 freestyle, unable to defend his championship.

Biondi broke the world record in the 100 freestyle on four occasions, his last mark standing for almost six years. He also broke the world record in the 50 freestyle three times, was an 18-time medalist at the Pan Pacific Championships, and was inducted into the International Swimming Hall of Fame in 1997.

11

Shane Gould

Country: Australia
Birth date: November 23, 1956
Events: Freestyle and individual medley
Olympic medals: Five

How good could Shane Gould have been? It's a question frequently posed about the Australian legend, who accomplished a great deal in a short period of time, then retired from the sport at her peak. Of course, there will never be a firm answer, so fans of the sport can only make an educated guess.

Between 1971 and 1972, as a teenager, Gould set 11 world records and became the toast of female swimming, the equivalent of what Mark Spitz was in men's swimming. At one point, Gould held every world record from the 100 freestyle through the 1500 freestyle and also was the world-record holder in the 200 individual medley. Coached by Forbes Carlile, Gould was immediately pegged for stardom.

"Shane, when she came to us as a 13-year-old from Brisbane, was a pretty good swimmer," said Carlile, regarded as one of the greatest coaches in history. "We picked her as a future champion. In fact, as far as I was concerned, it wasn't going to be if she broke Dawn Fraser's record for the 100 [freestyle], it was a question of when. She went on to hold all the world records in freestyle, which hadn't been done before and may not be done again."

Indeed, Gould lived up to the expectations of Carlile, first tying Fraser's seven-year-old world record as a 14-year-old, then breaking the mark as a 15-year-old. It was her performance at the 1972 Olympics in Munich, however, that was her finest moment. Although overshadowed by the seven gold medals won by Spitz, Gould collected five medals, including victories in the 200 freestyle, 400 freestyle, and 200 individual medley, all in world-record time. She added a silver medal in the 800 freestyle and was the bronze medalist in the 100 freestyle.

In some ways, Gould is an underappreciated star, largely because Spitz cast a huge shadow in Munich. Her achievements in Germany, had they been delivered in today's media-drenched world, would have led to a crush of attention. For her part, Gould was never one to enjoy the limelight.

Just as quickly as she ascended to the top of the sport, Gould left swimming not long into 1973 despite the likelihood that she would have dominated the first version of the World Championships, held later in the year. A 1977 inductee into the International Swimming Hall of Fame and *Swimming World Magazine*'s 1971 and 1972 Female Swimmer of the Year, Gould tired of the immense pressure under which she competed. She also wondered about what she was missing away from the pool.

"In some senses, it was like a big circus and I was one of the performers," Gould said. "I was like one of the trained seals. Then I started to think, is that all there is? You get to the top in your sport and you get told 'yeah, that's really good Shane,' and 'you're fantastic,' and I think, I'm not really good at school, and sometimes I don't wash the dishes. I fight with my sisters and I'm not fantastic in everything. So I started to question all the praises that were given and whether they were accurate.

"When I started swimming faster and breaking records and winning more events, I got more of the attention, and that sort of isolated me from other people. It then became a little bit more serious, and it wasn't quite so much fun. There were more expectations."

Gould remains the only female swimmer in Olympic history to win five individual medals in a single Olympiad. As further proof of her premature exit, Gould became the first woman to break the 17-minute barrier in the 1500 freestyle just before her retirement.

12

Don Schollander

Country: United States
Birth date: April 30, 1946
Event: Freestyle
Olympic medals: Six

Between the dominating reigns of Johnny Weissmuller and Mark Spitz, the United States had another legend of the sport to closely follow. His name was Don Schollander, a scholar whose aquatic talent set him apart from the competition but was matched by his intellectual attributes, which landed him as a student at Yale University.

A teenage star, Schollander burst onto the global scene with several world-record swims in 1962 and 1963. But just a few months before the 1964 Olympics in Tokyo, at the AAU National Championships, he etched himself as a big-time star in development. Schollander cruised to victories in the 100 freestyle, 200 freestyle, and 400 freestyle, revealing a combination of speed and endurance that hadn't been seen since Weissmuller. His performances in the 200 and 400 distances are what caught the eye of the rest of the world, as those events featured victories over Australian legend and Olympic champion Murray Rose. In the span of a few days, Schollander was the future of swimming for the United States.

"It may be a year or two before Schollander completely masters his art, but there is no doubt that he is already the finest combination of speed and durability that has ever stepped onto a block," wrote Coles Phinizy in a *Sports Illustrated* article. "If he decides to gamble across the board in the Olympic Trials in New York three weeks from now, he could very well end up representing the U.S. in every freestyle event at Tokyo. The principal reasons for his success are the usual ones: hard, honest work in a good racing stable, the Santa Clara Swim Club, under a good coach, George Haines."

It didn't take Schollander the perceived year or two to become a master of the pool. Rather, it was just a few weeks. At the Tokyo Games, Schollander became the first swimmer to win four gold medals at a single Games, prevailing in the 100 freestyle and 400 freestyle and as a member of the American 400 freestyle relay and 800 freestyle relay. His haul could have been greater, but Schollander was left off the 400 medley relay and the 200 freestyle, which might have been his best event, was not part of the Olympic program until the 1968 Olympics.

So dominating was Schollander that he was inducted into the International Swimming Hall of Fame in 1965 as a 19-year-old. Schollander was the first World Swimmer of the Year chosen by *Swimming World Magazine*, and he set 11 world records in the 200 freestyle between 1962 and 1968 and three world records in the 400 freestyle. While the middle distance was his prime area, he was also suited to the sprints and distance events. If not for concern over a too-demanding training schedule to prepare for the 1964 Olympics, Schollander might have been a factor for gold in the 1500 freestyle.

Schollander continued on after the 1964 Olympics and won three gold medals at the 1967 Pan American Games, a triumph in the 200 freestyle supported by a pair of relay victories. At the 1968 Olympics in Mexico City, Schollander was a member of the victorious 800 freestyle relay for the United States but had to settle for the silver medal in the 200 freestyle, clocking a time more than a second off his world record and finishing behind Australian Michael Wenden. It was the only shortcoming of an illustrious run.

"There are three things that make Don such a terrific swimmer," Haines said. "First, he is almost flawless mechanically. Second, he has a tremendous desire to win. Finally, he is a thoroughly intelligent competitor with a wonderful tactical sense."

13

Tamas Darnyi

Country: Hungary
Birth date: June 3, 1967
Event: Individual medley
Olympic medals: Four
World Championship medals: Five

Before Michael Phelps and Ryan Lochte became the names synonymous with the individual medley events, Hungary's Tamas Darnyi was the undisputed king of the all-encompassing disciplines. For much of the 1980s and into the early 1990s, Darnyi knew no equal when all four of swimming's strokes were combined.

Had the Eastern bloc countries not boycotted the 1984 Olympics in Los Angeles, perhaps Darnyi would have become a big name on the international circuit earlier than 1985. It was that year, however, in which Darnyi announced his arrival to the world by winning the 200 individual medley and 400 individual medley at the European Championships. A year later, at the World Championships, he confirmed his status as the number 1 medley swimmer by knocking off the reigning Olympic champion. In two meetings with Canada's Alex Baumann, Darnyi had no trouble beating his North American foe.

By the time the 1988 Olympic Games were held, Darnyi had set the first world records of his career and continued his dominance, which ultimately led to a nearly decade-long winning streak in both the 200 and the 400 individual medley. At the Seoul Olympics, Darnyi overwhelmed the competition as expected, winning the shorter medley by more than a second and the longer event by nearly three seconds, thanks to a world-record performance.

The Darnyi roll didn't let up, either. He doubled in the medley events at the 1989 European Championships, where he also prevailed in the 200 butterfly, and he won gold medals in each medley event at the 1991 World Championships, where Darnyi became the first man to break the two-minute barrier in the 200 individual medley. It all led to the 1992 Olympics in Barcelona.

At the 1992 Games, Darnyi became the first man to repeat as Olympic champion in either medley event, winning both. He followed with a fourth European title in the 400 medley in 1993, then walked away from the sport as the most decorated medley swimmer of all time. He achieved that status despite not having a single stroke that was dominant.

Not only did Darnyi overwhelm his competition, he set the standard for future Hungarian success in the medley events. From a country with a rich swimming tradition, Darnyi established the bar for athletes like Laszlo Cseh. Although Cseh came along during the Phelps-Lochte era and couldn't quite produce the same success as his American rivals, he left a strong mark on the sport, claiming several Olympic medals to go with world and European championships over the course of his career.

"Tamas has four pretty good strokes, but none are outstanding," said Jon Urbanchek, a highly regarded American coach who was born in Hungary. "What he lacks in natural talent he makes up for with incredible dedication. I don't think anyone in the free world could have put that much time into the sport."

Darnyi was named *Swimming World Magazine* Male Swimmer of the Year on two occasions, winning the honor in 1987 and 1991. After his retirement, Darnyi's last world record in the 400 individual medley lasted for more than three years.

14

Mary T. Meagher

Country: United States
Birth date: October 27, 1964
Event: Butterfly
Olympic medals: Four
World Championship medals: Nine

Madame Butterfly was the nickname bestowed on Mary T. Meagher at a young age, and what an appropriate moniker it was. Meagher was the best butterfly swimmer in the world in the late 1970s and into the 1980s, and no individual—man or woman—dominated a specific stroke in similar fashion.

Meagher emerged as a significant factor on the international scene in 1979 when she set three world records in the 200 butterfly, lowering the standard by nearly three seconds, an unheard-of amount of time. On the basis of those performances, Meagher was expected to be one of the stars of the 1980 Olympics in Moscow, but that scenario never unfolded when the United States boycotted the Games.

"The Olympics had always been my dream," she said. "And that is what they have remained—only a dream. I felt like hanging up the phone and crying."

Meagher briefly considered leaving the sport but decided to stay with it. At the 1981 U.S. Nationals, Meagher produced two of the finest efforts the sport has seen. In the 100 butterfly, she turned in a time of 57.93, becoming the first woman to break both the 59- and 58-second barriers. She also went 2:05.96 in the 200 butterfly, and at one point held the 11-fastest times ever recorded in the event. Both of Meagher's standards lasted for 18 years, including the assault on the record books that took place during the height of East Germany's systematic doping program.

After winning the gold medal in the 100 butterfly and the silver medal in the 200 butterfly at the 1982 World Championships, Meagher geared up for her first

Olympic opportunity. At the 1984 Games in Los Angeles, she won the gold medals that she likely would have secured had the boycott of 1980 not taken place. Meagher also helped the United States win gold in the 400 medley relay.

"I guess I'll always envision them as a kind of heaven, sort of a dream world," she said of the Olympics. "Only this dream world was real."

Continuing to compete after the 1984 Olympics, Meagher won six medals at the 1986 World Championships, highlighted by a victory in the 200 butterfly. She added bronze medals in the 100 butterfly and 200 freestyle, the latter event a testament to her versatility. Rather than retire, she kept training through the 1988 Olympics, where she won the bronze medal in the 200 butterfly.

Meagher was inducted into the International Swimming Hall of Fame in 1993 and was a multiple NCAA champion at the University of California, Berkeley. She was named *Swimming World Magazine* Swimmer of the Year in 1981 and 1985.

15

Ryan Lochte

Country: United States
Birth Date: August 3, 1984
Events: Multiple
Olympic medals: Twelve
World Championship medals: Twenty-seven

The era in which Ryan Lochte has competed has not been conducive to headline-grabbing ease. Because of Michael Phelps's prominence in the sport, Lochte spent a number of years overshadowed by his rival and frequently lost races to Phelps during their head-to-head matchups. But during the back half of his career, Lochte more than proved himself capable of slaying Phelps, and his stature in the sport significantly surged. Today, Lochte can be called one of the greatest of all time, not simply an also-ran during the Phelps phenomenon.

For the first few years of his international career, Lochte routinely took the backseat to his more prominent countrymen. In Phelps, Lochte couldn't get by a guy who was redefining what was possible in the sport. He would lose to Phelps in the 200 individual medley, 400 individual medley, and the 200 freestyle, with some of those defeats arriving at the Olympic Games or World Championships. Meanwhile, there was a time when Lochte couldn't get by fellow American Aaron Peirsol in the 200 backstroke.

Between the 2004 and the 2008 Olympics, Lochte suffered more setbacks than victories against his leading adversaries. He was the silver medalist to Phelps in the 200 individual medley at the 2004 Olympics and couldn't beat Phelps in either medley event at the 2007 World Championships or the 2008 Olympics. There were also losses to Peirsol, although the shift in momentum started when Lochte beat Peirsol for the gold medal in the 200 backstroke at the 2007 World Championships and the 2008 Games. It was an indication that he could get the job done against the best and on the big stage.

Rather than get down and develop doubt in his ability to ever surpass his U.S. teammates, Lochte was rewarded for plugging away. A huge part of Lochte's rise was related to a more demanding training program and a better diet. In addition, he wasn't afraid to battle Phelps and was convinced that Phelps was beatable, a thought process not shared by all.

"There were different things I added to my training," Lochte said. "I started doing Strongman workouts. I didn't get too big from them, but I got a lot stronger, and that helped me in the pool. The other thing was changing my eating habits. There was no more fast food or junk food. I cut out candy and soda. [Overall], I started seeing better results in my training. It was an important step."

While Lochte first saw the difference in his approach during practice, the public got a glimpse at major events. He was the world champion in the 200 individual medley and 400 individual medley at the 2009 World Championships, then won four individual events at the 2010 Pan Pacific Championships and was named World Swimmer of the Year, knocking Phelps from that throne.

At the 2011 World Championships, Lochte reaffirmed his status as the best swimmer in the world when he won the 200 freestyle, 200 backstroke, and both individual medley events, defeating Phelps in the 200 freestyle and 200 individual medley. It was huge momentum for the 2012 Olympic Games in London. Lochte actually relished his duels with Phelps, viewing the occasions as the chance to step up his performances.

"I love a challenge," said Lochte, a multiple NCAA champion for the University of Florida. "[Phelps] is the world's best swimmer ever, and I love racing him. It's fun to race a guy who will go toe-to-toe with you all the way to the end. I respect every-thing he's done, but I always believed I could beat him. I had to believe in myself."

Lochte and Phelps engaged in a split decision at the 2012 Olympics. With Phelps heading into his first retirement, Lochte won the first event of the Games, the 400 individual medley, in dominating fashion, with Phelps finishing off the podium in fourth place. However, Phelps got revenge in the 200 individual medley, leaving Lochte with the silver medal. The bigger shock, though, was Lochte earning only the bronze medal in the 200 backstroke, in which he was the defending champion.

With Phelps out of the sport, Lochte was left alone to carry the USA Swimming banner, and did so admirably. He added world titles in the 200 medley and 200 backstroke in 2013 and in 2015, he won his fourth consecutive world crown in the 200 individual medley, joining Australian Grant Hackett (1500 freestyle) as the only men to win world titles in a single event on four consecutive occasions.

The 2016 Olympiad was supposed to offer the chance at additional hardware, but the trip to Rio de Janeiro proved to be a disaster. Not only did Lochte finish fifth, and off the podium, in the 200 individual medley, his only gold medal was the result of a prelim contribution in the 800 freestyle relay. Then there was what transpired outside the pool.

On the surface, Lochte comes across as aloof and with a surfer-dude personality. He's a practical joker and a daredevil, enjoying a variety of extreme sports, and he took part in a reality show on cable television that painted Lochte as a goof and party guy. That identity was affirmed in Rio when Lochte became caught up in a contro-versy that dominated the headlines as much as any competitive action.

Following the last night of swimming action, Lochte went out with teammates and took part in a night of heavy drinking. By the next morning, Lochte told a story of being robbed at gunpoint, only to have the tale spiral in a range of directions—none positive for the American athlete. Ultimately, it was revealed that Lochte, along with fellow American swimmers Jimmy Feigen, Gunnar Bentz, and Jack Conger, had stopped to use a gas station restroom, only to find the bathroom locked. Along the way, Lochte tore a sign down from its perch and the group was confronted by Brazilian police.

After the police became involved is where the haziness of the incident arises. Lochte stated the officers pointed guns at the group of Americans and demanded money in a shakedown of sorts. Brazilian officials claim the officers were merely seeking restitution for the damages to the sign, and the Americans offered to make payment. However the events actually unfolded, Lochte was charged with reporting a false robbery and was the subject of scorn in Brazil and the United States.

Not only was Lochte vilified for tainting the Olympic Games, his sponsors moved quickly to distance themselves. Speedo and Ralph Lauren, longtime partners of Lochte's, dropped endorsement deals, and USA Swimming eventually levied a 10-month suspension that prevented Lochte from attempting to qualify for the 2017 World Championships.

"After Rio, I was probably the most hated person in the world," Lochte said. "There were a couple of points where I was crying, thinking, 'If I go to bed and never wake up, fine.' You can go from the highest of highs to the lowest of lows."

While the events of Rio will remain a bullet point in Lochte's career, deep down he's been anything but a clown around the pool. He set a singular goal to be the best in the sport, and he once delivered on that goal while establishing a lasting legacy.

"He's got a tremendous work ethic," said Gregg Troy, Lochte's college coach at the University of Florida. "He really likes to train, and he's very coachable. If you can identify a weakness, he'll work real hard to make a change."

Lochte also focused on enhancing the popularity of swimming, something Phelps made a priority. That goal is one of the reasons Lochte is continuing with the sport, a bid to the 2020 Olympics in Tokyo a specific target.

"My main goal is to make swimming bigger than what it is or what it was back in 2008, and the only way I can do that is by going and doing cameos, being on talk shows, doing all those little things to help bring people . . . into swimming more," Lochte said. "Honestly, the only time you ever hear about swimming is during the Olympics. I say to myself and to other people, why can't swimming be like the NBA or the NFL or something like that, because we do have those big championship meets once a year. So why can't we have that [attention]?"

16

Kornelia Ender

Country: East Germany
Birth date: October 25, 1958
Events: Multiple
Olympic medals: Eight
World Championship medals: Ten

Arguably the greatest female swimmer produced by East Germany, Kornelia Ender is both a success and a tragic story. From an achievement standpoint, she was a raging bull, dominating the sport over several events and distances and breaking numerous barriers. Yet she was also part—by no willingness of her own—of the systematic doping program that was implemented by East German coaches in the 1970s and 1980s. Thus, all Ender accomplished is tainted, the sport unaware of what she could have done based on sheer skill and not performance-enhancing assistance.

Barely a teenager at the 1972 Olympic Games in Munich, Ender showed glimpses of what was to come. She totaled three silver medals, two in relay competition and one in the 200 individual medley, where she nearly upended Australian Shane Gould, easily the number 1 female swimmer in the world. By merely staying with Gould, Ender demonstrated her vast talent.

The 1972 Olympics, though, were just the start of a five-year reign in which Ender nearly achieved unbeatable status. Between the 1973 World Championships and the 1975 World Championships, Ender collected 10 medals, eight of which were gold. She earned podium places in the 100 freestyle, 200 freestyle, 100 butterfly, and 200 individual medley, that variety revealing her versatility. Her efforts at the World Championships carried into the 1976 Olympics in Montreal.

While the American men dominated by winning all but one event, Ender was the showstopper on the female side and led the Wundermadchen dominance. The East

German was the gold medalist in the 100 freestyle, 200 freestyle, and 100 butterfly, setting world records in each event. She also helped her country to the gold medal in the 400 medley relay and to a silver medal in the 400 freestyle relay. Years later, Ender had to come to terms with what took place in her training.

"Now, after all this time, I still ask myself whether it could be possible they gave me things because I remember being given injections during training and competition, but this was explained to me as being substances to help me regenerate and recuperate," she said. "It was natural to think this way because the distance swimmers had more injections than we did as sprinters. It's very sad. The only losers in that are the athletes."

The medal count forged by Ender is just a small example of her dominance. During her career, she set world records in the 50 freestyle, 100 freestyle, 200 freestyle, 100 butterfly, 100 backstroke, and 200 individual medley, leaving just the breaststroke as a stroke in which she did not attain a global mark. However, the way she lowered the records is even more astounding.

In the 100 freestyle, Ender set 10 consecutive world records from 1973 to 1976, becoming the first woman to break the 58-, 57-, and 56-second barriers. In just three years, she lowered the world record in the event by nearly three seconds, a time drop that has never been matched over that distance in a similar time frame. Meanwhile, she was the first woman to crack the two-minute barrier in the 200 freestyle. Enshrined in the International Swimming Hall of Fame in 1981, Ender was named World Swimmer of the Year in 1973, 1975, and 1976. She established a stunning 23 individual world records.

At the revelation that she was provided performance-enhancing drugs by East German doctors and coaches, Ender expressed anger in a 1991 interview.

"It is easy for them to state these things now," she said. "The finger of blame is pointed at us, not them, and we knew nothing of these things they did. They deserve [punishment]. The medical men are the real guilty people. They know what they have done. When they gave us things to help us 'regenerate,' we were never asked if we wanted it. It was just given."

17

Alexander Popov

Country: Russia
Birth Date: November 16, 1971
Event: Sprint freestyle
Olympic medals: Nine
World Championship medals: Eleven

Alexander Popov is widely considered the greatest sprint freestyler in history and is the only man to win consecutive Olympic gold medals in the 50 freestyle and 100 freestyle. Aside from possessing vast talent, the Russian was one of the most intense performers of all time and frequently tried to intimidate his competition with a steely stare.

One year after capturing the 100 freestyle title at the 1991 European Championships, Popov shot to the top of his sport by winning gold medals in the 50 freestyle and 100 freestyle at the 1992 Olympic Games in Barcelona, in the process defeating American Matt Biondi. He added silver medals in a pair of relays.

Popov maintained his status as the world's premier sprinter at the 1994 World Championships, again sweeping the sprint events, and then repeated as champion of the 50 freestyle and 100 freestyle at the 1996 Olympic Games in Atlanta. His final Olympic medal, the ninth of his career, was a silver in the 100 freestyle at the 2000 Olympics in Sydney.

"When I go for competitions to Europe or America or even here in Australia, I am always looking for potential challengers," said Popov, who trained in Australia under coach Gennadi Touretski. "If I see any, I have to swim faster and make them feel sick. If they have a little potential, you must get on top of them and kill that enthusiasm right away so they will lose their interest in swimming."

Inducted into the International Swimming Hall of Fame in 2009, Popov nearly lost his life shortly after the 1996 Olympics. While walking with friends down a Moscow street, someone in Popov's group engaged in a verbal dispute with several watermelon vendors. An altercation ensued, and Popov was stabbed in the abdomen and had to undergo emergency surgery to treat the wound. Ultimately, he rebounded from the incident and continued to excel in the sprint events.

"You know, we probably could have gotten out of the situation if it had been handled differently," Popov said of the stabbing incident. "But they approached us, and somebody started talking with them, and they misunderstood us and started to fight. The men didn't know who I was. We were in the wrong place at the wrong time."

Popov was the gold medalist in the 100 freestyle and the silver medalist in the 50 freestyle at the 1998 World Championships and won crowns in both events at the 2003 World Championships. He also added several European titles and finished his career with 11 medals at the World Championships and 26 medals at the European Championships, including 21 gold medals.

At the 2000 Olympics, Popov medaled for the third consecutive Games in the 100 freestyle, claiming silver behind Dutchman Pieter van den Hoogenband. However, there was a misstep in the 50 freestyle, where Popov was a big favorite as the world-record holder. But as Americans Gary Hall Jr. and Anthony Ervin shared the title, Popov struggled to sixth place in a rare subpar performance by a man nicknamed "The Tsar."

Popov set just one world record each in the 50 freestyle and 100 freestyle, but both marks endured for lengthy periods. His clocking of 21.64 in the 50 freestyle at the 2000 Russian Olympic Trials stood as the global standard for nearly eight years. In the 100 freestyle, his 1994 performance of 48.21 stood as the world record for more than six years.

18

Debbie Meyer

Country: United States
Birth date: August 14, 1952
Event: Freestyle
Olympic medals: Three

Lost in the passage of time and the greatness of first Janet Evans and later Katie Ledecky, American Debbie Meyer probably does not receive the attention she deserves. In the late 1960s and during what was an abbreviated career, Meyer displayed a range that was extraordinary and propelled the teenage phenom to the top of her sport.

Adhering to a grueling training schedule, Meyer rose to prominence in the lead-up to the 1968 Olympic Games in Mexico City. At the 1967 Pan American Games, she registered a 10-second victory in the 400 freestyle and won the 800 freestyle by more than 15 seconds, margins that made her opposition appear to be competing in a separate race. During that season, she broke six of her 15 career world records, her marks spanning the 400 freestyle, 800 freestyle, and 1500 freestyle.

A year later was her crowning moment. At the 1968 Games, which marked the introduction of the 200 freestyle and 800 freestyle to the women's program, Meyer walked away with three gold medals, becoming the first swimmer to win three individual events at a single Olympiad. Each of her triumphs arrived in Olympic-record time, with her gold medal in the 800 freestyle highlighted by an 11-second decision.

Meyer seemed headed for a second Olympiad, her training after Mexico City geared toward preparation for the 1972 Games in Munich. En route to that destination, she set several more world records, the latest coming in the 400 freestyle at the 1970 U.S. National Championships. Yet less than a year before the 1972 Olympics, Meyer lost the desire to forge ahead and retired.

"I had every intent to swim in Munich, but seven months before the Games I decided that wasn't in my game plan," Meyer said. "It wasn't fun anymore. Competing wasn't exciting. I don't think there's any one thing [that stood out about my career]. I think just the total package. I loved every minute of it, even the days when I hated working out."

Inducted into the International Swimming Hall of Fame in 1977, Meyer concluded her career with 27 American records and 19 national championships. She was named World Swimmer of the Year by *Swimming World Magazine* in 1967, 1968, and 1969. She was also the 1968 winner of the Sullivan Award, given annually to the best amateur athlete in the United States.

Meyer returned to prominence in conjunction with Ledecky's showing at the 2016 Olympic Games in Rio de Janeiro. By capturing gold medals in the 200 freestyle, 400 freestyle and 800 freestyle, Ledecky equaled Meyer's trifecta from nearly 50 years earlier. At least for a brief moment, Meyer was again thrust into the spotlight.

"She reminds me so much of me 48 years ago," Meyer said, as Ledecky pursued her Rio triple. "It brings back so many wonderful memories of when I was swimming, things that this old brain has forgotten. I love watching her swim, absolutely love it. I love seeing that drive. I love seeing the way she attacks things. The way she swims is very much the way I tried to swim. She said I was her hero growing up. People don't remember what I did. That was 48 years ago. I was taken aback."

19

Roland Matthes

Country: East Germany
Birth date: November 17, 1950
Event: Backstroke
Olympic medals: Eight
World Championship medals: Five

There is little debate over the status of Roland Matthes as one of the best two back-stroke specialists in history, a distinction the East German athlete earned during the late 1960s and into the mid-1970s. Matthes excelled in Olympic and World Championship competition and redefined the backstroke events by significantly lowering the world records in the 100 and 200 distances.

Undefeated during a seven-year period from 1967 to 1974, Matthes posted the first major highlights of his career at the 1968 Olympics in Mexico City. He won the 100 backstroke by more than one second and was the only competitor to break the one-minute barrier. In the 200 backstroke, Matthes captured the gold medal by one second over American Mitch Ivey.

Four years later, Matthes continued to dominate the Olympic scene by again sweeping the backstroke events. Once more, he won both events by more than one second. A year later, at the first World Championships, he pulled off another double in the backstroke disciplines. He repeated as the world champion in the 100 backstroke in 1975 but managed just a fourth-place finish in the 200 backstroke while suffering from the effects of a stomach bug.

Matthes pursued a third consecutive Olympic crown in the 100 backstroke at the 1976 Games in Montreal, but by that time he had been surpassed as the elite backstroker in the world by the American John Naber. Still, Matthes managed to add another Olympic medal to his collection, winning the bronze medal in the 100 backstroke.

The dominance of Matthes can be seen in his world-record-setting ways. In the 100 backstroke, Matthes established seven global standards from 1967 to 1972, lowering the record from 59.1 to 56.3 seconds. His final record lasted for nearly four years. As for the 200 backstroke, Matthes set nine world records from 1967 to 1973, taking the mark down by an astonishing six seconds from 2:07.90 to 2:01.87.

Although the latter part of Matthes's career unfolded during the start of East Germany's systematic doping program, Matthes did not take part in the use of performance-enhancing drugs. His coach, Marlies Grohe-Geissler, did not believe in the cheating that was implemented at the top level of the sport.

"Described as the Rolls-Royce of backstroke swimming, Matthes, highly flexible and capable of turning his arms over his head stretched out with hands tied, covered a [50-meter] lap using some 10 strokes less than many of his rivals," wrote Craig Lord of *Swim News*. "It often appeared to observers as though Matthes was watching the clock and did just enough to set records. The reason: Incentives for the [German Democratic Republic's] 'ambassadors in tracksuits' included better homes and a fast-track up the waiting list for cars and other luxury items."

In addition to excelling in the backstroke, Matthes was a silver medalist at the European Championships in the 100 freestyle and 100 butterfly. Only American Aaron Peirsol is seen on par with Matthes in the backstroke events.

20

Vladimir Salnikov

Country: Soviet Union
Birth date: May 21, 1960
Event: Distance freestyle
Olympic medals: Four
World Championship medals: Six

Distance swimming is often associated with Australian excellence, but an argument can be made for Vladimir Salnikov as the finest distance freestyler in history. Although a segment of his career was short-circuited by political influence, the Soviet Union star put together a résumé for the ages, complete with world records spanning three distances.

Salnikov was a barrier-breaking performer whose introduction to the international stage was marked by a fifth-place finish in the 1500 freestyle at the 1976 Olympics in Montreal. From that point forward, Salnikov was almost untouchable in the distance events, taking his disciplines to heights that previously seemed out of reach.

The 1978 world champion in the 400 and 1500 freestyle events, Salnikov merely set the stage for what was to come at the 1980 Olympics. At a home Games in Moscow, Salnikov was the gold medalist in the 400 freestyle and 1500 freestyle, his winning time of 14:58.27 in the longer event marking the first time an individual broke the 15-minute barrier. The only element missing from Salnikov's virtuoso effort was a showdown with reigning champion Brian Goodell, who did not receive the opportunity to defend his title because of the U.S. boycott of the Moscow Games.

Once again the world champion in the 400 freestyle and 1500 freestyle at the 1982 World Championships, Salnikov soon understood the disappointment felt by Goodell. In 1984, the Soviet Union led an Eastern bloc boycott of the Olympic Games in Los Angeles, a decision that denied Salnikov his chance to repeat. Given his dominance at the time, additional gold medals would have been a likely outcome.

Continuing on to the 1988 Olympics, Salnikov was not considered a strong contender for a gold medal at the Seoul Games, deemed over the hill at age 28. However, the Soviet summoned some of his past magic and won the 1500 freestyle by more than two seconds, giving him victories in the event eight years apart. It was an accomplishment not overlooked by his fellow competitors.

"If [the 1980 Olympics] marked his entry into the club of sporting immortals, it was his Magnum Opus eight years on, beyond another Olympic boycott (this time affecting those on the other side of a political divide) and in the midst of a comeback written up as doomed to fail, that brought him universal acclaim and recognition," once wrote Craig Lord of *Swim News*. "When Salnikov, fresh from a second, stunning 30-lap Games victory, walked into the athletes' dining hall in the Olympic Village in Seoul 1988 a little shy of midnight on September 25, 1988—medal ceremony, drug testing, media interviews, and television appearances out of the way—some 300 fellow competitors, coaches, and officials from all sports spontaneously laid down their cutlery and gave a standing ovation to honor the 'Monster of the Waves,' as he was known in the Soviet Union."

During the course of his career, Salnikov set six world records in the 400 freestyle, four in the 800 freestyle, and three in the 1500 freestyle. His final world record in the 1500 freestyle remained on the books for nearly eight years.

21

Grant Hackett

Country: Australia
Birth date: May 9, 1980
Event: Distance freestyle
Olympic medals: Seven
World Championship medals: Nineteen

The latest and greatest of the Australian distance legends, Grant Hackett was untouchable in the 1500 freestyle for the majority of his career while also flourishing in the middle-distance events. However, a good portion of his career coincided with the reign of countryman Ian Thorpe, timing that frequently left Hackett in the background.

As Hackett made his way up the global distance ladder, his first major challenge was cracking the invincibility of Kieren Perkins, the fellow Australian who was the Olympic champion in the 1500 freestyle at the 1992 and 1996 Games. Achieving

that goal was a process for Hackett, who won the world title in the 1500 freestyle in 1998. Still, he needed to knock off Perkins on the biggest stage, an opportunity that afforded itself at the 2000 Olympics in Sydney.

With Perkins seeking a third consecutive Olympic crown, Hackett played the role of spoiler and taught his idol a lesson with a commanding five-second triumph.

Hackett's victory not only started a sterling run by Hackett but also marked the changing of the guard in distance swimming. Considering some gamesmanship by Perkins, it was an even more satisfying triumph for Hackett.

"You fall in love with the event but also the man who was creating these world records. He was an Australian icon. He was my hero," Hackett said of Perkins. "It's an interesting dynamic. You watch and admire him and the feats he has been able to accomplish, and then, suddenly, you're standing on the blocks with him as your number 1 rival. It's a weird shift. You go from idol to rival, and it takes a bit of adjustment, particularly when he tries to intimidate you the whole time. I respected him, but every time he said something, it just fired me up. I used it in the pool, used it in training and in competition, and it obviously worked for me. I had this misconception, probably, that he would be happy to see another Australian coming along in the 1500 and encourage it, but instead he looked on it as a rivalry and someone encroaching on his territory."

Hackett followed the Sydney Olympics with some of his best performances. At the 2001 World Championships, he set a world record in the 1500 freestyle that lasted a decade and added silver medals behind Thorpe in the 400 freestyle and 800 freestyle. Two years later, he was the world champion in the 800 freestyle and 1500 freestyle and again took silver to Thorpe in the 400 free.

Competing at the 2004 Olympics, Hackett repeated as the champion of the 1500 freestyle despite racing with a partially collapsed lung. That effort, because of the endurance-based nature of the event, is viewed as one of the gutsiest swims in history. Hackett, too, finished second in the 400 freestyle to Thorpe, although he gave his rival the best challenge of his career.

With Thorpe retired, Hackett finally had the distance spotlight all to himself at the 2005 World Championships in Montreal. Hackett won the 400 freestyle, 800 freestyle, and 1500 freestyle and earned a silver medal in the 200 freestyle. In the 800 freestyle, Hackett broke one of Thorpe's world records, a considerable achievement, and his world title in the 1500 freestyle was his fourth in a row, a feat never before accomplished in any event. The totality of that performance propelled Hackett to World Swimmer of the Year and allowed him to escape from Thorpe's overwhelming shadow, not that Hackett was frustrated playing second fiddle to Thorpe.

"It is great. It is an awesome feeling to be able to achieve something like that and to be the first person in history to do it," Hackett said. "For me, it is something that I have been focusing on. Now that it is over and I have completed it, it is really satisfying. And it's always nice to get a world record and great to get one that was [Thorpe's]. He's one of the greatest ever. Being the 1500 record holder, I wanted the 800, too. There's no reason to get uptight when people ask me about Ian. He deserves the recognition. It's an honor to do this."

The final two years of Hackett's initial run did not match what he was able to produce during his prime seasons, but he remained an international force. The Australian earned a silver medal in the 400 freestyle at the 2007 World Championships and was the silver medalist in the 1500 freestyle at the 2008 Olympic Games, where he came up short of becoming the first man to win an event at three straight Olympiads.

A comeback was made in 2015, with Hackett qualifying for the World Championships and earning a bronze medal as a preliminary swimmer in the 800 freestyle relay. But a push for another Olympic nod fizzled out a year later. More, Hackett found himself dealing with mental health issues that led to an incident with another passenger aboard a flight and Hackett's arrest after a disturbance at his parents' house. As a result of his personal-life struggles, and his use of sleeping pills, Hackett sought treatment at a rehab center. He's also forged a close friendship with Michael Phelps, who, like Hackett, has dealt with mental health issues.

"It's hard when you've done something that many people see as extraordinary, but as a person you're not," Hackett said. "It's almost like you're separated from the pack. You're having to try to grow as a person and work out who you are in this really difficult set of circumstances, under a microscope."

Hackett once held world records in the 200 freestyle, 800 freestyle, and 1500 freestyle and was an eight-time medalist at the Commonwealth Games and a 13-time medalist at the Pan Pacific Championships.

22

Murray Rose

Country: Australia
Birth date: January 6, 1939
Death date: April 15, 2012
Event: Distance freestyle
Olympic medals: Six

Murray Rose is revered as one of the best distance swimmers in history and one of the first in a long line of world-class distance freestylers from Australia. As a 17-year-old at the 1956 Olympics in Melbourne, Rose won gold medals in all three events he contested, in the process becoming the youngest swimmer in history to win three titles in a single Olympiad.

Aside from helping Australia win the gold medal in the 800 freestyle relay, Rose dominated his competition in the 400 freestyle and 1500 freestyle. He captured the gold medal in the 400 freestyle by more than three seconds and won his second individual title by winning the 1500 freestyle by nearly two seconds.

Four years later, Rose won three more Olympic medals, including a repeat of his championship in the 400 freestyle, again prevailing over Japan's Tsuyoshi Yamanaka by more than three seconds. However, he was unable to duplicate his gold medal in the 1500 freestyle, finishing in the silver-medal position behind countryman John Konrads. His third medal was a silver in the 800 freestyle relay.

"Murray Rose was certainly one of the greatest of all time," Konrads said after Rose's death in early 2012. "There's Mark Spitz in the sprints and so on and now Michael Phelps, but they're short-distance swimmers in the professional era. I think taking into consideration the amateur era, Murray was the greatest of all time."

During his career, Rose set world records in the 400, 800, and 1500 freestyles. His two world records in the 1500 freestyle were separated by eight years, a testament to Rose's longevity and ability to remain at the top of his sport. However, he was denied the chance to compete in the 1964 Olympics, where he likely would have added to his medal total.

A five-time NCAA champion at the University of Southern California, Rose graduated from the school in 1962 and briefly pursued a career in acting. But because he was based in the United States, Australian officials did not allow him to compete in their country's Olympic Trials, which put an end to the possibility of Rose competing in Tokyo.

Rose routinely spoke to younger swimmers about their pursuits and how to handle big occasions, such as competing in the Olympic Games. His insights were appreciated by Kieren Perkins, who joined Rose as a distance legend and multiple Olympic champion.

"We talked about what the actual Games itself would be like," Perkins said of Rose's mentoring. "Being a 1500-meter swimmer, the thing he left me with was just this notion around holding your rhythm and not letting the middle of the race get away from you and the aura of what it was you were a part of. And that was really quite significant for me because it was the difference between breaking world records and not. That was something that I carried with me really for the rest of my career."

23

Kristin Otto

Country: East Germany
Birth date: February 7, 1966
Events: Freestyle, backstroke, and butterfly
Olympic medals: Six
World Championship medals: Nine

Whether it was freestyle, backstroke, or butterfly, Kristin Otto had the discipline mastered, such was her extraordinary talent. How Otto is remembered on a historical basis, however, is up for debate. As gifted as the East German athlete was in the water, her accomplishments will always be tainted by the revelation that she was administered performance-enhancing drugs as part of a systematic doping program overseen by her coaches.

Emerging as the 1982 world champion in the 100 backstroke, a title that was complemented by a pair of relay gold medals, Otto was destined for an Olympic breakout at the 1984 Games in Los Angeles. But because of the Eastern bloc boycott orchestrated by the Soviet Union in retaliation for the U.S. boycott of the 1980 Olympics in Moscow, Otto was forced to wait for her Olympic moment.

Otto bided her time in impressive fashion, proving herself to be one of the most versatile performers of her era—and of all time. At the 1986 World Championships, Otto was a six-time medalist, including individual crowns in the 200 individual medley and 100 freestyle. She added silver medals in the 50 freestyle and 100 butterfly and set herself up for two years later, when she would shine at the 1988 Olympics in Seoul.

Becoming the first woman to win six gold medals in an Olympiad, Otto grabbed four individual gold medals, victories that were spread over three strokes. Aside from doubling in the 50 freestyle and 100 freestyle, Otto was triumphant in the 100 backstroke and 100 butterfly. She completed her six-for-six performance with a pair of gold medals in relay action, and she could have matched Mark Spitz's seven gold medals from Munich in 1972 had there been a third women's relay, as was the case with the men's program.

"She's the best because she works harder than the rest," said Wolfgang Richter, an East German coach. "She's tough [mentally]. She cannot stand to lose."

Working harder may have been an accurate assessment but only because Otto was part of a doping program that supplied her with an unfair advantage. Although she has steadfastly denied knowledge of performance-enhancing drug use during her career, documentation exists from the German Ministry for State Security (Stasi), which confirms that Otto was given illegal drugs to boost her athletic talent.

Additionally, several athletes who competed with Otto have publicly revealed her usage of steroids. Because of the paperwork confirming her doping involvement, Otto's profile at the International Swimming Hall of Fame, to which she was inducted in 1993, contains a disclaimer acknowledging her illegal practices. The drug use also calls into question where she should be ranked among the all-time greats or whether she should be considered at all.

"When she claims she cleaned up in Seoul in 1988 without taking anything, then I can only say she didn't win six golds by drinking buttermilk," said Rica Reinisch, a three-time Olympic gold medalist who herself was part of the East German doping program.

An 11-time medalist at the European Championships, including nine gold, Otto was named *Swimming World Magazine* World Swimmer of the Year on three occasions. She set two individual world records during her career in the 100 freestyle and 200 freestyle.

24

Aaron Peirsol

Country: United States
Birth date: July 23, 1983
Event: Backstroke
Olympic medals: Seven
World Championship medals: Twelve

A lively debate can be held when discussing the greatest male backstroker in history. Some will argue for the selection of East Germany's Roland Matthes, a star of the late

1960s and first half of the 1970s. Others will make a case for the American Aaron Peirsol, the undisputed king of the backstroke for the first decade of the new millennium. Wherever Peirsol falls, his career was extraordinary.

It's difficult to maintain consistency in the sport for lengthy time frames, but that's exactly what Peirsol managed to accomplish. From his Olympic breakthrough as a 17-year-old to his retirement a decade later, Peirsol was routinely atop the medals podium and threatening world records, always saving his best performances for the most pressure-packed moments.

At the 2000 Olympics in Sydney, Peirsol scored his first significant accomplishment, capturing the silver medal in the 200 backstroke behind countryman Lenny Krayzelburg. From that point forward, it was the laid-back Peirsol who ruled his stroke. By 2001, he had won his first world title, and by 2002, he had his first world record, both achievements in the 200 backstroke. He was considered, along with Michael Phelps, to be one of the leading forces for the United States for many years to come, and neither man slipped on that promise.

For his career, Peirsol won 12 medals at the World Championships, including 10 gold medals. He won three consecutive championships in the 200 backstroke in 2001, 2003, and 2005 and threepeated in the 100 backstroke in 2003, 2005, and 2007. While he originally broke out in the longer backstroke, he clearly demonstrated impressive speed to stand atop the 100 backstroke as well.

An NCAA champion at the University of Texas, Peirsol produced his best showings at the Olympic Games. In 2004 in Athens, he was the champion of the 100 backstroke and 200 backstroke, along with helping the 400 medley relay to victory. Peirsol's triumph in the 200 backstroke, however, was not without controversy, as he was initially disqualified before that ruling was overturned.

There was speculation that Peirsol's disqualification stemmed from some comments he made earlier in the meet. After American teammate Brendan Hansen finished second to Japan's Kosuke Kitajima in the 100 breaststroke, Peirsol accused Kitajima of cheating by using illegal tactics at two points during the race. Peirsol's disqualification temporarily handed Austrian Markus Rogan the gold medal, but after the ruling was voided, Rogan was bumped back to the silver medal. It was a decision the Austrian understood, and it also was what Peirsol obviously desired.

"I knew I didn't do anything wrong," Peirsol said. "It was a roller coaster. I am sad for those who thought they were on the podium and were then thrown out of it after my race was made valid."

At his third Olympiad, in 2008 in Beijing, Peirsol repeated a pair of his gold medals, successfully defending titles in the 100 backstroke and 400 medley relay. He had to settle for silver in the 200 backstroke, though, as countryman Ryan Lochte earned the gold medal. It was the identical finish to the previous year's World Championships, when Lochte snapped Peirsol's seven-year winning streak in the 200 backstroke.

After setting a world record on the way to gold in the 200 backstroke at the 2009 World Championships, a record that remains standing, Peirsol ended his career by winning the gold medal in the 100 backstroke at the 2010 Pan Pacific Championships. He retired having broken six world records in the 100 backstroke and seven world marks in the 200 backstroke. There was nothing left to prove.

"I ended up doing everything I set out to do," Peirsol said. "It was an amazing feeling to know that I was done when I was on that podium [at the Pan Pacific Championships]. I always told myself that when I was done, I would be done. When I look back on my career, I can smile."

25

Michael Gross

Country: West Germany
Birth date: June 17, 1964
Events: Freestyle and butterfly
Olympic medals: Six
World Championship medals: Thirteen

Germany's Michael Gross is one of the most imposing figures to ever walk the pool deck. Standing six feet seven and with a wingspan of nearly seven and a half feet, Gross literally towered over the majority of his opposition. His accomplishments, too, dwarfed what most athletes ever dream of achieving.

Nicknamed the Albatross, Gross burst onto the global scene at the 1982 World Championships, where he won five medals, including individual titles in the 200 freestyle and the 200 butterfly, events that became his trademark disciplines. The medals were the first of 13 won by Gross over the course of three World Championships. A year later, Gross set the first of his world records and walked away from the 1983 European Championships with five medals, highlighted by individual triumphs in the 200 freestyle, 100 butterfly, and 200 butterfly. It all set the stage for his first Olympiad.

Heavily hyped by the media heading into the 1984 Olympics in Los Angeles, Gross excelled with a four-medal performance that included world-record efforts in the 100 butterfly and 200 freestyle. His victory in the butterfly arrived over Pablo Morales, the favorite from the United States. His win in the 200 freestyle was by nearly two seconds.

"I think he's the best swimmer ever," gushed John Naber, a five-time medalist for the United States at the 1976 Olympics in Montreal. "If he were an American, he could win three relays plus four other golds. He's better than Mark Spitz."

As impressive as Gross was at the 1984 Games, he wasn't invincible, as was the case when Spitz won seven gold medals at the 1972 Olympics in Munich. Despite being the world-record holder, Gross was beaten to the wall in the 200 butterfly by Australian Jon Sieben, a relative unknown. It was a shocking loss that took some of the luster off his previous gold medals.

Gross continued to flourish after the Olympics, winning six gold medals at the 1985 European Championships and repeating as world champion in the 200 freestyle and 200 butterfly in 1986. He set three more world records in the 200 butterfly, his signature event. For all his success, Gross had a philosophical approach to his swimming.

"I'm never very nervous, especially before a big competition, because I tell myself that I have nothing to lose," Gross said. "I do my best, and if someone is better than me in the race, I still do not worry about him because I have done my best. If you know this, you will always be happy. It's not important to win only."

At the 1988 Olympics, Gross was forced to accept his outlook on the sport. He managed to win the gold medal that eluded him four years earlier in the 200 butterfly, but the 200 freestyle proved to be a disappointment. The world-record holder in the event, Gross didn't only fail to win the gold medal but also failed to medal at all, finishing fifth in a race won by Australian Duncan Armstrong.

Gross capped his career at the 1991 World Championships, winning four medals, including silvers in the butterfly events. With the 1992 Olympics just a year away, Gross could have easily hung on and been a factor in a third Olympiad. However, he decided to leave the sport and move his focus to new endeavors.

"The worst thing in life is to have no wishes, no goals, because then you have nothing to reach for, nothing to live for," said Gross, who was inducted into the International Swimming Hall of Fame in 1995.

Gross is one of only a few men in history to simultaneously hold three world records. At one point, Gross was the world-record holder in the 100 butterfly, 200 butterfly, and 200 freestyle. He was also a 19-time medalist at the European Championships, 13 of those medals being gold.

26

Inge de Bruijn

Country: Netherlands
Birth date: August 24, 1973
Events: Sprint freestyle and butterfly
Olympic medals: Eight
World Championship medals: Six

Most followers of the sport know Inge de Bruijn as a great of the sprinting ranks and one of the dominant performers of her era. What is frequently overlooked, however, is the nature of her story, a comeback tale with a fruitful ending. Now regarded as the finest Dutch female swimmer in history, de Bruijn faced a difficult stretch in her career in the mid-1990s, a slump so great that it threatened to derail her dreams. Rather than back down, though, de Bruijn fought her way to the top.

There were no medals for de Bruijn at her first Olympiad in 1992, but there were signs from the teenager that big things could be in the offing, such as four medals from the 1991 European Championships. Quickly, though, de Bruijn's career hit a pothole, and she failed to qualify for the 1996 Olympics in Atlanta. That setback led to de Bruijn's connection with coaching great Paul Bergen, a match that proved to be highly successful.

By 1999, de Bruijn was the European champion in the 50 freestyle and the 100 butterfly, and her career was again on the rise, hitting its pinnacle at the 2000 Olympic Games in Sydney. At her second Olympiad, de Bruijn was the toast of the women's swimming competition, capturing gold medals in the 50 freestyle, 100 freestyle, and 100 butterfly. She added a silver medal in the 400 freestyle relay.

"I'm floating on a big cloud," de Bruijn said. "I hope I don't land for a long time. I knew I could do great, but I didn't know if I would do three gold medals. It's easy for the outsiders to predict three gold medals, but you still have to do it. You're all alone up there. You've got to do it yourself."

Her confidence at an all-time high, de Bruijn surged forward after Sydney and captured five individual gold medals between the 2001 World Championships and the 2003 World Championships, including back-to-back victories in the 50 freestyle and 50 butterfly. She was the queen of sprinting and had no true rival.

At the 2004 Olympics in Athens, de Bruijn enjoyed further success by repeating as the champion of the 50 freestyle and adding a silver medal in the 100 freestyle and a bronze medal in the 100 butterfly. She also helped the Dutch to bronze in the 400 freestyle relay.

De Bruijn set four world records during her career in the 50 freestyle, lowering the mark by almost four-tenths of a second, and established two world records in the 100 freestyle. In the 100 butterfly, de Bruijn set three world records and took the global standard down by more than one second in 2000. Because of her success, de Bruijn was often the target of doping accusations, although she never failed a test for performance-enhancing drugs.

"You know the people are stupid, especially people who are into swimming, especially coaches who say that. They shouldn't be here," said Jacco Verhaeren, de Bruijn's Dutch coach. "If I thought anyone used drugs or whatever, I wouldn't be here. I think it's a little bit of jealousy. I don't know why they do that. It makes me sad, but that's it, and I don't want to think about it."

De Bruijn was inducted into the International Swimming Hall of Fame in 2009.

27

Natalie Coughlin

Country: United States
Birth date: August 23, 1982
Events: Multiple
Olympic medals: Twelve
World Championship medals: Eighteen

As the title of her book indicated, Natalie Coughlin was the Golden Girl of American swimming for more than a decade, etching herself as one of the best backstrokers in the history of the sport. But Coughlin, was a star beyond the backstroke, too, flourishing in the freestyle, butterfly, and individual medley. It's not surprising, then, to find her so high on this list.

Coughlin's emergence as an international star was supposed to take place in 2000. The first person in history to qualify for the U.S. Olympic Trials in every event, Coughlin was a developing force. But a shoulder injury incurred through overintensified training derailed Coughlin's upward surge and left her without a bid to the Sydney Games. Simultaneously, Coughlin questioned her love for the sport.

"The whole experience was incredibly trying," she said. "I ended up hating swimming. I didn't care. I wasn't happy, I wasn't upset. I was indifferent. I just thought, well, that's over with. I just wanted to go to college and have a different environment, a different everything."

Following those struggles, Coughlin became a top-flight performer. Attending the University of California, Berkeley, Coughlin developed a tremendous relationship—personal and professional—with coach Teri McKeever. Together, they accomplished just about everything they set out to achieve.

A year after her disappointing showing at the Olympic Trials, Coughlin was the gold medalist in the 100 backstroke at the 2001 World Championships, a medal that was the first of 20 she won at Worlds. During her career, she medaled individually at the World Championships in the 50 backstroke, 100 backstroke, 100 freestyle, and 100 butterfly. She was also the most reliable relay swimmer in the U.S. arsenal, helping 13 relays to the podium, including six to the top step.

As successful as Coughlin was at the World Championships, she was even greater at the Olympic Games. While her medal count is higher at the World Championships, the stage at the Olympics is much greater, and Coughlin never disappointed under considerable pressure and expectations.

At the 2004 Olympics in Athens, Coughlin walked away with a gold medal in the 100 backstroke and a bronze medal in the 100 freestyle in addition to being a member of three medal-winning relays. Four years later, she was even better. Not only did Coughlin repeat as champion of the 100 backstroke, but she again won bronze in the 100 freestyle and showed her versatility with a bronze-medal effort in the 200 individual medley. There were also three more relay medals. Her repeat in the 100 backstroke was certainly her highlight of the 2008 Games in Beijing.

"I didn't feel great going into this meet," Coughlin said. "The last few days, I wasn't feeling as strong as I was hoping to mentally. Regardless, I was able to get my head together and perform today. The 100 back has been progressing faster than any other female event, I think. For me to win gold in such a strong, strong event, I was really proud. I think that's why I was crying like a baby on the medal stand."

Coughlin had visions of adding several more medals at the 2012 Olympics, but struggles at the Olympic Trials limited her to racing only in the preliminary heats of the 400 freestyle relay. When the United States won the bronze medal in the final, Coughlin had the 12th Olympic medal of her career, a total that is tied for the most in history by a female swimmer.

At the collegiate level, Coughlin won 11 of a possible 12 individual NCAA titles and became the first woman in history to break the one-minute barrier in the 100 backstroke, accomplishing that feat in 2002. During her career, she set the world record in the 100 backstroke on five occasions and won 16 medals at the Pan Pacific Championships.

Like Michael Phelps on the male side, Coughlin became a recognizable figure outside the pool, appearing on the ninth season of the television show *Dancing with the Stars*. She's also been a guest judge on *Iron Chef America*, an appearance that was related to her passion for cooking.

28

Kosuke Kitajima

Country: Japan
Birth date: September 22, 1982
Event: Breaststroke
Olympic medals: Seven
World Championship medals: Eleven

Japan's Kosuke Kitajima is the greatest
male breaststroker in history and the
only man to repeat as the Olympic
champion in the 100 breaststroke
and 200 breaststroke in consecutive
Olympiads. One of the hallmarks of
his career was his ability to perform at
his best under pressure and when the
stakes were highest.

Kitajima first gained notice on the
international scene in 2000 and 2001.
After just missing a medal in the 100
breaststroke at the 2000 Olympics
in Sydney with a fourth-place finish, Kitajima earned a bronze medal
in the 200 breaststroke at the 2001
World Championships. In late 2002,
he etched himself as the man to beat in the breaststroke when he took down the
10-year-old world record of American Mike Barrowman in the 200 breaststroke.

The 2003 world champion in the 100 and 200 breaststroke events, Kitajima repeated that feat at the 2004 Olympic Games in Athens. While he won the 200 distance in commanding fashion, Kitajima's victory in the 100 breaststroke was controversial. Video footage of the race showed Kitajima using an illegal dolphin kick off the start and turn, a maneuver that ultimately enabled the Japanese swimmer to defeat American rival Brendan Hansen. Kitajima's tactics, which were not cited as violations by officials, agitated Hansen's teammates.

"He knew what he was doing. It's cheating," said Aaron Peirsol, who won Olympic titles in both backstroke events. "Something needs to be done about that. It's just ridiculous. You take a huge dolphin kick, and that gives you that extra momentum, but he knows that you can't see that from underwater."

Hansen regained the upper hand in the rivalry in 2005 and 2006, winning the 100 breaststroke and 200 breaststroke ahead of Kitajima at the World Championships and Pan Pacific Championships, respectively. Hansen also defeated Kitajima in the 100 breaststroke at the 2007 World Championships, although Kitajima was the world champion in the 200 breaststroke, an event Hansen missed because of illness.

However, at the 2008 Olympic Games in Beijing, Kitajima was unbeatable and demonstrated his talent of coming through at the biggest moments. He set a world record en route to winning the 100 distance and established an Olympic record in prevailing in the 200 breaststroke. Kitajima took a year off in 2009 but returned in 2010 to win his specialty events at the Pan Pacific Championships. He also won the silver medal in the 200 breaststroke at the 2011 World Championships.

Attempting to win three consecutive Olympic titles in each breaststroke discipline at the 2012 Games in London, Kitajima failed to medal in both events. However, he helped Japan win the silver medal in the 400 medley relay. For his career, Kitajima won seven Olympic medals—four individual and three in relay action—and 11 medals at the World Championships. He also set five world records.

"Kosuke does not have an imposing physical stature that defines his success," said Dave Salo, who coached Kitajima during the latter half of his career. "He is probably the most efficient breaststroke swimmer I have ever witnessed. His coach from Japan believes that his ankle speed is the source of his speed. I think that, coupled with his ability to hold his body core in the most efficient position, is the key to his success. He probably carries the least amount of drag of any breaststroke swimmer that I have worked with."

29

Duke Kahanamoku

Country: United States
Birth date: August 24, 1890
Death: January 22, 1968
Event: Freestyle
Olympic medals: Five

Most people know Duke Kahanamoku as the Father of Surfing, but as much as the Hawaiian did for that sport, he was equally famous for his swimming exploits. In freestyle events extending from the 50-yard distance to the 220-yard distance, Kahanamoku was far ahead of his time, even posting performances that were difficult for some of the sport's officials to believe.

Kahanamoku made his first international splash at the 1912 Olympic Games in Stockholm, where he easily won the gold medal in the 100 freestyle and was a member of the U.S. 800 freestyle relay, which won the silver medal. His victory in the 100 freestyle was not unexpected, however, as Kahanamoku had broken the world record in the event by more than four seconds the previous year. Because he broke the record by such an extensive margin, the AAU was skeptical of its legitimacy.

"He first startled the swimming world by shattering both the 50 and 100 yard world records on the anniversary of Hawaiian annexation day, August 2, 1911, just 12 days before his 21st birthday—doing 24.2 in the 50, or 1.6 seconds better than the record, and 55.4 in the 100, 4.6 seconds better than the record," reads Kahanamoku's International Swimming Hall of Fame profile. "Unfortunately the [officials were] all Hawaiian, and the times were so unbelievable that the Amateur Athletic Union, headquartered in New York, refused to recognize them in spite of the careful reports that were compiled showing that the course in Honolulu Harbor had been measured before the race and three times after; had been surveyed by a registered surveyor, that the swimmers were swimming against the tide; and that his nearest competitor, Lawrence Cunha, was 30 feet behind."

Kahanamoku didn't get the chance to defend his Olympic crown until the 1920 Games, as the 1916 Olympics were canceled by World War I. Despite the eight-year gap between Olympiads, Kahanamoku won the gold medal again in 1920. Four years later, he was the silver medalist in the 100 freestyle, finally falling from the top of the sport because of the emergence of Johnny Weissmuller. In 1920, he also helped the United States to the gold medal in the 800 free relay.

Had the 1916 Games not been canceled, Kahanamoku likely would have won the gold medal in the 100 freestyle, and with his victory in 1920, he would have won three straight titles in the event. That was a feat not accomplished until Australian Dawn Fraser pulled off the threepeat in the 100 freestyle in 1964. No man won three consecutive Olympic titles until Michael Phelps did so in the 200 individual medley and 100 butterfly in 2012, with Phelps making it four straight 200 medley wins with a triumph in Rio de Janeiro in 2016.

Following his swimming career, Kahanamoku became one of the world's most famous surfers, his popularity in that sport exceeding the prominence he gained in swimming. Kahanamoku is widely regarded as the man who took surfing from Hawaii and made it famous around the world.

30

Shirley Babashoff

Country: United States
Birth date: January 31, 1957
Event: Freestyle
Olympic medals: Eight
World Championship medals: Ten

At a glance, the career portfolio of American Shirley Babashoff is impressive, high-lighted by eight medals in Olympic competition and 10 medals in World Champi-onship action. Yet Babashoff's career could have been much more impressive had she not been the primary victim of the systematic doping program orchestrated by East Germany during the 1970s and 1980s.

One of the best freestylers in history, boasting range from the 100 distance through the 1500 distance, Babashoff frequently found herself standing below an East German woman on the medals stand and fully knowing that her competitors had used performance-enhancing drugs to defeat her.

At the 1972 Olympics, as a 15-year-old, Babashoff won a gold medal in the 400 freestyle relay and earned silver medals in the 100 freestyle and 200 freestyle, fin-ishing behind an American and an Australian. After that appearance, her struggles with the East German doping program began. At the 1973 World Championships, Babashoff captured four silver medals, with three of her finishes coming behind the East Germans.

Babashoff had greater success at the 1975 World Championships, winning gold medals in the 200 freestyle and 400 freestyle, but her silver medals in the 100 free-style and in two relay events were at the hands of East German athletes. She also won a bronze medal in the 800 freestyle, and her six-medal haul set Babashoff up for the 1976 Olympics.

The Olympic Games in Montreal, however, proved to be a heartbreaking affair for Babashoff. She won the silver medal in the 200 freestyle, 400 freestyle, 800 freestyle, and 400 medley relay, beaten out for the gold medal each time by East German athletes. The only positive was the stunning victory by the United States in the 400 freestyle relay, in which the Americans narrowly edged East Germany with Babashoff swimming the anchor leg.

In addition to falling to drug-enhanced opponents, Babashoff was vilified in the media for publicly accusing East Germany's athletes of using steroids. Babashoff was the first individual to openly levy accusations against the East Germans, and her decision to speak up was seen as sour grapes and earned Babashoff the nickname "Surly Shirley."

"They had gotten so big, and when we heard their voices, we thought we were in a coed locker room," Babashoff said of seeing and hearing the East German women. "I don't know why it wasn't obvious to other people, too. I guess I was the scapegoat. Someone had to blame somebody. Something bad had to happen, and it had to happen to me. I didn't get the gold. I got the silver, so I was a loser."

Years after her retirement from the sport and her induction into the International Swimming Hall of Fame in 1982, Babashoff was partially vindicated when it was officially revealed that East Germany had taken part in a systematic doping program. Still, the International Olympic Committee did not strike the results from the record books and did not award those who finished behind the East Germans with improved places and medals. To this day, Babashoff is bitter over the handling of the situation.

"Everyone should be compensated somewhat or just acknowledged," Babashoff said. "Even our own Olympic Committee should step up and have an event where they can invite those who are still alive and recognize them, perhaps with a commemorative medal, or at least say, 'We know that this has been hard for you.' They should at least acknowledge the women. Some people want to think that the issue is over. From our side of it, the whole issue has been shoved under the carpet. I think it is sad. So many women deserved their medals. They were cheated out of their medals at the Olympics. We would like to get what we earned. We were going for the medals, not the cash. We were amateurs. We worked so hard. We earned it, and it was stolen right in front of everyone's face, and no one did anything about it. It was like watching a bank robbery where they just let the crooks go and then say, 'It's okay.'"

31

Leisel Jones

Country: Australia
Birth date: August 30, 1985
Event: Breaststroke
Olympic medals: Nine
World Championship medals: Fourteen

Thanks to a combination of excellence and longevity, Australian Leisel Jones is revered as one of the premier women breaststrokers in history. She first broke onto the global scene as a 15-year-old at the 2000 Olympics in Sydney and was among the elite in her stroke from 2000 to 2004. From 2005 to 2008, however, Jones was the best of the breaststroke bunch.

After winning the silver medal in the 100 breaststroke at the 2000 Games, Jones was among the favorites for gold at the 2004 Olympics in Athens. But the Aussie didn't match the expectations that surrounded her as she was the bronze medalist in the 100 breaststroke and the silver medalist in the 200 breaststroke. Jones was not pleased with her results and outwardly displayed her disappointment, something that elicited criticism.

"Jones is suffering from having a swollen head, and unfortunately that is not going to get her very far in the sport, especially if she continues to handle herself the way she did," said Dawn Fraser, the Australian legend who won three consecutive Olympic titles in the 100 freestyle from 1956 to 1964. "In the trials, she turned her back on her rivals, and she did the same thing at the Olympics. She's got to be taught what to do in these situations because she came across like a spoiled brat, and that's unfortunate because people will remember that."

Jones's disappointment might have rubbed some the wrong way, but it clearly lit a fire. She was the world champion in the 100 breaststroke and 200 breaststroke in

2005 and followed with a sweep of the breaststroke events at the 2006 Commonwealth Championships. At the 2007 World Championships in Melbourne, she satisfied her home-nation fans by repeating as the champion in the 100 breaststroke and 200 breaststroke. During this run, Jones set world records in both events, standards that were more than a second clear of any rival.

At the 2008 Olympics, Jones vanquished the last of her demons by becoming an Olympic champion in the 100 breaststroke, holding off American Rebecca Soni. They swapped places in the 200 breaststroke, but Jones was elated with her victory. She also won a gold medal as a member of the 400 medley relay for the second straight Olympiad.

"A little bit of shock and probably more relief I guess," Jones said of her Olympic triumph. "It has been a long journey. It's been a long eight years. And I think just a lot of relief that the training was definitely worth it. I couldn't care less about the time. An Olympic gold is an Olympic gold."

Jones pursued a fourth consecutive medal in the 100 breaststroke at the 2012 Olympics but finished fifth in the final. However, she collected a silver medal in the 400 medley relay, the ninth Olympic medal of her career. That mark is tied with Ian Thorpe for the most by an Australian swimmer.

32

Yana Klochkova

Country: Ukraine
Birth date: August 7, 1982
Events: Individual medley and freestyle
Olympic medals: Five
World Championship medals: Six

Most of the swimming success from the former republics of the Soviet Union has come from Russia, which produced the likes of Alexander Popov and Denis Pankratov. But Ukraine, too, has played a role in the development of standouts, with multievent star Yana Klochkova leading the way.

Klochkova shot to the forefront of the sport in the late 1990s, when she emerged as a major factor in the individual medley events and 400 freestyle at the European Championships. After securing a silver medal in the 400 individual medley and a bronze medal in the 200 individual medley at the 1997 European Championships, Klochkova rose to gold medalist in both events at the 1999 version of the meet, where she also was the bronze medalist in the 400 freestyle. Her effort was merely a precursor of what was to come.

A tireless worker who felt destined to excel in the pool, Klochkova was one of the highlight performers at the 2000 Olympics in Sydney. In addition to sweeping the medley events, her 400 individual medley triumph arriving in world-record time, Klochkova picked up a silver medal in the 800 freestyle.

"I've never really thought of doing anything else," Klochkova said. "I've trained for a long time, but you have to if you want to be recognized as a top swimmer."

On top is where Klochkova remained. Between the Sydney Olympics and the 2004 Games in Athens, Klochkova was a five-time medalist at the World Championships, including four gold, and continued to pile up hardware from the European

Championships. For her career, she was a 16-time medalist at the European Championships, with 10 of those medals of the gold variety. But it was her performance at the 2004 Olympics that solidified her legendary status.

Holding off challenges from a pair of American stars, Amanda Beard and Kaitlin Sandeno, Klochkova repeated as the Olympic champion in the 200 individual medley and 400 individual medley, a feat that had never been accomplished. Thanks to her second sweep, Klochkova was named World Swimmer of the Year by *Swimming World Magazine*.

"At the moment when I realized I won, I felt great joy for my country and for myself too, of course," Klochkova said of her Olympic achievements. "When I think that my success raises the prestige of my country, I feel pride, joy, responsibility, and nostalgia. I knew I had a lot of fans in Ukraine who were glued to their television sets watching me perform. I knew I just could not disappoint them, and I struggled to the very last ounce of my strength to win. After such moments, you begin to see your country and yourself in a different light. At the award ceremony, they raised the Ukrainian flag and played the Ukrainian anthem. It felt great."

33

Claudia Kolb

Country: United States
Birth date: December 19, 1949
Events: Individual medley and breaststroke
Olympic medals: Three

At a time when the United States was producing what seemed to be a constant flow of fresh-faced teenage stars, Claudia Kolb fit that description almost perfectly. She broke away from the shadows at the 1964 Olympics and through the next Olympiad remained one of the headliners in the sport, becoming the best in the world in the individual medley events.

Kolb introduced herself to the world at the Tokyo Games, surging to a silver medal in the 200 breaststroke. Kolb wasn't thought to be much of a medal contender at the 1964 Games, and as the final of the 200 breaststroke unfolded, Kolb found herself out of medal position. But a surge over the final lap enabled the 14-year-old to close on the field and earn a place on the podium.

Four years later, at the 1968 Games in Mexico City, Kolb wasn't sneaking up on anyone. Kolb headed to that Olympiad off a sterling showing at the previous year's Pan American Games. In Winnipeg, Kolb stormed to victories in the 200 individual medley, 400 individual medley, and 200 butterfly, with the medley events also producing world records. In the 200 breaststroke, she added a silver medal.

"I was scared [in 1964], but nothing like I was four years later," Kolb said while recalling her Olympic appearances. "That was the worst thing I ever did. I was a heavy favorite, and when you start to realize that, you think anything you do that's less than first will not be good enough. I was a basket case. I cried. It was horrible. It was that way before any big meet. I never slept the first night. It used to panic me."

If Kolb's nerves were frayed, she hardly showed it. She made the medley events in Mexico City into a one-woman show, winning the 200 individual medley by more than four seconds and capturing top honors in the 400 individual medley by just under 14 seconds. She had no peer, and Kolb's performances were the perfect way to wrap up her Olympic career.

Enshrined in the International Swimming Hall of Fame in 1977, Kolb set five world records in the 200 medley and four world marks in the 400 medley during her career, her final standard in the shorter event lasting for more than five years. Kolb was the World Swimmer of the Year in 1967 and totaled 25 national championships.

34

Kieren Perkins

Country: Australia
Birth date: August 14, 1973
Event: Distance freestyle
Olympic medals: Four
World Championship medals: Three

The way he maneuvered through the water with a combination of power and grace, there was no need for Kieren Perkins to be brash with his words. Yet Perkins was known for letting his feelings be known. If nothing else, the Australian's performances were impressive enough to back up his verbal expressions.

Perkins is revered as one of the finest distance freestylers in history, one in a long line of extraordinary distance stars from Australia. Throughout the 1990s and into the beginning of the next millennium, Perkins was as good as it got in the longest of freestyle events. The silver medalist in the 1500 freestyle at the 1991 World Championships, he won the 400 freestyle, 800 freestyle, and 1500 freestyle at that year's Pan Pacific Championships, the springboard for what he would accomplish at the next year's Olympics.

At the 1992 Olympics, Perkins complemented a silver medal in the 400 freestyle with a gold medal and a world record in the 1500 freestyle, defeating countryman Glen Housman and Germany's Jorg Hoffmann, a bitter rival who had beaten Perkins at the previous year's World Championships. From that point forward, the rivalry belonged to the Aussie.

"Depending on how things are going, I'll look at the crowd, try to catch a peek at my parents," Perkins once said of his race management. "Because you swim so fast, your mind races. Your brain goes quicker. Bang. Bang. Something is going on. Your stroke is good. You are in the lead. The first 1000 in a race is okay. The last 500, you start to feel it. That's where you separate the men from the boys."

The victories continued to pile up following the 1992 Games as Perkins was the 1994 world champion in the 400 freestyle and 1500 freestyle, along with winning the 200 freestyle, 400 freestyle, and 1500 freestyle at the Commonwealth Games. Riding high, Perkins appeared headed for a historic performance at the 1996 Olympics in Atlanta. Instead, he had to battle just to earn the opportunity to defend his crown.

At the Australian Olympic Trials, Perkins failed to make the team in the 200 freestyle or 400 freestyle and barely qualified for the Games in the 1500 freestyle, as he placed second to Daniel Kowalski. Then at the Olympics, Perkins was the eighth and last qualifier for the final of the 1500 freestyle, and any chance of a repeat victory seemed gone. Perkins, however, dug deep and managed to win back-to-back titles, leaving Kowalski in the silver-medal position. The effort was a tribute to Perkins's mental toughness.

"It was at that stage of my career that I was a proven performer," Perkins said, recalling the final of the 1500 freestyle in Atlanta. "I wasn't a junior trying to work myself up. To get to a moment like that where for the first time you are questioning whether you can do it was quite confronting and challenging. What I'm proud of is that I was able to overcome that and come out the other side and still perform. It would have been really easy to give up and run away. It was tempting, and there were moments when it came into play. But even if I hadn't won, if I had been able to get home that night, look in the mirror, and say, yep, I couldn't have done that any better today, I would have been okay. That was the benchmark I always held myself to, and the fact I still delivered, that is far and away my greatest achievement."

Perkins wasn't at his peak in the years following the Atlanta Games, and he watched as countryman Grant Hackett rose to the top of the world in the distance events. Nonetheless, he regained enough of his past form to win the silver medal at the 2000 Olympics in Sydney behind Hackett. Perkins set world records in the 400 freestyle, 800 freestyle, and 1500 freestyle during his career and was the world-record holder in the longest distance from 1992 through 2001.

35

Ragnhild Hveger

Country: Denmark
Birth date: December 10, 1920
Death: December 1, 2011
Events: Freestyle and backstroke
Olympic medal: One

Perhaps more than any swimmer in history, Ragnhild Hveger is underappreciated because of circumstances beyond her control. A star for Denmark in the 1930s and 1940s, Hveger could have put together a glorious Olympic portfolio if not for poor timing. While Hveger competed in two Olympics, her peak days coincided with the cancellation of the Olympic Games in 1940 and 1944.

Hveger was nothing short of extraordinary in all freestyle events, the owner of the perfect blend of speed and endurance. It's not surprising, then, that she set world records from the 200 freestyle through the 1500 freestyle and was also a world-record holder in the backstroke. Her induction into the International Swimming Hall of Fame in 1966 was a simple decision.

At the 1936 Olympics in Berlin, Hveger captured the sole Olympic medal of her career, taking the silver in the 400 freestyle behind Rie Mastenbroek of the Netherlands. Hveger was just coming into her own at the Berlin Games, and two years later, she won the 100 freestyle and 400 freestyle at the European Championships.

Had World War II not canceled the Olympic Games in both 1940 and 1944, Hveger easily could have prevailed in the 100 freestyle and 400 freestyle, with the possibility of a third gold medal in the 100 backstroke. Of course, exactly what Hveger would have accomplished will never be known, part of her legacy left to interpretation. What is known is that she bypassed the 1948 Games, and by the time she returned for the 1952 Olympics, she was past her prime.

The duration of Hveger's world records speaks to her skill, which was far beyond that of her peers. She was the world-record holder in the 800 freestyle for 16 years, held the world record in the 200 freestyle and 1500 freestyle for 17 years, and was the owner of the global mark in the 400 freestyle for 19 years. In the 400 freestyle, which was her best event, she set the world record on eight occasions from 1937 to 1940. Her overwhelming success opened Hveger up to usage as a political pawn, although she was not against such a move.

"Such was her prowess that she was seized upon by the Germans during their occupation of Denmark and used for propaganda purposes," stated her obituary. "This rankled with many of her countrymen after the war had ended, as did the fact that [she] had also been happy to swim competitively in Germany."

Hveger was selected as one of the top-10 women swimmers of the 20th century in a 1999 vote overseen by *Swimming World Magazine*.

36

Pieter van den Hoogenband

Country: Netherlands
Birth date: March 14, 1978
Event: Freestyle
Olympic medals: Seven
World Championship medals: Ten

He was dubbed the Flying Dutchman, a more-than-appropriate nickname for a man who was a dominant freestyler for more than a decade. Pieter van den Hoogenband of the Netherlands will long be remembered for routinely producing top-flight performances, including one of the biggest upsets in the sport.

The fourth-place finisher in the 100 freestyle and 200 freestyle at the 1996 Olympics, van den Hoogenband showed early glimpses of stardom. Once he won four individual titles at the 1999 European Championships, that promise was confirmed. He had won the 50 freestyle, 100 freestyle, and 200 freestyle, and the next logical step was for the Dutch star to shine at the Olympic Games, the pinnacle of his sport. It only took until 2000 for that scenario to unfold albeit in slightly surprising fashion.

While van den Hoogenband was the class of the 100 freestyle, setting a world record that would last for more than seven years, he was not expected to capture the gold medal in the 200 freestyle in Sydney. That honor was supposed to go to Australian Ian Thorpe, who was competing in his home country, and in front of a raucous crowd. Van den Hoogenband, however, rose to the occasion, setting a world record in the semifinals, then matching that time to beat Thorpe in the final. The victory was the defining moment of the Dutchman's career, and left the jam-packed arena silenced.

"The whole year [Thorpe] was breaking world records, I was home training," said van den Hoogenband, who added a bronze medal in Sydney in the 50 freestyle. "He motivated me to train harder. Now, I won. It's amazing."

It was one of the few times van den Hoogenband got the best of Thorpe. Although Hoogie, which was another of his nicknames, beat Thorpe in a few meetings in the 100 freestyle, Thorpe was too much over the 200-meter distance, turning the rivalry into a one-sided affair. Not only did Thorpe defeat van den Hoogenband at the 2001 and 2003 World Championships, but he got his Olympic revenge at the 2004 Olympic Games in Athens. In a showdown that was dubbed "The Race of the Century," Thorpe not only relegated van den Hoogenband to the silver medal, but also beat Michael Phelps, who earned the bronze medal in what was one of his early ventures into the 200 freestyle.

Still, the 2004 Games produced prosperity for van den Hoogenband, as he defended his Olympic crown in the 100 freestyle. By defending his Olympic crown in the 100 freestyle, van den Hoogenband joined a club that featured legends like Duke Kahanamoku, Johnny Weissmuller, and Alexander Popov.

"I'm so happy, I feel like I'm drunk," van den Hoogenband said. "It's much harder to defend a title than to win it."

Although he won 10 medals at the World Championships during his career, he never won a gold medal, settling for eight silver medals and two bronze medals. All but two of those medals were in individual action. Meanwhile, van den Hoogenband was a 19-time medalist at the European Championships, including eight individual gold medals. He was the 2000 World Swimmer of the Year as chosen by *Swimming World Magazine*.

37

Jenny Thompson

Country: United States
Birth date: February 26, 1973
Events: Freestyle and butterfly
Olympic medals: Twelve
World Championship medals: Fourteen

Depending on which lens is used, Jenny Thompson's career can be viewed in multiple ways. From one vantage point, the American enjoyed a sensational run while piling up one of the highest Olympic-medal counts in history by a female swimmer. From the other perspective, Thompson's career was unfulfilled, her résumé featuring some glaring omissions. What can be agreed on is Thompson's rightful spot among the greats in her sport.

For almost two decades, Thompson was one of the elite performers in the pool. While she emerged on the international scene with a three-medal showing at the 1987 Pan American Games, including gold in the 50 freestyle, Thompson firmly made a name for herself by winning five medals between the 1989 and 1991 Pan Pacific Championships and through her world record at the 1992 U.S. Olympic Trials in the 100 freestyle.

From prodigy to American star, Thompson was expected to challenge for her first individual Olympic gold medal at the 1992 Games but had to settle for silver in the 100 freestyle and gold medals in two relays. Thompson's individual effort marked the first time—but not the last—in which she dealt with Olympic disappointment.

Because of a poor showing at the 1996 Olympic Trials, where she was favored to advance to multiple medal opportunities for the Atlanta Games, Thompson was limited to relay-only duty. For a woman who was a world-record holder, it was a bitter pill to swallow and the first example of pressure affecting Thompson's performances. Thompson did win three gold medals in relay action and used her shortcomings as a learning experience.

"I think the media pressure was getting to me," Thompson said. "I was putting too much pressure on myself. I was worried about my competitors. I wasn't being myself. I wasn't enjoying the sport. Winning was the only important thing. I really wanted to kill my competitors. I think, in a large way, it was a blessing. I learned so much about myself and my swimming. I've never lost the desire to win a race, but I do see it with a different perspective. Now I have much more joy. I enjoy the whole process, the crowds, the kids, my teammates cheering."

Thompson's change in approach paid off at the 1998 World Championships, where she won gold medals in the 100 freestyle and 100 butterfly. In addition, she broke one of the iconic world records in the sport in 1999 when she took down the 18-year-old standard of Mary T. Meagher in the 100 butterfly. It seemed that Thompson was on target for the 2000 Olympics in Sydney, a belief that was confirmed at the 2000 Olympic Trials, where Thompson prevailed in the 100 freestyle and 100 butterfly.

At the Sydney Games, though, Thompson struggled again. She added three more gold medals in relays but managed only a bronze medal in the 100 freestyle. Worse, she was the fifth-place finisher in the 100 butterfly despite entering the year as the world-record holder. That loss stung Thompson as much as any setback she had previously experienced.

"There's nothing more I could have done," Thompson said. "I think when I went into it, I felt good. I went in with a positive attitude, feeling good, feeling ready. I went for it. I was just trying too hard."

After taking some time off following the Sydney Games, Thompson returned to competition and piled up a few more accomplishments. She was the gold medalist in the 100 butterfly and bronze medalist in the 100 freestyle at the 2003 World Championships, then won two silver medals as a relay contributor at the 2004 Olympics in Athens. For all her demons in individual events at the Olympics, Thompson might be the finest relay swimmer the sport has seen. Of her 12 Olympic medals, eight are gold from relay duty. The United States knew it had an ace when it came to relay work.

Inducted into the International Swimming Hall of Fame in 2009, Thompson's Olympic-medal total was complemented by 14 medals at the World Championships and 34 medals at the Pan Pacific Championships. She was also an NCAA champion at Stanford University and retired with a fine perspective of her swimming days.

"It's time for me to stop looking at what I don't have and look at what I do have," Thompson said in 2000. "I have a tremendous amount in my life to be grateful for and happy about. And winning these medals is just a small part of that."

38

John Naber

Country: United States
Birth date: January 20, 1956
Events: Backstroke and freestyle
Olympic medals: Five
World Championship medal: One

During the mid-1970s, American John Naber was one of the world's finest swimmers, known primarily for dominating the backstroke events. Naber, also an elite freestyler, was the man who ended the lengthy reign of East Germany's Roland Matthes as the premier backstroker in the world.

By winning the bronze medal in the 200 backstroke at the 1973 World Championships, Naber revealed his talent and set himself up to shine at the 1976 Olympic Games in Montreal. In his first and only Olympiad, Naber emerged as the star of the swimming events, capturing five medals, including four gold.

Naber not only dethroned Matthes, the two-time defending champion, in the 100 backstroke, but also won the event by nearly one second and set a world record of 55.49. Naber was even more impressive in the 200 backstroke, prevailing in a world record of 1:59.19, marking the first time anyone had eclipsed the two-minute barrier. Each of those world records endured for seven years, an illustration of Naber's ahead-of-his-time skill.

A gold medalist as a member of the American 400 medley relay and 800 freestyle relay, Naber picked up a fifth medal in Montreal in the 200 freestyle, and it took a world record by teammate Bruce Furniss to leave Naber in the second-place position. Had Mark Spitz not won seven gold medals at the previous Olympiad, Naber's accomplishments would have been more appreciated.

"John is always so friendly, and that makes it hard to swim against him," said Bruce Hardcastle, a former rival of Naber's. "I sometimes think he does it for a purpose. Like before a race, he'll say, 'Let's you and I go one-two.' I know he means I'm the one finishing second. That's when I tell myself, 'Hey, maybe this guy's not that nice.'"

As the University of Southern California won four consecutive NCAA championships during Naber's time at the school, the Illinois native won 10 individual NCAA titles, a total that remains a school record. Naber won the 100 backstroke and 200 backstroke in each of his four seasons and added a pair of victories in the 500 freestyle. Outgoing in his demeanor, Naber was also an introspective athlete who viewed the big picture.

"My determination was about 110 percent more than anybody else I've ever known," Naber said. "And for anyone who has the courage to set high goals for themselves, I encourage them to try. But the success in swimming is the journey, not the destination."

39

Kirsty Coventry

Country: Zimbabwe
Birth date: September 16, 1983
Events: Backstroke and individual medley
Olympic medals: Seven
World Championship medals: Eight

What Kirsty Coventry has done for her homeland is difficult to measure. She has proven that despite a lack of tradition in a particular sport, an athlete can flourish on the largest stage behind a combination of hard work and focus. More important, her performances—at times—have encouraged citizens of Zimbabwe to forget about the racial strife that exists in the African nation.

Starting with the 2004 Olympics, Coventry was one of the most consistent and successful female swimmers in the world, a backstroke and individual medley specialist who racked up dozens of medals at the international level. While she trained in the United States, where she attended college at Auburn University, she never forgot about her homeland.

Coventry made her first considerable noise at the 2004 Olympic Games in Athens, where she won the gold medal in the 200 backstroke and added a silver medal in the 100 backstroke and a bronze medal in the 200 individual medley. Her exploits made her a national hero and briefly quelled the racial hostility in Zimbabwe as citizens got caught up celebrating her achievements.

"I've been very lucky with the community in Zimbabwe being behind me and backing me up," Coventry said. "It's such an honor, such a great honor. I'm very proud to be Zimbabwean and to represent Zimbabwe. I've always tried not to read too much or involve too much politics in my sport. You know, if you look at other countries like South Africa and what a rugby game can do to unify a country, that's how I kind of want to look at and approach my sport in swimming."

One of the headlining female performers at the 2005 World Championships, Coventry packaged gold medals in both backstroke events with silver-medal outings in the individual medley disciplines. She added silver medals in the 200 backstroke and 200 individual medley at the 2007 World Championships and carried that momentum into the 2008 Olympics in Beijing.

At the 2008 Games, Coventry appeared destined to be the bridesmaid of the meet as her first three events—the 400 individual medley, 100 backstroke, and 200 individual medley—yielded silver medals. However, Coventry was golden again in the 200 backstroke, repeating as champion in world-record time. She earned that victory by nearly one second over rival Margaret Hoelzer of the United States, a former college teammate at Auburn.

Coventry checked in with another gold medal in the 200 backstroke at the 2009 World Championships, and the five-time Olympian managed to final in three events between the 2012 and 2016 Olympic Games. For her career, she set three world records in the 200 backstroke, including breaking the 16-year-old mark of Hungary's Krisztina Egerszegi at the start of the 2008 season.

"I'm proud that I was able to represent my country for so many years at such a high level, the Olympic movement and the Olympic stage—especially when Zimbabwe was going through hard times," Coventry said. "Just because you might be from a landlocked country in Africa and didn't have the same opportunities as some other people in first-world countries, it doesn't matter as long as you keep pushing yourself and working hard."

40

Sun Yang

Country: China
Birth Date: December 1, 1991
Events: Freestyle
Olympic medals: Six
World Championship medals: Fourteen

The sole Chinese athlete in the top-100, Sun Yang emerged as one of the world's premier middle-distance and distance freestylers beginning in 2009. Prior to Sun, only a handful of Chinese male swimmers ever made a dent on the international scene, while the country's female program was dogged by revelations of performance-enhancing drug use.

Sun enjoyed a rapid ascent to the top of the sport and has not looked back in the decade since his emergence. After finishing eighth in the final of the 1500 freestyle at the 2008 Olympic Games, Sun claimed a bronze medal in the 1500 freestyle at the 2009 World Championships in Rome. But it was his showing at the 2010 Asian Games that truly marked his breakthrough. To go with a gold medal in the 1500 freestyle, and a near world-record effort, Sun won silver medals in the 200 freestyle and 400 freestyle.

Racing at the 2011 World Championships, held in his home nation in Shanghai, the Chinese star won double gold in the 800 freestyle and 1500 freestyle, the longer event producing his first world record, and took the silver medal in the 400 freestyle. The outing set the stage for the 2012 Olympic Games in London, where Sun was the titlist in the 400 freestyle and 1500 freestyle, and the silver medalist in the 200 freestyle. His gold medal in the longest event arrived in world-record time on the final day of the competition, an exclamation point of sorts.

Sun's success continued at the next two editions of the World Championships as he swept gold medals in the 400, 800, and 1500 freestyles at the 2013 version of the meet, and secured gold medals in the 400 and 800 freestyles in 2015, where he also was the silver medalist in the 200 freestyle. He took that momentum into the 2016 Olympic Games in Rio de Janeiro, where he was the champion of the 200 freestyle and silver medalist in the 400 freestyle. By winning the 200 free in Rio, Sun became the only male swimmer to win Olympic crowns in the 200 freestyle, 400 freestyle, and 1500 freestyle, a tribute to his range in the freestyle disciplines.

Sun's career has not been without its share of controversies, most notably the three-month doping ban he served in 2014 for use of a drug that was on the banned list of the World Anti-Doping Agency. After a Chinese doctor prescribed Sun the stimulant Trimetazidine for the treatment of a heart condition, it was learned that the medication had been added to WADA's list of banned substances. As a result, Sun was given a three-month ban by the Chinese Anti-Doping Agency (CHINADA), although the ban was not made public until after Sun served the penalty. Sun and CHINADA came under scrutiny for the violation, particularly due to China's history of doping violations in the sport.

"I have taken many doping tests during years of training and competition and I had never failed one before," Sun said. "I was shocked and depressed at that time, but at the same time it made me cherish my sporting life even more. I will take it as a lesson and be more careful in the future."

Sun also courted controversy in 2015 and 2016, both times at the year's marquee event. At the 2015 World Championships, Sun was accused by Brazilian officials of assaulting one of their female swimmers, Larissa Oliveira. According to reports, Sun and Oliveira collided while in the practice pool, with Sun getting physical with Oliveira after the collision. FINA, the sport's world governing body, looked into the incident and declared there was no need to pursue it further.

Meanwhile, at the 2016 Olympic Games, Sun was accused of splashing Australian rival Mack Horton while the swimmers moved through warmup sessions in the practice pool. Horton called Sun a "drug cheat" due to the Chinese athlete's positive doping test. When the two met in the final of the 400 freestyle, Horton edged his rival for the gold medal, Sun settling for silver. The Chinese Swimming Association was not pleased with Horton's assertions.

"We are aware of the harsh criticism from Australian swimmer Mack Horton, and the personal attack on Sun Yang," said a statement by the federation. "We think his inappropriate words have greatly damaged sporting ties between China and Australia, and damaged the image of Australian athletes. These comments lack manners, and we strongly ask that Horton apologize."

At the 2017 World Championships, Sun earned a measure of revenge against Horton when he won gold—his third straight—in the 400 freestyle, more than two seconds ahead of Horton in the silver-medal position. Sun also added gold in the 200 freestyle.

41

Helene Madison

Country: United States
Birth date: June 19, 1913
Death date: November 27, 1970
Event: Freestyle
Olympic medals: Three

Among the early-era stars of women's swimming was the American Helene Madison, who emerged as a standout in each of the freestyle events, a testament to her versatility. Although her career was short lived and could have been much more celebrated, her accomplishments continue to be appreciated.

Just five years after coach Ray Daughters identified vast talent in Madison, a 14-year-old when she started competitive training, she became one of the most decorated Olympians of the 1932 Games in Los Angeles. At that Olympiad, Madison shared top female billing with track star Babe Didrikson thanks to gold-medal performances in the 100 freestyle and 400 freestyle and as a member of the U.S. 400 freestyle relay.

"None among the 200,000 that day burst with more pride than Ray Daughters, who first spotted Madison as a gangly 14-year-old in the summer of 1927, taking part in the Seattle Post-Intelligencer's annual Swim Carnival at Green Lake," wrote Seattle-area historian David Eskenazi. "Madison, who lived a block from the lake and had been participating in Seattle Parks Department swim programs since the age of six, had done nothing to distinguish herself from other girls her age and was devoid of technique. But Daughters focused on her height—5-11—big bones, and the way she naturally navigated the water."

Daughters's eye proved to be on target as Madison set world records in freestyle events ranging from the 100-meter distance to the 1500-meter distance. She would have been a leading contender for gold medals at the 1936 Olympics in Berlin, but her decision to turn to an acting career after the 1932 Games sacrificed her amateur status and made her ineligible. Madison also lost her amateur status because of professional swimming gigs in which she would race for prize money.

A 1966 inductee into the International Swimming Hall of Fame, Madison was undefeated in the freestyle events at the 1930, 1931, and 1932 U.S. National Championships.

42

Adolph Kiefer

Country: United States
Birth date: June 27, 1918
Death date: May 5, 2017
Event: Backstroke
Olympic medal: One

As a teenager, Adolph Kiefer became one of the first backstroke stars, dominating that event each time he entered the water. A standout on the Illinois high school scene, Kiefer won the state title in the 100-yard backstroke as a 16-year-old, simultaneously becoming the first man to break the one-minute barrier in the event.

At the 1936 Olympic Games in Berlin, the 17-year-old Kiefer won the gold medal in the 100 backstroke by almost two seconds. It was expected to be the first of several gold medals in the event for Kiefer, who was still developing. However, the development of World War II forced the cancellation of the 1940 Olympics and the 1944 Games.

"Kiefer didn't reach his peak for almost a decade later," wrote legendary sports journalist Frank Deford. "Had there been the Tokyo Olympics of 1940 and the London Games of 1944, Sonny Boy Kiefer would surely have won them in a breeze. He'd be to the backstroke what Pablo Casals was to the cello. But it was wartime, and Kiefer became a naval officer who helped write the guidelines that taught thousands of American sailors to swim."

Kiefer was also hurt by the fact the 200 backstroke was not an Olympic event during his competitive days. Nonetheless, he put together an extraordinary career that included world records on a regular basis in a variety of backstroke distances. None of his world records were broken until four years after his retirement, and Kiefer also won a national title in the three-stroke individual medley.

Among the first class of inductees into the International Swimming Hall of Fame in 1965, Kiefer invented several swimming devices, including lane lines, which negated waves, and a variety of swimsuits. In 2007, Kiefer was given the Gold Medallion by the International Swimming Hall of Fame, an award that honored his accomplishments in the pool and out of it. Kiefer served on the President's Council on Fitness, Sports and Nutrition under three presidents.

"Adolph's selection for the Gold Medallion is long overdue," said Bruce Wigo, the onetime chief executive officer of the International Swimming Hall of Fame. "Not only was he an Olympic Champion and world record holder, but he was instrumental in saving thousands of lives during World War II and for the past fifty years has been a giant in the swimming pool and water safety industry."

43

Penny Heyns

Country: South Africa
Birth date: November 8, 1974
Event: Breaststroke
Olympic medals: Three

At her peak, South Africa's Penny Heyns was unbeatable and put together one of the finest years the sport has seen in recent times. A versatile breaststroker, Heyns excelled over the 50-, 100-, and 200-meter distances and was inducted into the International Swimming Hall of Fame as part of the class of 2007.

Heyns started to emerge on the international scene during the 1994 and 1995 seasons, winning the bronze medal in the 100 breaststroke at the 1994 Commonwealth Games. A year later, she was the gold medalist in the 100 breaststroke and the silver medalist in the 200 breaststroke at the Pan Pacific Championships. It all set the table for the 1996 Olympic Games in Atlanta.

A 1992 Olympic participant, Heyns made her second Olympiad one to remember as she prevailed in both the 100 breaststroke and the 200 breaststroke at the 1996 Games. Each triumph was over American Amanda Beard, and Heyns became the first South African to medal in the Olympics since that country's readmission to the competition in 1992. Prior to the Barcelona Games, South Africa was prohibited from Olympic competition for 32 years because of its apartheid practices.

"I didn't grow up with a dream about Olympic gold," Heyns said. "It's interesting that different people have asked me if I had [dreamed] about winning at the Olympics. But the answer is no because in South Africa, we were so isolated all those years. I never thought about the Olympic Games. Even in 1992, when I knew there was a chance we would go, I swam that season thinking, 'Oh, well! I'll just do the best I can, and if South Africa is invited to participate, and I make the team, I'll go!' But even Barcelona wasn't the wonderful, overwhelming experience that it should have been."

Following the Atlanta Games, Heyns encountered a rough season followed by the greatest stretch of her career. At the 1998 World Championships, Heyns failed to medal in her prime events. By 1999, though, she was on a tear. Aside from breaking four world records in the 200 breaststroke, Heyns set three of her five career world records in the 100 breaststroke. She also set a global standard in the 50 breaststroke and was the Pan Pacific champion in each breaststroke discipline.

Heyns's farewell to the sport was the 2000 Olympic Games in Sydney. Although she was unable to replicate her feats from Atlanta, Heyns was the bronze medalist in the 100 breaststroke. She remains the only female to win both the 100 breaststroke and the 200 breaststroke at the same Olympics.

44

Gary Hall Jr.

Country: United States
Birth date: September 26, 1974
Event: Sprint freestyle
Olympic medals: Ten
World Championship medals: Six

From a family with a rich swimming tradition, Gary Hall Jr. established himself as one of the best sprint free-stylers in history. His father, Gary Hall Sr., won one medal each at the 1968, 1972, and 1976 Olympics. Also competing in three Olympiads, Hall Jr. was a 10-time Olympic medalist and one of only nine swimmers to win 10 or more medals in Olympic competition.

Hall focused on the 50 freestyle and 100 freestyle during his career but excelled greatest in the 50 freestyle, an event that measures the fastest man in the pool. At the 1996 Olympics in Atlanta, Hall Jr. won the silver medal in

his primary event, placing behind Russia's Alexander Popov, widely considered the greatest sprinter in history. At the next two Olympic Games, however, Hall Jr. was the champion of the 50 freestyle.

At the 2000 Games in Sydney, Hall shared the gold medal in the 50 freestyle with U.S. teammate Anthony Ervin. Four years later, at the Athens Games, Hall stood on the top step of the medals podium alone. Hall's Olympic accomplishments also include a silver medal in the 100 freestyle at the 1996 Olympics and a bronze medal in that event at the 2000 Games. He also won five relay medals—three gold, one silver, and one bronze.

Hall's career was defined largely by his boisterous personality. He wasn't afraid to boast during media interviews, and he brought a larger-than-life persona to the starting blocks, including the wearing of boxing shorts and a robe over his swimsuit. More cerebral in his approach, Popov did not like Hall's over-the-top ways, at one point declaring that his rival "talks too much." Not one to back down, Hall declared Popov to be "immature."

Popov ultimately got the best of Hall during their matchups. While they split their duels in the 50 freestyle in Olympic competition, Popov bettered Hall in the 100 freestyle at the 1996 Olympics and beat him in both the 50 freestyle and the 100 freestyle at the 1994 World Championships in Rome. Popov also held the world record in the 50 freestyle from 2000 to 2008 and was the world-record holder in the 100 freestyle from 1994 to 2000. Hall never set an individual world record.

In addition to not sitting well with Popov, Hall's outspoken nature served as motivation for the Australian 400 freestyle relay at the 2000 Olympics. Prior to the final of the relay, which the United States had never before lost in Olympic competition, Hall predicted that the United States would "smash [the Australians] like guitars." The statement was part of a larger-context piece in which Hall spoke highly of Australia, but that fragment of the interview was highlighted. As the race unfolded in front of a partisan Aussie crowd, Hall was caught on the anchor leg by Ian Thorpe, prompting the Australians to celebrate their triumph by strumming air guitars on the pool deck.

"We whispered in each other's ears, 'Let's do the air guitars,'" said Michael Klim, who led off the Australian relay. "That wasn't planned, nor had we spoken about it. It hadn't been mentioned at all, but on the spur of the moment, we did it. But I must say, Gary Hall was the first swimmer to come over and congratulate us. Even though he dished it out, he was a true sportsman."

As much as Hall's flamboyance irked his competitors and some fans of the sport, he also was viewed as an inspiration. In 1999, Hall was diagnosed with type 1 diabetes, and doctors initially told him he would not be able to continue his career. Hall refused to accept that fate and learned to deal with his disease while still competing at a high level. He became a spokesman for the disease and for maintaining a healthy lifestyle while managing the effects of diabetes.

"The quality of life a person with diabetes can have really comes down to the individual and the management that individual can provide," Hall said. "Other people have been able to successfully manage this disease and avoid very serious complications that stem from this disease, so it can be done. If there are complications, it's difficult to blame anybody but yourself."

45

Rebecca Soni

Country: United States
Birth date: March 18, 1987
Event: Breaststroke
Olympic medals: Six
World Championship medals: Six

Through a sharp trajectory between 2008 and 2012, Rebecca Soni emerged as one
of the best breaststrokers in history. While many breaststroke specialists focus on

a particular distance, Soni proved herself to be a major factor from the 50-meter breaststroke through the 200-meter breaststroke, which was her best event.

Although she was known at the national level, Soni didn't make her first significant mark until the 2008 season, which she capped with a stellar showing at the Olympic Games in Beijing. After earning the silver medal in the 100 breaststroke behind Australian Leisel Jones, Soni pulled off a shocking triumph in the 200 breaststroke, setting a world record and defeating Jones, who was thought to be unbeatable. Soni also won silver as a member of the American 400 medley relay.

Following her Olympic debut, Soni was the undisputed queen of the breaststroke, winning the gold medal in the 100 breaststroke at the 2009 World Championships and the 100 breaststroke and 200 breaststroke at the 2010 Pan Pacific Championships. At the 2011 World Championships, her victories in the 100 breaststroke, 200 breaststroke, and 400 medley relay were complemented by a bronze medal in the 50 breaststroke.

The best performances of Soni's career, however, came at the 2012 Olympic Games. Although she was edged in the final of the 100 breaststroke and forced to settle for the silver medal, Soni overwhelmed the opposition in the 200 breaststroke. She set a world record in the semifinal round, only to return with another world record in the final, becoming the first woman to break the 2:20 barrier with a time of 2:19.59. It was a goal that Soni had been chasing for several years.

"I'm so happy," Soni said. "I didn't try to focus on medals or records. I just wanted to swim one more race the way I knew I could. It's been my goal since I was a little kid to swim under 2:20. When my coach told me you're going to be the first woman to go under 2:20, I've been chasing it ever since, and I'm so happy."

Soni, a multiple NCAA champion for the University of Southern California, set one world record in the 100 breaststroke and three in the 200 breaststroke. She was named World Swimmer of the Year by *Swimming World Magazine* in 2010 and 2011.

46

Tom Dolan

Country: United States
Birth date: September 15, 1975
Events: Individual medley and freestyle
Olympic medals: Three
World Championship medals: Two

Whether as a youngster at the Curl-Burke Swim Club or as a competitor for the University of Michigan, Tom Dolan developed a reputation for embracing grueling workouts, training sessions that would make most high-level swimmers surrender under the high intensity. It was his willingness to endure pain that made Dolan one of the finest individual medley performers in history.

Dolan was the best 400 individual medley swimmer in the world during the second half of the 1990s and into the new millennium. That identity was first formed at the 1994 U.S. National Championships, where Dolan set an American record. By the end of the year, he had won the gold medal in the 400 individual medley at the World Championships in Rome, a victory that was sweetened by a world-record time. It was the perfect jump start toward the 1996 Olympics.

"My aim with Tom was to get him ready for 1996," said Jon Urbanchek, Dolan's coach at the University of Michigan. "The Atlanta Olympics were my goal, and I thought he could be the number 1 I.M.er by then. He beat me by almost two years. I thought the road would be longer, but it took a lot less time."

Once Dolan generated momentum, he was unstoppable. Aside from winning six individual NCAA championships at Michigan, he captured back-to-back gold medals in the 400 individual medley at the Olympic Games. In 1996, he narrowly edged Michigan teammate and training partner Eric Namesnik, with whom Dolan had a frosty relationship. Four years later, Dolan broke the world record to retain his title and again led a gold–silver finish for the United States, this time ahead of Erik Vendt by nearly three seconds. For good measure, he picked up the silver medal in the 200 individual medley.

As much as Dolan is defined by his prowess in the 400 individual medley, he also established himself as an elite swimmer in the distance-freestyle events. He won three national titles in the 400 freestyle, four in the 800 freestyle, and one in the 1500 freestyle. His four championships in the 400 individual medley were complemented by a pair of crowns in the 200 individual medley.

All of Dolan's success came despite his struggles with a severe case of exercise-induced asthma. Dolan would regularly have breathing problems during practice and in his races, a combination of his asthmatic condition and a narrower-than-normal esophagus. However, he fought through the difficulties and learned how to manage his condition without sacrificing results.

"It can really get bad in our workouts," Dolan said. "There will be a real tightness in my chest, and I won't be able to get a lot of air. But my coach says it actually helps me in meets because it increases my ability to withstand stress.

"I don't know if I became a better person for going through the health problems I had, but I became a different person. I realized that the path you take is immensely more important than the final goal. It was an outlook I wish I'd had my whole career."

47

Lorraine Crapp

Country: Australia
Birth date: October 1, 1938
Event: Freestyle
Olympic medals: Four

In the mid-1950s, as Murray Rose carried the mantle for men's swimming in Australia, that role for the women was handled by a twosome that is typically linked. While Dawn Fraser's name is one of the biggest in the sport's history, she had plenty of help from Lorraine Crapp in elevating the reputation of women's swimming in her homeland.

During her career, Crapp was one of the premier freestylers in the world, demonstrating range from the 100-meter distance through the 800 freestyle. She was so dominant and ahead of her time that she was expected to set a world record nearly each time she competed. On some occasions, Crapp set multiple world records in a single race, her split times at certain distances counting for the record book.

The first woman to break the five-minute barrier in the 400 freestyle, Crapp put her name on the map at the 1954 British Empire and Commonwealth Games, where she was the gold medalist in the 100 freestyle and 400 freestyle. This performance was not only an introduction of sorts but also the launching point for Crapp's most successful Olympic appearance.

"Lorraine Crapp, with 23 world records, was and is the first great swimmer of the modern era of Australian swimming," states her International Swimming Hall of Fame profile. "Miss Crapp burst into prominence in 1954 with her eleven-minute 880 [freestyle] and heralded the coming of a new wave of Aussie world-record swimmers to dominate their own 1956 Melbourne Olympics."

At the 1956 Games, Crapp won the 400 freestyle by almost eight seconds over Fraser. However, it was Fraser, en route to three straight titles, who prevailed in the 100 freestyle. Together, they helped Australia win the gold medal in the 400 freestyle relay. At the 1960 Olympics, Crapp added the final Olympic medal of her career, a silver in the 400 freestyle relay.

It was unfortunate the 200 freestyle was not an Olympic event at the 1956 Games, for Crapp and Fraser would have engaged in an epic matchup. The women had exchanged the world record during the year, and a duel would have been the perfect meeting point of Fraser's sprinting speed and Crapp's endurance.

Crapp set at least one world record in each event from the 100 through the 800 and cut more than 10 seconds off some of the previous records in the longer events. Her International Swimming Hall of Fame induction took place in 1972.

48

Ethelda Bleibtrey

Country: United States
Birth date: February 27, 1902
Death date: May 6, 1978
Events: Freestyle and backstroke
Olympic medals: Three

Among the first superstars of women's swimming, Ethelda Bleibtrey made her mark in the late 1910s and early 1920s as a freestyle and backstroke standout. Like many of the freestylers of her era, she was equally versed in the sprint events and distance disciplines. What separated Bleibtrey was her ability to also flourish in another stroke.

Originally involved in the sport as therapy for her polio condition and to keep a friend company, Bleibtrey quickly turned into an elite athlete. One of the defining moments of her career and a performance that legitimized her status was a victory over Australian legend and 1912 Olympic champion Fanny Durack during Durack's American tour in 1919.

At the 1920 Olympics in Antwerp, Bleibtrey won a gold medal in every female event contested, walking away with three Olympic titles. In addition to winning the 100 freestyle and 300 freestyle, Bleibtrey was a member of the U.S. squad that took first place in the 400 freestyle relay.

Bleibtrey's Olympic accolades could have been greater if not for the limitations of the time period. She would have likely been the gold medalist in the 100 backstroke if it was contested, and she would have been a factor at the 1924 Olympics had Bleibtrey not turned professional, consequently removing herself from Olympic competition.

In national-championship competition, Bleibtrey displayed her versatility by winning every event from the 50-yard distance through the mile. Inducted into the International Swimming Hall of Fame in 1967, Bleibtrey wasn't without her controversial moments. She was once arrested for swimming without stockings, which was against the law. However, her decision to do so led to women typically racing without stockings.

"I have my memories," she said, "and I guess some of those other people remember too. I owe a great deal to swimming."

49

Mike Burton

Country: United States
Birth date: July 3, 1947
Event: Distance freestyle
Olympic medals: Three

For Mike Burton, a near tragedy wound up being one of the best circumstances in his life. Involved in a bicycle accident with a truck as a young teenager, Burton suffered injuries that forced him away from sports involving physical contact. Consequently, he developed an affinity for the pool and became one of the world's greatest distance freestylers.

During the 1960s and 1970s, Burton was a standout in the 400 freestyle and 1500 freestyle. He burst onto the international scene in 1967 behind strong showings at the Pan American Games and World University Games, where he combined for six medals, including a pair of victories in the 1500 freestyle, an event that turned into his specialty.

The momentum that Burton generated in 1967 carried over to the next year's Olympic Games in Mexico City. Burton breezed by his competition in the distance freestyles, winning the 400 freestyle by nearly three seconds and making the 1500 freestyle seem like a solo swim. So dominant was Burton over the 30-lap event that he prevailed by almost 20 seconds. The combination of his success and appreciation for the Olympic movement has not been forgotten.

"Behind every athlete in the Olympic Games, there's a story about how they got there and what they went through to get there," Burton said. "To me, that's more impressive than anything else. If you weren't ready to compete after walking into the stadium [for the Opening Ceremony], you were never going to be ready. The adrenaline high you got from doing that lasted the entire Games. It was a very inspiring moment in my life, and I wasn't going to miss that for anything."

Burton stayed with the sport after Mexico City, his sights set on defending his championship in the 1500 freestyle. However, it proved to be a much more difficult task than anticipated. At the Olympic Trials, Burton narrowly qualified for the final and then earned the last invitation to the 1972 Games in Munich. A medal, much less a repeat, seemed out of the question.

Burton, though, rallied at his second Olympiad. Although he didn't enjoy the same margin of victory as four years earlier, he won by almost six seconds over Australian Graham Windeatt and set a world record of 15:52.58. It was the fifth and final world record of his career, and the victory was the most satisfying of his swimming days.

"It was probably the most physically exhausting and emotionally exhausting race of my career," Burton said. "I went out and took an early lead but lost the lead and with 300 meters got it back and won the race. As soon as I hit the wall, I turned and looked at the scoreboard and saw a world record. When I saw my coach, I just broke down crying. I was so happy and so exhausted. It was a final great swim. It's a special medal for me."

Burton also set two world records in the 800 freestyle, a non-Olympic event for men, and was a 1977 inductee into the International Swimming Hall of Fame. He remains the only American to repeat as Olympic champion in the 1500 freestyle.

50

Arne Borg

Country: Sweden
Birth date: August 18, 1901
Death date: November 7, 1987
Event: Distance freestyle
Olympic medals: Five

Tabbed as the best male swimmer in Swedish history, Arne Borg is widely considered to be one of the world's first stars in the distance-freestyle events. During his career, Borg set world records in the 400 freestyle, 800 freestyle, and 1500 freestyle, his most successful performances coming in the longest of the events.

From 1923 to 1927, Borg set five world records in the 1500 freestyle and became the first individual to cover the distance in under 20 minutes, accomplishing that feat at the 1927 European Championships in Italy. In setting that world record, which lasted for nearly 11 years, Borg cut nearly one minute off the previous record.

A five-time Olympic medalist, Borg got off to a slow start in his Olympic career. At the 1924 Games in Paris, he was the silver medalist in both the 400 freestyle and the 1500 freestyle when he was expected to win at least one gold medal. He also won a bronze medal as a member of Sweden's 800 freestyle relay.

At the 1928 Olympics in Amsterdam, Borg captured his elusive gold medal when he defeated Australia's Andrew Charlton in the 1500 freestyle, marking a reversal of the finish from the 1924 Games. Borg and Charlton also dueled in the 400 freestyle but got caught up racing each other and failed to keep an eye on Argentina's Alberto Zorrilla, who surprisingly won the gold medal. Charlton settled for the silver medal, with Borg taking the bronze.

Borg was a five-time champion at the European Championships, including a victory in the 100 freestyle in 1927 that proved his worth in the shortest freestyle event of the time. Although Borg was regarded as a peer to American Johnny Weissmuller, he was not liked by his competitors.

"Arne Borg did not have a style of swimming that one would consider normal and logical," says his International Swimming Hall of Fame profile. "Borg swam without a distinct rule. At times, he pulled only, or if not, he would use a two-beat kick. At other instances, he used a four- or six-beat kick. Sometimes, a few meters before the turn, he would prolong his stay underwater for 10 or 12 meters. This act of showing off made this swimmer very unpopular."

51

Charles Daniels

Country: United States
Birth date: March 24, 1885
Death date: August 9, 1973
Event: Freestyle
Olympic medals: Seven

The first great American swimmer was Charles Daniels, who was also the world's best in the sport during the first decade of the 1900s. Like many of the freestyle swimmers in the early days of swimming competition, Daniels excelled at all distances while representing the New York Athletic Club.

A winner of 33 national championships, Daniels made his Olympic splash at the 1904 Games in St. Louis, where he won five medals. That total was the most by an American until Mark Spitz won seven medals—all gold—at the 1972 Olympics in Munich. In addition to winning the 220-yard freestyle and the 440-yard freestyle, Daniels helped the United States to a win in the 200-yard freestyle relay. He checked in with a silver medal in the 100-yard freestyle and a bronze medal in the 50-yard freestyle.

Daniels cut sizable amounts of time from the previous world records and set global standards in every freestyle event from 25 yards through the mile. Much of this success was due to his transformation of the freestyle into a powerful stroke in which he relied not only on the arms but also on the lower body.

"Daniels was the best in nearly all freestyle events he entered over a six-year period," stated a Yahoo! article on Daniels's often overlooked talent. "The front crawl technique was going through major changes at the time. Daniels is credited with bringing about advancements resulting in superior usage of the legs when kicking, including an accelerated number of beats per stroke cycle. Daniels's crawl technique was very similar to the freestyle stroke used today."

At the 1906 Olympics in Athens, which are no longer considered official, Daniels won the 100-meter freestyle. It was a gold medal he would repeat at the 1908 Olympics in London, where he also collected a bronze medal as a member of the U.S. 800 freestyle relay. The totality of his accomplishments made Daniels one of the inaugural members of the International Swimming Hall of Fame, which inducted its first class in 1965.

52

Donna de Varona

Country: United States
Birth date: April 26, 1947
Event: Individual medley
Olympic medals: Two

There wasn't a more dominant athlete in the individual medley during the first half of the 1960s than Donna de Varona, who made world-record-setting efforts a norm. A relay-only swimmer at the 1960 Olympics in Rome, when she was a mere 13-year-old, de Varona built a strong foundation over the next few years in order to excel at the 1964 Games. Her blueprint worked perfectly.

Establishing world records in the 200 individual medley and the 400 individual medley, de Varona was the undisputed queen of the multistroke events. During her career, she set seven world records in the 200 individual medley and six world marks in the 400 individual medley. It was the longer event in which she enjoyed the finest moment of her career, a gold medal at the Olympic Games in Tokyo in 1964.

Heavily favored to win the 400 individual medley, de Varona had no problem delivering under pressure, as she prevailed by more than five seconds and set an Olympic record. She also secured a gold medal as a member of the American 400 freestyle relay and was the fifth-place finisher in the 100 butterfly. Had the 200 individual medley been contested, de Varona likely would have won a third gold medal.

"I think I was lucky to go and get up there twice," de Varona said of standing on the top step of the medals podium. "One was with great relief because I was expected to win. One was with a lot of joy because I was a part of a relay. I love being part of a team, and swimming can be a very lonely sport. That's what I like seeing on the pool deck. They understand they're competing for America as well as the individual golds. It connects you in a global world when you make an Olympic team, and it's about the journey, and I think you have to focus more on that."

By the time de Varona retired, she had lowered the world record in the 400 individual medley by 25 seconds and had dropped the global mark in the 200 individual medley by more than 10 seconds. She was inducted into the International Swimming Hall of Fame in 1969 and won 18 national championships in a variety of events before embarking on a career in broadcasting.

53

Mike Barrowman

Country: United States
Birth date: December 4, 1968
Event: Breaststroke
Olympic medal: One
World Championship medal: One

The majority of the athletes featured in this collection excelled either in multiple events or over multiple distances within the same stroke. However, American Mike

Barrowman was so dominant in the 200 breaststroke that he warranted inclusion in the top 100 despite focusing on a single event.

Barrowman revolutionized the 200 breaststroke, not only by adopting a new technique for the event but by lowering the world record to a point that previously was considered out of reach. Working with Hungarian coach Jozsef Nagy, Barrowman made the wave technique, in which the athlete lunges forward with greater emphasis, a successful new style. It was proven by Barrowman and Nagy that athletes using the wave technique were less tired in the latter stages of races.

A three-time NCAA champion at the University of Michigan, Barrowman turned his style into gold. After finishing in a disappointing fourth place in the 200 breaststroke at the 1988 Olympics, Barrowman embarked on a mission to attain victory at the 1992 Games. En route to that gold medal, he set five world records from 1989 to 1991 and won the 1991 world championship in a world-record time.

The crowning moment of his career, though, was the championship final of the 200 breaststroke at the 1992 Olympics. Leading from the start, Barrowman clocked a time of 2:10.16, a world record that lasted for more than 10 years. He was so dominant that he defeated his rivals by more than one second, including former world-record holder Nick Gillingham of Great Britain.

"Barrowman became the showman of the stroke," reads Barrowman's International Swimming Hall of Fame inscription. "Through the technical use of physics and the practical use of borrowing the same head and shoulder characteristics of a cheetah running, Barrowman turned this stroke into the fastest in the world. On land, he re-popularized the use of medicine balls, taken from the 1950s, to increase quickness, particularly in the recovery phase of the stroke. Dryland work, but not weight training, was a very important part of his total training. His secret to success was none other than good old hard work."

Swimming World Magazine's World Swimmer of the Year in 1989 and 1990, Barrowman also had some success in the 100 breaststroke, although it did not measure up to what he achieved in the 200 breaststroke. His finest achievement in the shorter event was a gold medal at the 1991 Pan Pacific Championships.

Barrowman began working with Nagy when the swimmer was a 17-year-old and long has paid tribute to his coach's approach, which was highly critical. Barrowman used the harshness of the relationship as motivation.

"Everything I do is bad," Barrowman said. "Everything I do, 100 people have done better. Girls have done it better. Some people couldn't handle it. But it works for me."

54

Dara Torres

Country: United States
Birth date: April 15, 1967
Events: Sprint freestyle and butterfly
Olympic medals: Twelve
World Championship medal: One

The year was 1984, and Dara Torres was at McDonald's Swim Stadium, competing in the Los Angeles Olympic Games. Fast-forward 24 years, and Dara Torres was at the Water Cube, representing the United States at the 2008 Olympics in Beijing. She won medals on each occasion and at other Olympic stops in between, establishing a mark of longevity that probably will never be replicated.

One of the best pure sprinters the sport has seen, Torres was a star during her teenage years and a star as a 40-year-old athlete who proved, as the title of her book claims, that age is just a number. What she accomplished during the latter portion of her career is what is best known, as she produced some of her finest performances and served as an inspiration to middle-age women. Still, the other chapters of her aquatic days are equally impressive.

Torres's career can be broken down into three stages, the first spanning from 1984 to 1992. During that era, she was a three-time Olympian and firmly established herself as one of the elite sprinters in the world. She set three world records between 1983 and 1984 in the 50 freestyle and was quickly dubbed as the future of American swimming, partly because of her talent and partly because of an outgoing personality and good looks, something that made her marketable. She was never the type to stay static.

"You need a lot of hyperness to get you going for sprint events," she said. "You can't just sit there moping. I can never do that anyway. Most of my hobbies are sports—windsurfing and jet-skiing—not just sitting around reading books."

During her first three Olympiads, Torres collected four Olympic medals—all in relay action. Despite her early success, she was unable to land a berth in the 50 freestyle for the 1988 and 1992 Games. Meanwhile, the 50 freestyle was not an Olympic event at the 1984 Games, which was the best chance at an individual medal during the opening phase of Torres's career.

Following the 1992 Olympics, Torres left the sport and entered into a life that included commercial appearances, modeling, and broadcasting duties. She missed the 1996 Olympic Games during her seven-year retirement but eventually decided to make what would be her first comeback, a return that paid major dividends. Torres quickly became one of the big names in the sport, as she excelled at the 2000 Olympic Trials and Olympic Games in Sydney. In Australia, Torres was a five-time medalist, winning two gold medals in relay action and the first individual medals of her Olympic career: bronze medals in the 50 freestyle, 100 freestyle, and 100 butterfly. Her first comeback, too, included an American record in the 50 freestyle.

"I've never seen anything like that in my life, in any sport, to be out of the sport for seven years and to come back like that," said her coach, Richard Quick. "It's all a surprise to me, really, not just the record. Not that I wasn't confident, but if you had asked me a year ago if she would be breaking records and swimming like that, I wouldn't have believed you."

Another seven-year retirement followed the Sydney Games, but once again Torres got that itch to return. The second time, however, was far more stunning. In a sport dominated by teenagers and athletes in their early 20s, Torres was a 40-year-old mother trying to defy the odds of Mother Time. Somehow, she managed to succeed. After a few impressive tune-up efforts that proved that her return was legitimate, Torres secured an invitation to a fifth Olympiad, an accomplishment even more impressive considering that her appearances were over the span of seven Olympiads.

She was the talk not only of the swimming world but of general sports fans as well. At the 2008 Olympics, Torres won three silver medals: one in the 50 freestyle and two as a member of American relays. Her silver medal in the 50 freestyle was by a hundredth of a second, a poor finish the only thing separating Torres from the first individual gold medal of her Olympic career. Nonetheless, she improved her career total to 12 Olympic medals, tied for the most by a female swimmer. She also was an inspiration to many 40-something women.

"If it helps anyone else out there who is in their middle-aged years and they put off something they thought they couldn't do because they were too old or maybe thought that because they have children they can't balance what they want to do and be a parent, then I'm absolutely thrilled," she said.

Torres nearly qualified for a sixth Olympics in 2012 but came up a little short in the 50 freestyle as a 45-year-old. That race, at the U.S. Olympic Trials, was the final competitive outing of her career. It was also the latest evidence of her ability to turn back the aging process. Because of her unprecedented success, Torres has been dogged with allegations of performance-enhancing drug use. She has taken the accusations in stride and even participated in a program that tested her more frequently than other athletes.

"I'm an open book," Torres said in 2008. "DNA test me, blood test me, urine test me. Do whatever you want. I want to show people I'm clean. So if anyone says it now, I just take it as a compliment."

During her career, Torres set American records in the 50 freestyle, 100 freestyle, and 100 butterfly and was an NCAA champion at the University of Florida.

55

Sybil Bauer

Country: United States
Birth date: September 18, 1903
Death date: January 31, 1927
Event: Backstroke
Olympic medal: One

How talented was Sybil Bauer? To this day, she is believed to be the only woman in history to have broken a world record held by a man. Unfortunately, Bauer's accomplishments were cut short because of her death at the age of 23, and it is difficult to gauge exactly what she could have achieved if illness hadn't befallen her at such a young age.

Bauer was the first female star of the backstroke events, dominating and breaking world records at every distance during the 1920s. She was exceptional as a sprinter but also excelled as an endurance swimmer. She made her biggest mark at the 1924 Olympic Games in Paris, where she was the gold medalist in the 100 backstroke, winning the event by more than four seconds. Had there been a 200 backstroke at the time, she would have easily won that event, too.

From 1921 to 1926, Bauer won six consecutive national titles in the 100 backstroke, and she established 23 world records during her career. In addition to swimming, she was a standout basketball player and field hockey player for Northwestern University. She lost her life after a battle with cancer, ending the chance that she would repeat as Olympic champion at the 1928 Games.

"Sybil's early passing is saddening beyond human expression," reads her profile at the International Swimming Hall of Fame, to which she was enshrined in 1967. "Had she lived a hundred years, she could hardly have added anything important to her glorious athletic career, nor strengthened her hold upon the hearts of all who knew her. She was champion of women swimmers, the greatest of all in her field, and as such she will always be remembered."

Bauer is recognized as the lone female to break a men's world record, accomplishing the feat in Bermuda in 1922. Swimming the 440-yard backstroke, Bauer covered the distance in 6:24.8, four seconds faster than the men's world record. Although the mark was never officially ratified because the swim was unsanctioned, the effort is widely recognized as a defining performance in the sport's history.

56

Petra Schneider

Country: East Germany
Birth date: January 11, 1963
Events: Freestyle and individual medley
Olympic medals: Two
World Championship medals: Four

Whether it is proper to include East Germany's Petra Schneider on this top-100 list is debatable because of the revelations that Schneider was part of a systematic doping program implemented by East German coaches during the 1970s and 1980s. However, on the basis of her accomplishments alone, Schneider is an automatic selection, and this list is focused on identifying the 100 swimmers who achieved the most in the sport.

Schneider was best known for her prowess in the individual medley events and for her talent in the 400 freestyle. After winning the bronze medal in the 400 individual medley at the 1978 World Championships, where American Tracy Caulkins won gold, Schneider became unbeatable in the medley events. She won the gold medal in the 400 individual medley at the 1980 Olympics and won both medley events at the 1982 World Championships, with Caulkins the bronze medalist in each discipline.

But it was the manner in which she prevailed that was stunning and that led to beliefs (later proven) that Schneider was benefiting from the use of performance-enhancing drugs. Schneider not only won the 400 individual medley at the 1980 Olympics by more than 10 seconds but also lowered the world record in the event by nearly five seconds from 1980 to 1982, her best time of 4:36.10 serving as the global standard for 15 years. During her career, Schneider denied the use of steroids.

"For me, swimming is the most beautiful of all sports," she said. "Although I have been training for very many years and have taken part in a great number of competitions, I always find something new in this sport. And this I'm sure is greatly to the credit of my coach, Eberhard Mothes, who [oversees] my training sessions at the sport club in Karl-Marx-Stadt and never fails to come up with something interesting or challenging in the course of the work. I am the kind of person who likes being expected to achieve as much as I possibly can."

Schneider was named *Swimming World Magazine*'s World Swimmer of the Year in 1980 and 1982 and was also the silver medalist in the 400 freestyle at the 1980 Olympics. After her career and following the admission to the systematic doping within the East German sports machine, Schneider called for the elimination of her past records.

"My record was influenced by doping," Schneider said. "It's a record of the past. I'd like the current list to be reset at zero."

57

John Hencken

Country: United States
Birth date: May 29, 1954
Event: Breaststroke
Olympic medals: Five
World Championship medals: Three

At the 1976 Olympics in Montreal, the American men put together the greatest team display in the history of the Games. They won 12 of the 13 events contested, their only loss coming in the 200 breaststroke, where John Hencken captured the silver medal behind Great Britain's David Wilkie. Despite the shortcoming of Hencken, his career was nonetheless spectacular.

Between the 1972 Olympics in Munich and the 1976 Olympics, Hencken collected five medals, including three gold. In addition, he set 12 world records: seven in the 100 breaststroke and five in the 200 breaststroke. He is considered one of the two best breaststrokers in American history, ranking first on some lists and second behind Brendan Hansen in other discussions.

His first Olympiad produced a gold medal in the 200 breaststroke and a bronze medal in the 100 breaststroke. Four years later, he was the gold medalist in the 100 breaststroke, took silver in the 200 breaststroke, and contributed to the United States winning the gold medal in the 400 medley relay. Along the way, he took part in one of the best rivalries in the sport: repeated duels with Wilkie.

While Hencken was convincingly better in the 100-meter distance, he and Wilkie exchanged blows in the 200 breaststroke. The gold–silver finish of Hencken and Wilkie at the 1972 Olympics was reversed at the 1976 Games when Wilkie came out on top and dropped Hencken's world record by an astounding three seconds. Wilkie also got the best of Hencken in the 200 breaststroke at the 1973 World Champion-ships, the rivals again producing a gold–silver outcome.

During an era in which swimmers' careers ceased in their early 20s, Hencken was an anomaly. He continued to race beyond the 1976 Olympics and, as a 26-year-old, qualified to contest both breaststroke events at the 1980 Games in Moscow. Three years older than any other member of Team USA, Hencken never got the chance to compete in another Olympiad because of the American boycott put into effect by President Jimmy Carter.

A five-time NCAA champion for Stanford University, Hencken continued to compete after 1980 with his sights set on the 1984 Olympic Trials. Ultimately, he abandoned that attempt, but he challenged the idea that careers end after college graduation.

"I believe it's a myth that swimmers are over the hill after college," Hencken said. "They should be able to continue improving until at least 30, but that's up to the individual. Obviously, certain priorities change. Some people stop enjoying the sport when it competes with family and job obligations. At that point, it's no longer worth the time and energy."

58

David Wilkie

Country: Great Britain
Birth date: March 8, 1954
Events: Breaststroke and individual medley
Olympic medals: Three
World Championship medals: Five

As David Wilkie rose to prominence in the breaststroke events during the 1970s, Great Britain was mired in a severe drought. Not since Henry Taylor in 1908 had a British man left the Olympic Games with a gold medal in swimming. Because of this futility, the pressure on Wilkie to deliver was magnified. Ultimately, he got the job done and became a national sporting hero.

Wilkie is still renowned as one of the best breaststroke specialists in history, particularly over the 200-meter distance. Although he was an elite performer in the 100 breaststroke, Wilkie separated himself from the competition over the longer distance. The gap he created was never more apparent than at the 1976 Olympic Games in Montreal.

Dueling with longtime American rival John Hencken, Wilkie turned what was expected to be a stroke-for-stroke battle in the 200 breaststroke into a rout. Pulling away from Hencken in comfortable fashion, Wilkie lowered the world record by more than three seconds, an obscene amount of time in a sport where a tenth or a hundredth of a second is the usual dent put in world marks.

For Wilkie and Hencken, it was a closing chapter of a rivalry that endured for several years. While Wilkie bested Hencken in the 200 breaststroke in Montreal, Hencken got the final say in the 100 breaststroke, as the men flipped their finishing order. Meanwhile, four years earlier at the 1972 Olympics, Wilkie placed behind Hencken in the 200 breaststroke.

Wilkie's success was not limited to the Olympics. He was the world champion in the 200 breaststroke in 1973 (another victory over Hencken) and added a bronze medal in the 200 individual medley. At the 1975 World Championships, Wilkie flourished even more, sweeping the breaststroke events.

Although Wilkie's best event was the 200 breaststroke, in which he held the world record for six years from 1975 to 1981, he also set a global standard in the 200 individual medley. The combination of his breaststroke and medley exploits made him an easy choice for induction into the International Swimming Hall of Fame in 1982. An NCAA champion at the University of Miami and born in Sri Lanka, Wilkie almost gave up on the sport because of difficult training conditions on his arrival in Scotland.

"Wilkie swiftly decided competitive swimming wasn't up his street," stated a 2009 retrospective on Wilkie. "It had lost its fun since he came to Scotland—thanks in no small part to the inhospitable weather. Thankfully Frank Thomas, his coach, was able to see Wilkie's potential, and encouraged him to stick at it."

History followed.

59

Tracey Wickham

Country: Australia
Birth date: November 24, 1962
Event: Distance freestyle
World Championship medals: Two

Without any Olympic medals to her credit, one might wonder why or how Tracey Wickham warrants inclusion among the top-100 swimmers in history. That's easy: She still rates as an all-time great in the distance-freestyle events, and that hole in her portfolio is a consequence not of athletic talent but rather of extenuating circumstances.

In the late 1970s, Wickham was the female answer to the legendary distance stars whom Australia routinely produced on the male side. At the 1978 World Championships, she obliterated the competition in the 400 freestyle and 800 freestyle en route to gold medals. While she won the shorter distance by nearly one second, it was her four-plus-second triumph in the 800 freestyle that illustrated the gap she had created between herself and the rest of the world.

The 1978 season didn't just produce a pair of world titles, as Wickham also cruised to Commonwealth Games gold medals in the 400 freestyle and 800 freestyle and added a silver medal in the 200 freestyle. Making the year even more impressive, she set three world records—one in the 400 freestyle and two in the 800 freestyle—and her final marks endured as the global standards for nearly nine years.

What is missing from her career, though, is an Olympic medal. Although Australia did not boycott the 1980 Olympics in Moscow as a country, a number of Australian athletes opted to follow the precedent set by the United States and boycotted the Games on a personal level, including Wickham, who was the overwhelming favorite for gold medals in each of the distance-freestyle events. Her decision received significant attention, the majority of which was critical. Today, Wickham cites nonpolitical reasons for her decision to bypass what would have been the biggest competition of her life.

"My reasons for not going were purely personal, not political," Wickham said in a 2011 interview. "My parents had just divorced, Dad was in America, and Mum had hardly any money, and there I was a champion of the world. And I had glandular fever and didn't know it. I couldn't work out why my times were down. I knew two things: I was nowhere near peak condition, and Australia expected me to win gold. I had been hoping [Australia wouldn't go] so I wouldn't have to make a decision. When I finally did, it suited people to blame me, and I became the villain. The press crucified me."

60

Hendrika Mastenbroek

Country: Netherlands
Birth date: February 26, 1919
Death date: November 6, 2003
Events: Freestyle and backstroke
Olympic medals: Four

Hendrika Mastenbroek of the Netherlands was an early star in women's swimming, packaging a sterling career despite its brevity. She can be credited for paving the road to lofty success for Dutch swimming, particularly among women. More than 70 years after her competitive days, the Netherlands remains a force in the sport.

As a 15-year-old at the 1934 European Championships, Mastenbroek set the groundwork for what would be the crowning achievement of her career. She was the European champion in the 400 freestyle and 100 backstroke, titles that were complemented by a silver medal in the 100 freestyle. She added another gold medal in the 400 freestyle relay.

The 1936 Olympics, however, was where Mastenbroek affirmed her status as a legend. As was the case at the European Championships, Mastenbroek took home four medals, including three gold. She was the champion of the 100 freestyle and 400 freestyle, along with helping the Dutch prevail in the 400 freestyle relay. Her silver medal was in the 100 backstroke. In the 400 freestyle, Mastenbroek earned a satisfying triumph.

Racing against Denmark's Ragnhild Hveger, Mastenbroek felt slighted before the final of the 400 freestyle when Hveger offered chocolates to her teammates and several competitors. Mastenbroek was hoping for an offer of candy as well, but when Hveger did not reach out, she used the incident as motivation. Mastenbroek pulled away from her rival down the stretch, waiting for the right moment to surge, and registered a victory of more than a second.

"In a smother of foam the race was over. . . . Miss Mastenbroek came up from behind as if Miss Hveger had been standing still instead of putting every ounce of energy into the final spurt," wrote Albion Ross in the *New York Times*. "Her victory today was not due as much to the reserve of strength in her stocky, powerful body as to her excellent tactics."

Inducted into the International Swimming Hall of Fame in 1968, Mastenbroek set nine world records during her career, six in the backstroke and three in the free-style.

61

Tim Shaw

Country: United States
Birth date: November 8, 1957
Event: Freestyle
Olympic medal: One
World Championship medals: Three

One year before his initial Olympic dance, Tim Shaw was destined to define himself as the greatest distance freestyler in history. He was as dominant as anyone had been in the sport and had set world records over a variety of distances but soon fell victim to an overload of training. Ultimately, Shaw didn't meet the expectations placed on his shoulders. Still, he will go down as a distance legend.

At the 1975 World Championships, Shaw was racing in another dimension. He won the 200 freestyle, 400 freestyle, and 1500 freestyle and was poised to replicate the feat at the 1976 Olympics in Montreal. However, Shaw never got the chance to compete in the Olympics while at full power. Because of overtraining under the direction of his coach, Dick Jochums, Shaw battled anemia in the lead-up to the 1976 Games. Although he managed a silver medal in the 400 freestyle, it was far from what was anticipated.

"Everything I know about coaching, I learned on Tim Shaw's body," Jochums said in the book *Gold on the Water*. "All my theories, all my mistakes. I will love Tim Shaw until the day I die more than any swimmer I will ever coach, and you know what? I ruined him as a swimmer. The one who will always mean more than anyone else. First I made him. Then, I broke him."

During the 1974 and 1975 seasons, Shaw set nine world records over four free-style events and was twice named World Swimmer of the Year. His global marks stretched over the 200 freestyle, 400 freestyle, 800 freestyle, and 1500 freestyle, a testament to his middle-distance and distance skill.

Inducted into the International Swimming Hall of Fame in 1989, Shaw won seven national championships and three NCAA championships. After his swimming career, he shifted his focus to water polo and won a silver medal as part of the American squad at the 1984 Olympics in Los Angeles. Shaw is not bothered by the turn of events that prevented Olympic glory.

"My coach, Dick Jochums, believed in Greek philosophy," he said. "He always felt true victories were won by battles with yourself, that no matter how you've mastered the moment, the [laurel] wreath dies. He convinced me that you can leave the past behind rather than continue to grasp at something you tried to accomplish."

62

Galina Prozumenshchikova

Country: Soviet Union
Birth date: November 26, 1948
Death date: July 19, 2015
Event: Breaststroke
Olympic medals: Five

Five decades have passed since Galina Prozumenshchikova emerged as an international sensation in the breaststroke events. As a result, her name is often left off the list of finest athletes in her sport, the Soviet Union star's longevity over three Olympiads a forgotten characteristic of her excellence.

During an era in which the majority of swimmers, especially females, competed in one Olympiad and then moved into the next stage of life, Prozumenshchikova was an anomaly. She not only soared to the top of her sport but also managed to maintain her status as an elite performer over three Olympiads. Even today, with more opportunities for extended careers, qualifying for the Olympics on three occasions is a difficult task.

Prozumenshchikova was best known for her talent in the longer breaststroke event, in which she medaled at three consecutive Olympiads. After winning the gold medal in the 200 breaststroke as a 15-year-old at the 1964 Olympics in Tokyo, Prozumenshchikova followed with bronze medals in the discipline at the 1968 Games and the 1972 Olympics. Her final medal in the event might have been her most impressive considering that she had given birth just a few years earlier and was the rare female athlete to return to competition after becoming a mother.

The Soviet's international success, however, was not limited to the 200 breaststroke. At both the 1968 Olympics and the 1972 Games, she was the silver medalist in the 100 breaststroke, losing by a tenth of a second at the 1968 Games. At the

European Championships, Prozumenshchikova was twice the champion of the 200 breaststroke and added one title in the 100 breaststroke.

As further evidence of her dominance in the 200 breaststroke, Prozumenshchikova set four world records from 1964 to 1966, lowering the global standard by an astounding eight seconds during that span. She also set the world record in the 100 breaststroke in 1966, although that mark lasted for just five months.

63

Yoshiyuki Tsuruta

Country: Japan
Birth date: October 1, 1903
Death date: July 24, 1986
Event: Breaststroke
Olympic medals: Two

The reign of Japanese breaststrokers has been a norm in the sport for nearly a century, with the country regularly producing Olympic medalists such as Kosuke Kitajima, a four-time gold medalist. The man who started the tradition was Yoshiyuki Tsuruta, who established himself as the premier breaststroke specialist during the 1920s and 1930s.

Tsuruta captured the most prestigious medal of his career at the 1928 Olympic Games in Amsterdam. In one of the most anticipated races of the early Olympic movement, Tsuruta battled Germany's Erich Rademacher, the world-record holder. Ultimately, Tsuruta produced a comfortable victory, defeating his rival by nearly two seconds. Tsuruta and Rademacher were so far ahead of the rest of the world that the bronze medal was won with a time more than five seconds slower than Rademacher.

Four years later, Tsuruta made history at the 1932 Olympics in Los Angeles. Battling countryman Reizo Koike, Tsuruta repeated as the gold medalist, prevailing this time by a little more than one second. He became the first individual to win back-to-back Olympic titles in the 200 breaststroke and remained as the sole man to accomplish that feat until Kitajima emerged as the winner in 2004 and 2008.

Tsuruta, who was inducted into the International Swimming Hall of Fame in 1968, remained involved in swimming after his competitive career concluded and held a number of leadership positions. He was once the director of the Japan Swimming League and also served as the head of the Ehime Swimming School.

At the end of the 20th century, Tsuruta was selected as one of the top-25 male swimmers in history by *Swimming World Magazine*.

64

Charles Hickcox

Country: United States
Birth date: February 6, 1947
Death date: June 14, 2010
Events: Individual medley and backstroke
Olympic medals: Four

A member of the Indiana University dynasty that ruled the collegiate ranks under the watch of coach James "Doc" Counsilman in the 1960s, Charles Hickcox became one of the world's finest all-around swimmers, flourishing in the individual medley events and the 100 backstroke and 200 backstroke. He competed at a time when he was surrounded at Indiana by the likes of Mark Spitz and Gary Hall Sr., individuals who also rank among the top-100 swimmers of all time.

The 1967 season proved to be Hickcox's launching pad for the next year's Olympic Games. At the Pan American Games, Hickcox secured a gold medal in the 100 backstroke and a silver medal in the 200 backstroke. That effort was complemented by an even more impressive performance at the World University Games in Tokyo, where Hickcox won gold medals—behind world-record outings—in both backstroke events. For good measure, he helped the United States to victory in the 400 medley relay and 800 freestyle relay.

By the time the 1968 Olympics rolled around, Hickcox had transitioned from a backstroke specialist into a multievent threat. He left the Mexico City Games with gold medals in the 200 individual medley and 400 individual medley and as a member of the American 400 medley relay. His backstroke prowess remained evident through his winning a silver medal in the 100 backstroke.

A seven-time NCAA champion for Indiana, Hickcox set world records in each medley event and both backstrokes during his career and was a 1976 inductee into the International Swimming Hall of Fame. Counsilman once theorized that Hickcox's best stroke might have been the butterfly, but he never got to test that skill at a major international event because of his focus on the backstroke and individual medley.

Hickcox, a captain at Indiana, was known as a leader both at the collegiate level and for Team USA and was named World Swimmer of the Year by *Swimming World Magazine* in 1968.

"Charlie has an unusual amount of talent for swimming," Counsilman said in 1969. "It's easy to understand the concept of intelligence, but it's a more nebulous thing in athletes when you say a guy has ability. Ability is coordination, flexibility in the ankles, a big heart. Charlie varies from a lot of athletes with ability in that he works hard, too. He has the ability to punish himself. On top of this he's very coachable. I think he's the best all-around swimmer of all time."

65

Ann Curtis

Country: United States
Birth date: March 6, 1926
Death date: June 26, 2012
Event: Freestyle
Olympic medals: Three

One of the best American female swimmers of the first half of the 20th century, Ann Curtis was a dominant force on the world stage despite not having a full opportunity to prove her worth. Although Curtis's best events were the distance freestyles, her versatility was on display when she raced over the shorter freestyle distances.

Curtis made her biggest mark at the 1948 Olympic Games in London, winning gold medals in the 400 freestyle and as a member of the U.S. 400 freestyle relay. She also added a silver medal in the 100 freestyle. Had the Olympic program featured the 200 freestyle and 800 freestyle at the time, Curtis would have added additional medals. The cancellation of the 1944 Olympics due to World War II also hindered her medal count, as Curtis would have contended for multiple podium finishes.

"Nobody ever worked harder to get where she is," said Curtis's coach, Charlie Sava. "Since she got [to the top], she kept right on plugging, because she's always afraid. Real champions are always afraid they'll lose."

Losing, however, was a foreign concept to Curtis. Under the guidance of Sava, Curtis put in more practice yardage than almost any woman in the sport, a total so high that other coaches questioned the decision. Yet that approach worked for Curtis, a winner of the Sullivan Award, given annually to the top amateur athlete in the

United States. Curtis won more than 30 national championships during her career and was the high-point scorer at Nationals on seven occasions.

Following her career, she opened a swim school in California and competed as a masters swimmer. She was inducted into the International Swimming Hall of Fame in 1966 and is credited with breaking 56 American records.

66

John Konrads

Country: Australia
Birth date: May 21, 1942
Event: Freestyle
Olympic medals: Three

Although born in Latvia, John Konrads became an Australian legend in the freestyle events, especially in the distance disciplines. Konrads was known for being half of a sibling duo with his sister Ilsa, establishing numerous world records during the late 1950s and early 1960s.

Konrads's international breakthrough came at the 1958 Empire Games, where he won three gold medals, including victories in the 400 freestyle and 1500 freestyle. That year also marked the first of Konrads's world records, the initial standard coming in the 800 freestyle. For his career and as a demonstration of his versatility, Konrads set world records in the 200 freestyle, 400 freestyle, 800 freestyle, and 1500 freestyle.

The crowning moment of his career was the final of the 1500 freestyle at the 1960 Olympic Games in Rome. Squaring off with countryman and defending Olympic champion Murray Rose, Konrads won the gold medal by more than two seconds, with Rose taking the silver medal. Konrads's strength over the last half of the race proved to be the difference.

"It was the win I wanted most because of Australia's history in the event," Konrads said of the 1500 freestyle. "The Olympic gold medal is the high of all highs, but I don't think anyone has really clear memories about winning. It's just an environment of everything that you've always strived for, and you can't put it into words. It's pride, joy, relief. Actually, a lot of it is relief—thank Christ it's over."

The victory in the 1500 freestyle followed a disappointing finish by Konrads in the 400 freestyle. Despite being the world-record holder, Konrads managed only a bronze medal in a race won by Rose. Making the defeat even tougher to accept was the fact Konrads finished six seconds off his best time. The loss still stings, more than 50 years later.

"[In the 400 freestyle], all I had to do was go 2.9 seconds worse than my personal best to get a gold," said Konrads, who added a bronze medal in the 800 freestyle relay. "Even though 99 percent of the time I'm at ease with it, when down times come or when depression sets in, they're the sort of things that you cover. And you know, it's hard to really square away with major . . . yeah, failures."

Konrads, who raced in the preliminaries of the 800 freestyle relay at the 1964 Olympics, and his sister were inducted into the International Swimming Hall of Fame in 1971. He has spoken out about his longtime battles with depression, hoping to help others affected by the disorder.

67

Karen Muir

Country: South Africa
Birth date: September 16, 1952
Death date: April 1, 2013
Event: Backstroke

The glaring omission from Karen Muir's portfolio is an Olympic gold medal or a medal of any color. However, it was not a lack of skill that prevented Muir from achieving the ultimate feat in her sport. Rather, she was the victim of politics and the ban placed on South Africa by the International Olympic Committee during her career.

Muir is considered one of the best backstroke specialists in history and the most precocious. As a 12-year-old in 1965, Muir became the youngest swimmer to break a world record when she covered the 110-yard backstroke in 1:08.7. It was the first of many world records for Muir, who would have been the favorite for the gold medal at the 1968 Olympics had she been allowed to compete. But because of South Africa's apartheid policies, Muir was not able to measure up against the best in the world.

"It has been a bit too much and I still cannot really believe that I am holder of the world record," Muir said of her first global standard. "It's like something out of a fairytale. Everyone has been very kind and wonderful, but I am glad that the fuss is finished."

Muir's timing was unfortunate, as the ban against South Africa did not take effect until after the 1960 Games, not long before Muir emerged on the international stage. However, the ban was not lifted until the 1992 Olympics, leaving Muir and fans of the sport to wonder how successful she could have been competing against the best competition in the biggest sporting event in the world.

"[Muir] has the greatest potential of any swimmer in the world," said South African coach Alex Bulley after Muir set her first world record. "There is no limit to what she can do."

Muir set two world records in the 100 backstroke and four world records in the 200 backstroke, including several marks during the 1968 Olympic year. A 22-time South African champion between the backstroke, freestyle, and individual medley, Muir also won U.S. and British national championships and held the world record in the 100 backstroke for more than four years.

68

Alex Baumann

Country: Canada
Birth date: April 21, 1964
Event: Individual medley
Olympic medals: Two
World Championship medals: Two

Born in the former Czechoslovakia, Alex Baumann moved to Canada when he was a child, a move that was a major boon for Canadian swimming. During the first half of the 1980s, Baumann was the premier individual medley performer in the world, cementing that status at the 1984 Olympics in Los Angeles.

Despite being hampered by injuries for a good portion of his career, particularly difficulties with his shoulders, Baumann broke his first world record as a 17-year-old in 1981, lowering the standard in the 200 individual medley. It was a major accomplishment not only for Baumann but also for Canadian swimming, which had not boasted an Olympic champion in the sport since 1912. Suddenly, that drought looked like it would end.

Although injuries forced Baumann to miss the 1982 World Championships, he rebounded later in the year by winning the 200 individual medley and 400 individual medley at the Commonwealth Games. Two years later, he turned that momentum in Olympic gold medals. Swimming with a heavy heart following the deaths of his father and brother, Baumann first won the 400 individual medley in world-record time, then set a world mark to win the 200 individual medley. He won both events by more than one second.

"I think after 72 years, it's about time," remarked Baumann, in reference to ending Canada's winless streak in the Olympics.

Baumann repeated as Commonwealth Games champion in both medley disciplines in 1986, but he was unable to remain on top of the world. At the World Championships, Baumann picked up the silver medal in the 200 individual medley and the bronze medal in the 400 individual medley while watching Hungary's Tamas Darnyi emerge as the number one force in the events, a distinction that Darnyi would keep into the 1990s.

"The deaths of his father and older brother left profound gaps in his life, but [coach Jeno Tihanyi] played a major role in keeping him focused on his goals," reads Baumann's International Swimming Hall of Fame profile. "Perhaps his single most admired quality was his disciplined approach to swimming. He always gave 100 percent. Every swim was a race. Nothing was wasted. Alex was a bit of a prankster, but never lost his humbleness and feel for his teammates and others. His self-determination to excel, coupled with a swimming program geared to his style, were the keys to his success."

69

Fanny Durack

Country: Australia
Birth date: October 27, 1889
Death date: March 20, 1956
Event: Freestyle
Olympic medal: One

Australian Fanny Durack was one of the first female stars in the sport, excelling in all freestyle events and holding the world record in various distances. She capitalized on her popularity by competing around the world and receiving newspaper billing for her swimming exploits.

In 1912, when women's swimming was added to the Olympic program, Durack became the first female champion by winning the 100 freestyle. Durack was so dominant and ahead of her time that she captured the gold medal by more than three seconds over Mina Wylie, her Australian teammate. By the time she won her gold medal, Durack was on the decline of her career. She would have been better suited if swimming had been added as a women's sport in either 1904 or 1908.

Durack set 11 world records during her career, and most of her records endured for nearly a decade, including a nine-year reign in the 100-yard freestyle from 1912 to 1921 and an eight-year reign in the 100-meter freestyle from 1912 to 1920. She also held the world record in the 220-yard freestyle for six years and was a world-record holder in the 500-meter freestyle and the one-mile swim, her performance in the longest event standing as the global best for 12 years.

As a way to make a living and draw interest to women's swimming, Durack would travel the world and face challenges from a variety of competitors. In addition to racing her opponents, Durack would take on challenges for making the deepest dive and staying underwater for the longest period of time. Durack initially used a stroke similar to the dog paddle but eventually graduated to a stroke that resembled today's freestyle.

"Miss Durack is no believer in special training for swimming," stated a 1914 article in the *Sydney Morning Herald*. "Swimming itself is a sufficiently all-round exercise to keep her fit, and she gets plenty of practice with the Eastern Suburbs Club. As a child she was very fond of dancing, and won a cakewalking competition at the Sydney Town Hall in 1902. She also won medals for tennis and calisthenics at school, but nowadays swimming crowds out all other recreations and exercises as far as she is concerned."

70

Susie O'Neill

Country: Australia
Birth date: August 2, 1973
Events: Freestyle and butterfly
Olympic medals: Eight
World Championship medals: Seven

Given the nickname Madame Butterfly, Susie O'Neill was one of Australia's finest female swimmers throughout the 1990s and 2000s, obviously excelling in the butterfly events. However, her moniker does not do her justice, as O'Neill was more than a one-event wonder. O'Neill might be one of the most underappreciated Australian women swimmers of all time.

O'Neill made her first significant impact at the international level during the 1990 and 1991 seasons, piling up medals at the Commonwealth Games and Pan Pacific Championships in addition to garnering a relay silver at the 1991 World Championships. However, it was at the 1992 Olympics in Barcelona where O'Neill really broke through, winning the bronze medal in the 200 butterfly, the event that became her signature.

Over the next several years, O'Neill became one of the biggest stars in the sport, although her profile was overshadowed by some of her better-known Australian teammates. She was the silver medalist in both butterfly events at the 1994 World Championships and won the gold medal in the 200 butterfly at the 1998 World Championships. In between, she was the champion of the 200 butterfly at the 1996 Olympics in Atlanta, a meet that also produced silver medals in two relays.

By the time O'Neill got to compete at the 2000 Olympics, held in her home nation, she was the undisputed queen of the 200 butterfly. Not only was she the two-time defending world champion and the reigning Olympic champion, but she

157

had broken Mary T. Meagher's iconic world record, which was on the books for more than 18 years. As the 2000 Games neared, O'Neill was viewed as unbeatable.

However, O'Neill suffered one of the biggest upsets in the sport in the final of the 200 butterfly in Sydney, beaten to the wall by American Misty Hyman. Despite winning the gold medal in the 200 freestyle in Sydney and adding silver medals in two relays, O'Neill was severely stung by her inability to win her prime event. It's a setback that still hurts.

"My initial reaction when people talk about Sydney is that it was the Olympics where I lost my main race, my gold medal," she said. "I won the 200 freestyle, but I have almost dismissed that over the last 10 years. I never really wanted to do [the 200 freestyle]. They [the national team coaches] tricked me into it. Then straight after that race, I had to do a 200 butterfly semifinal, and I was only thinking about that. I would still swap those two medals. I would way prefer the gold in the 200 butterfly and silver in the 200 freestyle."

Inducted into the International Swimming Hall of Fame in 2006, O'Neill captured 35 Australian championships during her career and was a 15-time medalist at the Commonwealth Games and a 13-time medalist at the Pan Pacific Championships.

71

Brian Goodell

Country: United States
Birth date: April 2, 1959
Event: Distance freestyle
Olympic medals: Two
World Championship medal: One

A great in distance swimming, Brian Goodell emerged as an international star as a teenager. A member of the American squad that won every event but one at the 1976 Olympics in Montreal, Goodell headlined the distance contingent for the United States and was part of a pair of gold–silver finishes.

That Goodell became a double-Olympic champion was not surprising based on his silver medal in the 1500 freestyle at the 1975 World Championships. Goodell took that momentum and turned it into victories in the 400 freestyle and 1500 freestyle at the Olympics, both triumphs arriving in world-record time.

A nine-time NCAA champion at the University of California, Los Angeles, spanning the 500 freestyle, 1650 freestyle, and 400 individual medley, Goodell was expected to further bolster his status in the years following his Olympic gold medals. In some ways, Goodell raised his profile, thanks to additional world-record performances in the 400 freestyle and 1500 freestyle. A high-intensity approach was a huge key to his success.

"He had a will to win that I've seen in few other athletes," said Ron Ballatore, Goodell's college coach. "He can summon up those hidden reserves and turn it on when somebody is after him."

Through a pair of events out of Goodell's control, he never matched his success of 1976. A case of strep throat derailed Goodell's qualifying attempts for the 1978 World Championships, where Goodell would have been a favorite for the gold medal alongside Soviet Vladimir Salnikov. Worse, the boycott of the 1980 Olympics in Moscow by President Jimmy Carter prevented Goodell—at the peak of his career— from defending his Olympic crowns. After Carter's decision to boycott the Games, Goodell retired.

Goodell's unfortunate circumstances prevented the sport from enjoying what could have been a spectacular rivalry between the American and Salnikov. The men changed the landscape of distance swimming and would have pushed each other to higher levels had they had the chance to duel.

"I just avoided him," Goodell said of once attending an event with President Carter. "I don't like seeing him—in person, on TV, in the newspaper. He's always got something critical to say about somebody else, but when it comes to criticism of the boycott, he can't take it. He's the victim. He can't take being criticized for the most harebrained thing I've ever heard of. . . . I was 17 in Montreal. In Moscow, I would have been 21 and in the prime of my career. And zippo. [Carter] screwed with everybody's lives. I could have made some pretty good coin. It did really screw me up."

72

Lenny Krayzelburg

Country: United States
Birth date: September 28, 1975
Event: Backstroke
Olympic medals: Four
World Championship medals: Three

The story of Lenny Krayzelburg is a feel-good tale. He was a Ukrainian immigrant who benefited from the early tutelage of the Soviet Union's sports system before settling in the United States as a teenager and eventually soaring to the top ranks of his sport, including status as an Olympic champion.

Identified as a potential swimming champion as a youth in the Soviet Union, Krayzelburg attended a sports school beginning as a nine-year-old, splitting 12-hour days between the classroom and the pool. Ultimately, his family decided to move to the United States, and despite a few early bumps in finding the proper training program, Krayzelburg continued to develop as a standout backstroker.

From 1997 through 1999, Krayzelburg put himself in position to become an Olympic champion. At the 1997 and 1999 Pan Pacific Championships, he won both backstroke events and led off the U.S. gold-medal-winning 400 medley relay. Meanwhile, he set world records in each of his individual events at the 1999 version of the meet. Sandwiched in between the Pan Pacific Championships was the 1998 World Championships, where Krayzelburg also doubled in the backstroke disciplines.

By the time the 2000 Olympics rolled around, Krayzelburg was among the biggest favorites for gold-medal performances. In the 100 backstroke, he got to the wall ahead of Australian Matt Welsh. He was even more impressive in the 200 backstroke, placing ahead of American teammate Aaron Peirsol, a rising star who looked up to and received mentoring from Krayzelburg. Also guiding the Americans to gold in the 400 medley relay, Krayzelburg didn't forget his roots.

"This is Mount Everest," Krayzelburg said. "It's great to know for the rest of your life you had this journey and it is completed. That is the most beautiful thing. In the States, people are afraid to challenge kids at a young age. They grow them slowly. In Russia, at nine years old, you have no choice. You either accept it, or you give up."

Following the 2000 Olympics, Krayzelburg faded from prominence, only to return in time to qualify for the 2004 Olympics in Athens. Although he missed winning the bronze medal in the 100 backstroke by just two one-hundredths of a second, he won a gold medal in the 400 medley relay after swimming the backstroke leg for the United States during the preliminary round.

73

Gunnar Larsson

Country: Sweden
Birth date: May 12, 1951
Events: Individual medley and freestyle
Olympic medals: Two
World Championship medal: One

More than 40 years had passed without a Swedish gold medalist in the pool when Gunnar Larsson trekked to the 1972 Olympics in Munich. Those Games, of course, are remembered for the exploits of Mark Spitz, who stormed to a record seven gold medals and seven world records. Larsson, however, made some noise of his own, especially for his homeland.

Four years after flaming out of the preliminary rounds in the 200 freestyle, 400 freestyle, and 1500 freestyle at the 1968 Olympics in Mexico City, Larsson had undergone a transformation. While he continued to dabble with the distance-freestyle events, he had become—first and foremost—an individual medley performer. It was at the 1970 European Championships where he put this multievent skill on display.

In addition to winning the 400 freestyle, consequently continuing to prove himself in the freestyle, Larsson doubled as the 200 individual medley and 400 individual medley champion against the best competition in Europe. Equally important, his world record in the 200 individual medley sent a message that he would be a significant factor at the 1972 Olympics.

At the Munich Games, Larsson again doubled as the titlist in the medley disciplines, setting another world record in the 200 distance. Still, the meet will be remembered for what unfolded in the final of the 400 individual medley. Engaging in a down-to-the-wire battle with American Tim McKee, Larsson won the gold medal in the closest finish in Olympic history and one that will never be replicated.

"The final was too close to call, so the fans looked to the electric timing," stated a recap of the race by the website *Sports Reference*. "Both Larsson and McKee had finished in 4:31.98, a seeming tie. But the electric timer could measure to the [thousandth] of a second, and when that was done, Larsson had the gold medal—4:31.981 to 4:31.983. After Munich, this would not be allowed again, as it was shown that this was less than the thickness of one coat of paint on the wall, and minute differences in the lanes could affect this result. All future international swimming races would be decided only to the [hundredth] of a second, and if swimmers were tied at that margin, they were declared tied."

Following his Olympic triumphs, Larsson hung around long enough to become the gold medalist in the 200 individual medley at the first World Championships, held in 1973. The Swede was inducted into the International Swimming Hall of Fame in 1979.

74

Martha Norelius

Country: United States
Birth date: January 20, 1908
Death date: September 23, 1955
Event: Freestyle
Olympic medals: Three

One of the trailblazers of American female swimming, Martha Norelius etched a fine career as a versatile freestyler, although her talents shone more brightly as the distance of her events increased. Coached and trained by her father, Charles, who was an Olympian for Sweden at the 1906 Olympics, Norelius carried the family's Olympic banner.

Forceful with her stroke, Norelius won her first Olympic gold medal at the 1924 Games in Paris. Setting an Olympic record, she won the 400 freestyle by more than one second and finished ahead of Helen Wainwright and Gertrude Ederle, the latter one of the great female swimmers in history and the first woman to cross the English Channel.

Norelius was even more impressive in her second Olympic appearance, leaving the 1928 Games in Amsterdam with two gold medals. In addition to helping the United States to victory in the 400 freestyle relay, Norelius successfully defended her championship in the 400 freestyle. It marked the first time an American woman was a repeat Olympic champion.

"Martha was considered the first woman to swim with and like the men," states her International Swimming Hall of Fame profile. "She used Johnny Weissmuller's high head position, arched back and a heavy six-beat kick, hydroplaning over the water. Her father trained her to see how few strokes she could swim a length of the pool in—39 or 40 strokes a minute—then speed it up for competition. . . . Norelius was the world's fastest woman swimmer for eight years and at any distance."

Because she gave an exhibition alongside professionals, she lost her amateur status and any chance of competing at the 1932 Olympics in Los Angeles had she decided to pursue that event. During her career, she set world records in the 200 freestyle, 400 freestyle, 800 freestyle, and 1500 freestyle but is best known for her excellence over the 400-meter distance, where she set four world records in 1927 and 1928, including in her second Olympic win.

75

Katinka Hosszu

Country: Hungary
Birth Date: May 3, 1989
Events: Multiple
Olympic medals: Four
World Championship medals: Thirteen

Katinka Hosszu has been one of the more polarizing figures in the sport in recent years, a tale of two careers the best way to describe the performances of the Hungarian multi-event star. A 2008 Olympian in both medley events, in which she failed to qualify for the final, Hosszu emerged on the worldwide stage at the 2009 World Championships in Rome, a gold medal in the 400 individual medley complemented by bronze medals in the 200 medley and 200 butterfly.

Hosszu continued to flourish the following year at the European Championships, where she won titles in the 200 individual medley and 200 butterfly, to go with a silver medal in the 400 individual medley. Hosszu's international success coincided with her time at the University of Southern California, where she was coached by Dave Salo and captured several NCAA Championships. It appeared that Hosszu was poised to excel at the 2011 World Championships and, more importantly, at the 2012 Olympic Games in London.

Hosszu, however, sputtered in 2011 and 2012, unable to reach the podium at either competition. Her showing at the Olympics was most frustrating, as she just missed a medal with a fourth-place finish in the 400 medley, to go with a sixth-place effort in the 200 medley. In the 200 butterfly, Hosszu failed to advance out of the semifinals. The shortcomings in London triggered a coaching change for Hosszu, who left the guidance of Salo and began working with Shane Tusup, a former USC swimmer who eventually became Hosszu's husband.

Despite not having a coaching background, Tusup jump-started Hosszu's career beginning in 2013, and the partnership has never looked back while attaining high-level success. Under Tusup's watch, Hosszu has won three consecutive world titles in the 200 individual medley and 400 individual medley, and has also earned medals at the World Championships in the 200 backstroke and 200 butterfly. More, she has been the dominant performer on the World Cup circuit, racing double-digit events on a regular basis to earn the moniker "The Iron Lady," and earning millions of dollars in the process.

The defining moment of Hosszu's career was the 2016 Olympic Games in Rio de Janeiro, where Hosszu captured gold in the 200 medley and 400 medley, and added another title in the 100 backstroke. Her world record in the 400 medley was eye-popping in nature, the previous standard viewed as untouchable. She also took silver in the 200 backstroke, where she was upset by American Maya DiRado and denied the chance to join East Germany's Kristin Otto (1988) as the only women to win four solo gold medals in the same Olympiad.

"I felt a lot of pressure going into London, and I was super-nervous before the final," Hosszu said of her 2012 struggles. "I remember not enjoying it. I just wanted it to be over. I was, I guess, more scared even than nervous. I was just afraid what happens if I don't win. After I started working with Shane, after London, we decided that we were just going to keep racing and keep improving and when I get to Rio, I'm just going to have fun and I'm just going to basically get up on the block and just have a fun race."

Since uniting with Tusup as a 23-year-old, Hosszu has established personal-best times in every event on the swimming program. To set personal records in each event is an anomaly in itself, but is considered even more startling considering that those personal marks have arrived at the age of 23 and beyond. Simply, the arc of Hosszu's career is abnormal when weighed against history, consequently leading to doping allegations. The fact that Hosszu races as frequently as she does, and is able to recover rapidly between events, has also raised eyebrows.

In a 2015 column published by *Swimming World Magazine*, a longtime leading publication in the sport, author Casey Barrett accused Hosszu of doping, despite the Hungarian having never failed a drug test. The accusations led to Hosszu filing a lawsuit against Barrett and *Swimming World*'s parent company, Sports Publications Inc. The lawsuit was eventually dismissed, and Hosszu has continued to be the subject of doubt when it comes to her performances and career surge under Tusup. For her part, Hosszu has steadfastly denied ever being involved in a doping program.

"I never took performance-enhancing substances," Hosszu said. "I would not sell my soul for money, fame or victory. Cheating is completely alien to me, as is shrugging off a self-serving attempt to undermine my credibility by someone completely unknown to me."

76

Anthony Ervin

Country: United States
Birth Date: May 26, 1981
Events: Sprint Freestyle
Olympic medals: Four
World Championship medals: Three

There are two ways to look at the career of Anthony Ervin. Through one set of lenses, many ask the obvious question: What could have been? Through another vantage point, many state: At least we got that second glimpse. In no way has Ervin's career been conventional, but in every way, it has possessed intrigue and drama.

When Ervin started his collegiate career at the University of California-Berkeley in 1999, there were lofty expectations attached to his name. Nonetheless, the speed with which Ervin ascended to the top of the sprinting realm was alarming—NCAA titles in the 50 and 100 freestyle events jump-starting his 2000 campaign and a year to remember.

As part of a training group known as The Race Club, which was coached by sprint guru Mike Bottom, Ervin had daily opportunities to push himself against some of the best sprinters in the sport. There were regular clashes with Gary Hall Jr., an eventual 10-time Olympic medalist, and routine face-offs with Polish Olympian

Bart Kizierowski. Simply, Ervin found himself in the best position to prime himself for the 2000 Olympiad, and he certainly took advantage of that prep work.

After placing second behind Hall at the 2000 Olympic Trials in Indianapolis, Ervin headed to the Olympic Games in Sydney as a medal possibility. But with Hall as the champion of the U.S. Trials and two-time defending Olympic champion Alexander Popov of Russia lurking, Ervin wasn't exactly tabbed as a leading challenger for gold, especially with the one-lap sprint known to belong to veteran performers. Then again, maybe the fact that Ervin was a tested 19-year-old played into his favor.

Posting an identical time to that of Hall, 21.98, Ervin walked away from the 50 free with the shared title of fastest man in water and the distinction of being the first man of African-American descent to earn Olympic gold in the pool. The gold medal was Ervin's second piece of hardware in Sydney, complementing the silver medal he won as a member of the American 400 freestyle relay earlier in the week. That the victory was shared with Hall, his training partner, made the victory that much sweeter.

"I have always been proud of my heritage," Ervin said. "But I don't think of it in terms of first of this, first of that. It is like people are trying to pin it down to one definitive thing. I never thought about it. In the nature of American society today, I would think having diverse blood would not be a big deal."

The summer following his gold in Sydney, Ervin firmly entrenched himself as the world's premier sprinter, with titles claimed in the 50 freestyle and 100 freestyle at the World Championships in Fukuoka, Japan. At the time, there was chatter that Ervin had the potential to etch himself as the finest sprinter the sport had seen. Instead, he traveled a different road.

While Ervin won a silver medal in the 50 freestyle at the 2002 Pan Pacific Championships, he failed to advance out of the event's prelims at the 2003 World Championships and an eight-year hiatus from competition followed. With guitar in hand, Ervin bounced around the country, picking up odd jobs and giving swim lessons on occasion. But there was no sign of the athlete who swiftly broke onto the global scene and soared to the top.

"It became time to go back and reclaim some of the stuff I had sacrificed along the way," Ervin said of his hiatus. "I was kind of shot down this tunnel. As a youth, as most people are, you're not really given a ton of options for a variety of reasons. When something sticks, people often stay with it. For whatever reason, I couldn't do that. I was convinced the grass would be greener somewhere else. Or, at the least, if I did make the journey that I would see the other side of that horizon, whatever was there. I think everybody's got that to a certain degree. But I certainly had a lot of angst and resistance toward being pushed in the direction I had always been going. I really just needed freedom, so I took it."

It wasn't until 2011, when Ervin got the itch again, that he climbed a starting block and again put his vast talent on display. Upon his return to the pool, there was no way to predict a positive outcome to Ervin's comeback. And then his times started to come down, and announce themselves as faster than Ervin had ever been before. After qualifying for the 2012 Olympics, where he finished fifth, Ervin was sixth in the 50 free at the 2013 World Championships and ninth at the 2015 World Champs.

The fairytale part of the comeback was written in 2016, when the Olympic Games made their way to Rio de Janeiro.

Having made it through the gauntlet that is the United States Olympic Trials, Ervin looked sharp from the onset in Rio. After contributing a prelim leg to the United States' 400 freestyle relay, which went on to win gold in the final, Ervin qualified third in the prelims of the 50 free and second in the semifinal round. He saved his best performance for the final, a mark of 21.40 supplying a victory of .01 over reigning Olympic and world champ Florent Manaudou of France.

At the age of 35 and 16 years after he captured his first Olympic title in the event, Ervin was again on top of the sprinting world. Ervin's age made him the oldest Olympic swimming champion in history.

"It's surreal, kind of absurd," Ervin said. "When I touched, turned around and saw the one next to my name, I kind of smiled and laughed. Then I wanted to show a little bit of emotion for the effort I'd put in—for my friends, for my family, for those watching at home and in the stands. It's been an incredible journey to think that after 16 years I'm back on the podium at the Olympic Games. But all the credit is to the love and support of my people, my family, my friends, my teammates, my coaches, my country."

77

Brooke Bennett

Country: United States
Birth date: May 6, 1980
Event: Distance freestyle
Olympic medals: Three
World Championship medals: Two

The ascension of Brooke Bennett to international standout in the distance-freestyle events was not an easy one. Surging onto the global scene as the career of the legendary Janet Evans came to a close, Bennett was routinely compared to her American compatriot. Fortunately for Bennett, she had enough talent to establish her own identity.

From the mid-1990s into the 2000s, Bennett became the number one distance performer in the world and engaged in several showdowns with Evans early in her career. At the 1996 Olympics, Bennett was the gold medalist in the 800 freestyle as Evans contested the last event of her Olympic career, finishing sixth. Bennett did not initially warm herself to Evans because of several comments she made, including the assertion that Evans was concerned about a challenge to her grip on distance swimming. Eventually, though, Bennett paid homage to Evans, easing off her brash remarks.

"Even 20 years down the road, everyone is going to remember Janet," Bennett said. "She will always be the queen of distance swimming. Hopefully, I'll move up now that I've won a gold medal, but Janet's been there since 1988. She's won gold medals and national titles and set world records—all the things that I haven't done yet."

Although Bennett was unable to break Evans's world records, she equaled her rival in a few categories. While Evans was the Olympic champion in the 800 freestyle in 1988 and 1992, Bennett managed to repeat her title in the event in 2000. That year, Bennett also captured the gold medal in the 400 freestyle, joining Evans as a woman who swept the distance events in an Olympiad.

Despite several injuries to her shoulders, Bennett tried to win a third consecutive Olympic crown in the 800 freestyle. However, a third-place finish in the event at the 2004 U.S. Olympic Trials denied her the opportunity to defend her previous two gold medals.

Bennett's career also included a gold medal in the 800 freestyle at the 1998 World Championships, where she also took the silver medal in the 400 freestyle. Additionally, she was a seven-time medalist at the Pan Pacific Championships, including six gold medals spread between the 400 freestyle, 800 freestyle, and 1500 freestyle.

78

Denis Pankratov

Country: Russia
Birth date: July 4, 1974
Event: Butterfly
Olympic medals: Three
World Championship medals: Four

His career overlapping with that of countryman Alexander Popov, it was easy for Denis Pankratov to fly below the radar. While Popov, perhaps the greatest sprinter in the history of the sport, was garnering all the headlines, Pankratov simply went about his business as a dual-threat butterfly specialist. By the end of his career, he had put together quite a résumé.

Pankratov gradually worked his way to the top of his events, following a blueprint that saw him initially break through as a European champion at the junior level. He followed with a sixth-place finish in the 200 butterfly at the 1992 Olympics, then proved himself as a significant player at the 1994 World Championships in Rome. In addition to capturing the gold medal in the 200 butterfly, Pankratov was the bronze medalist in the 100 butterfly and powered Russia to silver medals in the 400 medley relay and 800 freestyle relay, the latter proof of his skill beyond the butterfly.

Establishing himself as the front-runner for gold at the 1996 Olympics, Pankratov broke world records in each butterfly distance during the 1995 season, his mark in the 200 distance standing as the global standard for five years. Indeed, Pankratov delivered on his promise at the Atlanta Games, sweeping the 100 butterfly and 200 butterfly, with the shorter distance producing a world record. He added a silver medal in the 400 medley relay.

Known for his extraordinary underwater skill that enabled Pankratov to stay submerged for more than half a lap, he was dealt a blow to his approach in 1998. A rule change was implemented that prohibited athletes from staying underwater for more than 15 meters. Suddenly, Pankratov's advantage over his competition was neutralized. Pankratov was diplomatic in addressing the change.

"I think it's a shame for the spectators that the underwater kick has been restricted because it was something spectacular to watch," he said. "But I don't think it will make the records harder to reach. The swimmers who have mastered the technique will still use it in training. For me, the underwater was especially important to prepare my leg movements and get my body into the correct position. The most important thing in butterfly is the legs."

A three-time individual champion at the European Championships and a 2004 inductee into the International Swimming Hall of Fame, Pankratov competed in a third Olympiad at the 2000 Games in Sydney. He was unable to repeat his success from Atlanta, however, placing seventh in the 200 butterfly.

79

Norman Ross

Country: United States
Birth date: May 2, 1896
Death date: June 19, 1953
Event: Freestyle
Olympic medals: Three

Better known during the later stages of his life for his work as a disc jockey, Norman Ross was initially one of the leading swimmers in the world. He won five gold medals at the 1919 Allied War Games, a performance that was the jump start to Olympic success the next year. One of the biggest swimmers of his era, Ross measured in at six feet two and 210 pounds.

At the 1920 Olympics in Antwerp, Ross highlighted action in the pool by winning individual gold medals in the 400 freestyle and 1500 freestyle. He prevailed in the shorter distance by more than two seconds and registered a 13-second triumph in the 1500 freestyle. He added another gold medal as a member of the American 800 freestyle relay. He also competed in the 100 freestyle but failed to win a medal in an event that was extremely short for the distance-based competitor.

"Ross certainly qualifies as one of the world's all-time great swimmers, but it is as a showman and leader of swimmers that he is best remembered," reads his profile at the International Swimming Hall of Fame. "A master of psyching [out] other swimmers, he also [pressured] the Olympic officials by calling a strike which the Olympic athletes won for a better ship home than the 'cattle boat we went over on.'"

Ross won 18 national championships during his career and set a variety of records in the freestyle events, including a global mark in the 200 freestyle that lasted for more than three years. He was inducted into the International Swimming Hall of Fame in 1967 and was one of the first distance swimmers to use a scissor kick while racing. Ross might have been able to win several medals at the 1916 Olympics, but those Games were canceled because of World War I.

80

Petria Thomas

Country: Australia
Birth date: August 25, 1975
Event: Butterfly
Olympic medals: Eight
World Championship medals: Seven

It's hard enough to make a mark as a professional athlete, particularly one who has the ability to shine on the Olympic stage. Now try to imagine succeeding at the highest level while battling depression. That was the scenario encountered by Petria Thomas, a butterfly star for Australia during the 1990s and into the new millennium.

Despite dealing with bouts of depression, especially in the mid-1990s, Thomas had so much talent that she was still able to develop into one of the best performers in her sport. From 1994 through 1998, Thomas collected a bundle of international medals, from the silver medal she captured in the 200 butterfly at the 1996 Olympics to medals at the Commonwealth Games and the World Championships.

"I just felt hopeless. I felt useless as a person," Thomas said of her depression. "I didn't see a future, and I was only young at the time. Even though I had my swimming, my shoulders were starting to hurt at that stage. In a sense, swimming is all I felt like I had in my life. If I wasn't swimming, I didn't know what the hell else I was supposed to be doing, so that scared me. Whether it was right to feel that way or not, that's the way I felt at the time, and it was tough to get through, but I just took each day at a time and tried to make the most of it."

Through 2000, Thomas was overshadowed by her countrywoman and butterfly rival, Susie O'Neill. It was O'Neill who was the Olympic champion and world-record holder, and that status left Thomas in the background. Eventually, though, Thomas roared to the forefront and never looked back until her retirement.

The bronze medalist in the 200 butterfly at the 2000 Olympics, Thomas followed with a pair of world titles in 2001 in the 100 butterfly and 200 butterfly. There was also a sweep of the butterfly events at the 2002 Commonwealth Games, where Thomas totaled seven medals. Then came her biggest success, achieved at the 2004 Olympics in Athens.

Competing in the final competition of her career, Thomas piled up four medals, three of which were gold, and captured an individual Olympic title for the first time when she prevailed in the 100 butterfly. Her other golds were in relay duty, and she was the silver medalist in the 200 butterfly. It was the perfect way to cap her career and sent Thomas away from the sport on a high note.

"I think there probably wasn't a day in training where I sort of sometimes didn't wonder whether it was all worthwhile, whether I could keep myself going through everything, but you know, I suppose I'm glad I did," she said. "It took a lot of persistence and perseverance and a lot of great people around me telling me that I could do it and I could get there. It's been an amazing team effort I think, more than anything. There's so many people who have helped me and never given up on me, and I hope they can share in my moment and be happy as well as I am. They really deserve to be happy because they've helped me get this result."

Thomas was inducted into the International Swimming Hall of Fame in 2010 and ended her career with eight Olympic medals, seven medals at the World Championships, and 12 medals at the Commonwealth Games.

81

Amanda Beard

Country: United States
Birth date: October 29, 1981
Events: Breaststroke and individual medley
Olympic medals: Seven
World Championship medals: Three

Certain images from the sport's past are easily recalled, such as Mark Spitz with his seven gold medals from the 1972 Olympics draped around his neck. Another is the image of 14-year-old American Amanda Beard walking the deck at the 1996 Olympics in Atlanta with her teddy bear, Harold, tucked under her arm. Beard was a rising star at the time, an innocent teenager with a huge upside. Still, it was hard to predict that she would put together a multi-Olympic career that was filled with plenty of positives along with several struggles.

Beard made a huge splash on the international scene at the Atlanta Games, leaving a home Olympiad with three medals. There was a gold medal as a member of the U.S. 400 medley relay and silver medals in the 100 breaststroke and 200 breaststroke. After the Games, she was a celebrity and destined for big things.

"Right after those Olympics, I started to grow," she said. "In a year and a half, I gained six or seven inches and 25 pounds. I found that you have to get used to a new body, just like gymnasts and figure skaters do. You have to learn to swim again. It took a while to figure out whether I should continue. At that point, I didn't like swimming, and I didn't care if I won. I stopped for three months. Then I realized I wanted to do it, but it was hard getting used to having a new body in the water. It took three years."

Ultimately, Beard got back to the Olympic stage, and while she didn't match the success she found in Atlanta, her bronze medal in the 200 breaststroke at the 2000 Games in Sydney was as satisfying. It was a medal that was unexpected. It was also a performance that fully jump-started a once-stagnant career.

Leading to the 2004 Olympics in Athens, Beard earned the first world title of her career, taking gold in the 200 breaststroke in world-record time at the 2003 World Championships. That medal was complemented by a silver medal in the 100 breaststroke.

The next summer, Beard set another world record in her prime event and captured the first individual gold medal of her Olympic career, prevailing in the 200 breast-stroke at the 2004 Games in Athens. She added a silver medal in the 200 individual medley, proof of her talent beyond the breaststroke events. With all that success, Beard became an in-demand athlete for sponsorship and modeling gigs, along with speaking engagements.

"I don't think I'll be able to wipe the smile off my face for a while," Beard said of her 200 breaststroke triumph.

Beard qualified for a fourth Olympics in 2008, but she failed to advance to the finals of the 200 breaststroke. She continued to compete through 2012 as well, but her attempt to qualify for the London Olympics came up short. In 2012, Beard released a tell-all autobiography that revealed a number of battles she dealt with during her life, including drug abuse, self-mutilation, and bulimia.

Beard also made a big splash when she posed nude for *Playboy* magazine in 2007. The decision to appear in the men's magazine received mixed reactions. While critics accused Beard of not being a wholesome role model for young girls, supporters argued that Beard was displaying a body of which she was proud and that was the result of her dedication to training.

82

Andrew Charlton

Country: Australia
Birth date: August 12, 1907
Death date: December 10, 1975
Event: Distance freestyle
Olympic medals: Five

One of the early-era distance stars, Andrew Charlton, known more commonly as "Boy" Charlton, deserves some of the credit for generating the love affair between Australia and its distance swimmers. He was a standout at two Olympiads and posted one of the biggest upsets—at the time—at the 1924 Olympics in Paris.

As the athletes lined up for the start of the 1500 freestyle at the Paris Games, few expected anyone but Sweden's Arne Borg to capture the gold. After all, Borg was the world-record holder and a European icon, while Charlton was nothing more than a 16-year-old with much to prove. Prove something is exactly what Charlton did.

Not only did the Australian youngster teach Borg a lesson, beating him by nearly 35 seconds, but Charlton cut more than one minute from the world record, bringing it to 20:06.6. In a matter of 20 minutes, Charlton became one of the sport's elite figures, standing alongside the likes of Johnny Weissmuller.

"Known as the 'Manly Flying Fish' for his hometown of Manly, Australia, Charlton was self-taught and largely untrained, but tireless," states his profile at the International Swimming Hall of Fame. "He, more than all other swimmers combined, put Australia back on the Olympic swim map after World War I."

Charlton's victory in the 1500 freestyle was complemented by a bronze medal in the 400 freestyle, an event that was a sprint for the Aussie. He was defeated in that race by Weissmuller and Borg. Charlton, too, garnered a silver medal as a member of the Australian 800 freestyle relay.

Four years later, Charlton and Borg clashed again at the Olympics, this time in Amsterdam. In the 1500 freestyle, Borg got his revenge with a 10-second triumph over Charlton. In the 400 freestyle, Charlton finished ahead of Borg, but the men got so caught up racing each other that they lost track of Argentina's Alberto Zorrilla, who went on to win the gold medal.

Inducted into the Hall of Fame in 1972, Charlton's sole world record in the 1500 freestyle, which was reclaimed by Borg, was complemented by three world records in the 800 freestyle.

83

Gary Hall Sr.

Country: United States
Birth date: August 7, 1951
Events: Butterfly and individual medley
Olympic medals: Three

As unfair as it might be, considering the depth of what he accomplished during his career, Gary Hall Sr. is more frequently linked to others rather than lauded for what he achieved. On the one hand, he is known as the father of Gary Hall Jr., a 10-time Olympic medalist and one of the best sprinters the sport has known. On the other hand, he is known as the Indiana University teammate of Mark Spitz, the Olympic icon who wowed at the 1972 Games in Munich.

Hall Sr., though, is much more than a supporting character. In the late 1960s through the middle of the 1970s, Hall was one of the most accomplished swimmers in the world and for one period was probably the number one guy. A member of the high-powered championship squads at Indiana University, Hall stood out in a variety of events, excelling in both butterfly disciplines and as a 200 individual medley and 400 medley performer. He once held world records in each medley distance and the 200 butterfly, even beating Spitz's world record in the latter event.

"Right now, Gary is the best all-round swimmer in the world, past or present," said Indiana University manager Mark Wallace at the 1971 NCAA Championships. "Except for the breaststrokes, he could have won any race he wanted."

Inducted into the International Swimming Hall of Fame in 1981, Hall was a medalist in three Olympiads, including a silver medal in the 400 individual medley at the 1968 Games in Mexico City, where Hall was edged by teammate Charles Hickcox. Four years later, he landed another silver medal, this time finishing behind Spitz in the 200 butterfly at the Munich Games. He rounded out his career with a bronze medal in the 100 butterfly at the 1976 Olympics in Montreal, again beaten to the wall by American teammates.

As impressive as it was to medal in three separate events at three Olympics, Hall's lack of an individual gold medal is what separates him from being ranked higher on this list. His best years, 1969 and 1970, happened to fall in between Olympiads, and during Olympic action, he simply couldn't overcome a variety of fellow Americans. Yet it can also be argued that Hall benefited—especially at Indiana—from being surrounded by a stacked roster.

"There's no friction," Hall said in 1971. "We're all so versatile that we don't have to swim against each other all the time. I think working out together helps us all get better."

84

Cynthia Woodhead

Country: United States
Birth date: February 7, 1964
Event: Freestyle
Olympic medal: One
World Championship medals: Five

The singular Olympic medal on Cynthia Woodhead's résumé is one of the most misleading statistics in the sport. It does nothing to capture the excellence of the American swimmer, a teenage sensation whose precocious talent is still talked about today. It's not unusual for Woodhead's name to arise in conversation each time a teenager supplies a breakout performance, for the woman nicknamed "Sippy" remains a measuring stick.

From the late 1970s into the 1980s, Woodhead was one of the finest freestylers in the world, excelling from the 50-meter distance through the 800-meter event. While she could sprint with the best and hang with the elite of the distance group, Woodhead shone brightest in the 200 freestyle, where she set three world records during her career, the last enduring for more than four years.

At the 1978 World Championships, Woodhead was among the star performers. Aside from capturing the gold medal in the 200 freestyle and as a member of two American relays, Woodhead was the silver medalist in the 400 freestyle and the 800 freestyle. Her efforts laid the groundwork for what was supposed to be a banner showing at the 1980 Olympics, where Woodhead would have been a contender for medals in four freestyle events and in two relays.

At the peak of her career at the time of the 1980 Games in Moscow, Woodhead never got the chance to put her skills on display. American president Jimmy Carter ordered a boycott of the Olympics, denying Woodhead the chance to put together—

perhaps—one of the best Olympic performances ever by a female swimmer. It was a decision that stung.

"I was very depressed and disillusioned by the whole thing," Woodhead said. "It was tough enough being a teenager, plus this. And there was nobody to relate to. So I used to just walk out of school and leave. Somehow, my parents, my teachers, everyone dealt with it. They knew that I didn't want anyone to see me cry."

Unlike some of the other Americans affected by the boycott, Woodhead opted to continue her career. However, she ran into a few bumps. Not only was she sliding from top form, but she didn't get the chance to compete at the 1982 World Championships, that year's season interrupted by a combination of illness and injury. She bounced back enough to win the gold medal in the 200 freestyle and the silver medal in the 400 freestyle at the 1983 Pan American Games.

A year later, Woodhead earned her Olympic opportunity, although she qualified for the 1984 Games in Los Angeles only in the 200 freestyle. That race produced a silver medal and conflicting feelings. Although she was pleased to have finally received an Olympic medal, Woodhead knew that her best Olympic hopes were behind her, lost in a political decision.

"It was awful. Those four years [between Moscow and Los Angeles] felt like 10," Woodhead said. "It seemed like everything went wrong. But I felt I owed it to myself to compete in 1984, make the team, and actually go to an Olympics, so I pressed on. I enjoyed it, but I didn't. It felt like I was watching a movie and wishing I could have been there in my top form, at my peak. It certainly wasn't a highlight of my life."

Woodhead was the World Swimmer of the Year in 1979, thanks largely to victories at the Pan American Games in the 100 freestyle, 200 freestyle, and 400 freestyle. An 18-time U.S. national champion, Woodhead was inducted into the International Swimming Hall of Fame in 1994.

85

Zoltan Halmay

Country: Hungary
Birth date: June 18, 1881
Death: May 20, 1956
Event: Freestyle
Olympic medals: Nine

He was not the first Olympic swimming champion, but there is little debate Zoltan Halmay was the first major star of the sport. The Hungarian put together an extensive résumé that spanned four Olympiads and wide-ranging distances in the freestyle events. It can even be argued that Halmay—more than a century after his competitive days—is the most versatile freestyler in history.

One of the early pioneers of Hungary's rich tradition in the sport, Halmay made his Olympic debut at the 1900 Games in Paris. There, he was the silver medalist in the 200 freestyle and 4000 freestyle and won a bronze medal in the 1000 freestyle. The wide range of Halmay's events revealed his prowess not only in shorter disciplines but also as an endurance performer.

Although Halmay boasted versatility, he was suited best for the sprints. At the 1904 Olympics in St. Louis, Halmay delivered a sprinting clinic by winning the 50-yard freestyle and 100-yard freestyle, the victory in the 100 distance over American star Charles Daniels. Revenge belonged to Daniels at the 1908 Olympics, however, as he had surged ahead of Halmay and broke the world record. Halmay added another silver medal in the 800 freestyle relay.

Halmay had actually fallen behind Daniels two years earlier when the rivals met at the 1906 Olympics in Athens. Those Games have since been declared unofficial, as they were merely the 10-year anniversary of the first Olympiad and not part of the normal four-year rotation. Still, it was a big competition, and Halmay met his match in the 100 freestyle when Daniels came out on top. Halmay did win a gold medal in the 4-by-250 relay, an event that was never held in another Olympiad.

"Halmay swam mostly with his arms, without any leg movements, but in 1905 he set what is considered the inaugural record for 100 meters," states his profile on *Sports Reference*. "The record remained unbeaten for more than four years, a remarkable length of time during a period of rapid development in the sport."

86

Henry Taylor

Country: Great Britain
Birth date: March 17, 1885
Death date: February 28, 1951
Event: Freestyle
Olympic medals: Five

Inducted into the International Swimming Hall of Fame in 1969, Henry Taylor was one of the first stars of the sport and is widely considered the most accomplished British swimmer in history. Taylor medaled in three Olympiads: 1908, 1912, and 1920. He was also a medalist at the 1906 Olympics, but those Games are no longer considered official.

Known to practice during his lunch break and in any waterway he could find at night, Taylor won three medals at the 1908 Olympics in London, taking top honors in the 400 freestyle and 1500 freestyle and as a member of the British 800 freestyle relay. His three-medal haul remains an Olympic record for a British swimmer. When Rebecca Adlington won two gold medals at the 2008 Olympic Games in Beijing, it marked the first time since Taylor competed in which a British swimmer won multiple gold medals.

A world-record holder in the half-mile swim, Taylor added bronze medals in the 800 freestyle relay at the 1912 Olympics and at the 1920 Games. He likely would have won medals at the 1916 Olympics, but the event was canceled because of World War I. At the 1906 Olympics held in Athens, Taylor was the gold medalist in the one-mile swim, earned the silver medal in the 400 freestyle, and picked up a bronze medal in the 1000 relay.

Taylor was a regular in match races and competed in distance swims, winning the 13-mile Morecambe Bay Race on eight occasions. In various competitions, Taylor won more than 300 medals during his career. However, his life outside of the pool was difficult, and he was poor at the time of his death.

"He was the star of the Chadderton Swimming Club and at the age of 21, his success got him noticed nationally, when he was selected for the Intercalated Games in Athens in 1906—an unofficial multi-sports event, held to mark the tenth anniversary of the first Modern Olympics, which saw athletes from all over the world take part," stated a BBC article. "It wasn't expected that Henry would be amongst the medals, but his canal training must have paid off as he took gold in the one mile freestyle. That success, coupled with him setting the world record for the 880 yards later that year, meant Henry was an obvious pick for the British 1908 London Olympics team."

87

Adam Peaty

Country: Great Britain
Birth Date: December 28, 1994
Event: Breaststroke
Olympic medals: Two
World Championship medals: Six

Of the 100 athletes on this top-100 list, few—if any—are as one-dimensional as Great Britain's Adam Peaty, who is solely defined by his prowess in the 50 breaststroke and 100 breaststroke. But what Peaty lacks in range, he certainly makes up for with dominance, his supremacy in his events at the level of Michael Phelps, Mark Spitz, and Katie Ledecky in their disciplines.

The 2014 season served as Peaty's launching point to stardom, as he had the opportunity to race at a pair of high-profile international competitions. At that year's Commonwealth Games, Peaty walked away with a gold medal in the 100 breaststroke and a silver medal in the 50 breaststroke, the events a split decision between Peaty and South African Cameron van der Burgh, the 2012 Olympic champion in the 100 breaststroke. That Peaty was able to upend the reigning Olympic champ was a major step toward Peaty establishing himself as the man to beat in his events.

A few months after his Commonwealth Games success, Peaty captured four gold medals at the European Championships. Individual victories in the 50 breaststroke and 100 breaststroke were complemented by first-place finishes in the 400 medley relay and mixed medley relay. By the end of the year, Peaty was a well-known name in the sport.

Peaty's roll continued into 2015 as he set a world record in the 100 breaststroke at the British Trials for the World Championships, his time of 57.92 marking the first time a swimmer cracked the 58-second barrier. At the World Championships, Peaty won double gold in the 50 breaststroke and 100 breaststroke, his victory in the longer event arriving over van der Burgh and officially signaling a changing of the guard.

Consistently swift times and dominating triumphs made Peaty the overwhelming favorite for the gold medal in the 100 breaststroke at the 2016 Olympic Games in Rio, and Peaty did not fold under the pressure. Rather, he rose to the occasion, posting the three-fastest times in history during the three rounds of competition. Peaty opened with a world record of 57.55 during the preliminaries, came back with a mark of 57.62 in the semifinals, and lowered the world record again in the final with a clocking of 57.13. The silver medal went to van der Burgh, more than a second and a half back in 58.69.

"I can't even put it into words how much that swim meant to me," Peaty said of his Olympic-gold swim. "Going down that last 50, I was aware that I was in front, but not by that much. I touched the wall, looked to my left and I was like, 'where is everybody?' That swim for me was probably the best executed. The perfect race."

Peaty was again untouchable at the 2017 World Championships, as he repeated as champion of both the 50 breaststroke and 100 breaststroke. Again, Peaty was racing the clock more than he was racing the other seven men in the final, his winning time of 57.47 more than a second swifter than the silver-medal effort of American Kevin Cordes. In the 50 breaststroke, Peaty was .53 ahead—an unthinkable margin for a one-lap race—of Brazilian Joao Gomes.

Although Peaty has indicated the desire to branch out into the 200 breaststroke as his career continues to take shape, his legacy is surely sound for what he has done over the 50- and 100-meter distances. Despite the sport being more competitive than ever, Peaty owns surreal historical margins over his nearest competitors. In the 50 breaststroke, no one has been within .57 of Peaty, while the gap between Peaty and his closest all-time pursuer in the 100 breaststroke sits at 1.33 seconds. More, as the curtain closed on 2017, Peaty owned the 11-fastest performances in history.

"People say to me I've won the grand slam of swimming, got all the world records and stuff like that," Peaty said. "But for me that doesn't make me comfortable. I am not comfortable being the best. I want to be the best by a large margin. I still haven't got that margin yet. My motivation is off the charts and what I want to achieve is up there."

88

Libby Trickett

Country: Australia
Birth date: January 28, 1985
Events: Freestyle and butterfly
Olympic medals: Seven
World Championship medals: Fifteen

In the 30-plus years since the retirement of Dawn Fraser, Australia waited for its next sprint queen. During the mid-2000s, that role was occupied by Libby Trickett. Excelling in the 50 freestyle, 100 freestyle, and 100 butterfly, Trickett was a well-rounded sprinter and the go-to performer for Team Australia.

Trickett made her first international impact at the 2003 World Championships, winning bronze medals in the 50 freestyle and as a member of the 400 freestyle relay. The next year's Olympic Games were also impressive, with Trickett capturing bronze in the 50 freestyle and helping Australia to the gold medal in the 400 freestyle relay.

Still, Trickett was just starting to shine. She won five medals at the 2005 World Championships and followed with seven medals, including five gold medals, at the 2006 Commonwealth Games. By this time, she was equally proficient in the 50 freestyle and 100 freestyle and had added the 100 butterfly to her arsenal. It all came together at the 2007 World Championships.

Racing in her home country with the event held in Melbourne, Trickett was the dominant female of the World Championships, even if she was overshadowed by Michael Phelps. She won both sprint-freestyle events, prevailed in the 100 butterfly, and powered Australia to gold medals in the 400 medley relay and 400 freestyle relay. All that was missing from her résumé was an Olympic gold medal. She took care of that gap a year later.

En route to a four-medal performance, Trickett was the gold medalist at the Beijing Games in the 100 butterfly and as a member of the Australian 400 medley relay and added a silver medal in the 100 freestyle and a bronze medal in the 400 freestyle relay. The only shortcoming for Trickett was a fourth-place finish in the 50 freestyle.

"It's more than I could have dreamed," Trickett said of her gold medal in the butterfly. "I'm more than anything relieved. Before the race I felt like I was going to vomit. I was probably that nervous. But then just before I walked out, I had an amazing sense of calm. I just said to myself, more than anything, I just want to walk away with absolutely no regrets. My ultimate dream was to win an individual gold medal at an Olympics. To have done that, everything else is just icing on the cake."

Trickett added three more medals at the 2009 World Championships, including a bronze in the 100 freestyle, then retired from the sport. But after a brief break, she returned and qualified for the 2012 Olympics, where she claimed a gold medal for racing in the preliminaries of the 400 freestyle relay. For her career, Trickett set world records in the 50 freestyle and 100 freestyle and became the first woman to break the 53-second barrier in the 100 freestyle.

89

Ada Kok

Country: Netherlands
Birth date: June 6, 1947
Event: Butterfly
Olympic medals: Three

During the 1960s, Ada Kok established herself as one of the premier butterfly swimmers in the world, excelling in both the 100-meter and the 200-meter distances. One of the elite performers in Dutch history, Kok was also a standout in the middle-distance freestyle events and a factor in two Olympiads.

At the 1964 Olympics in Tokyo, Kok settled for the silver medal when she was beaten by American Sharon Stouder in the 100 butterfly. Stouder and Kok were viewed as equal contenders for the gold medal and later exchanged the world record in the event. Kok added a second silver medal as a member of the Dutch 400 medley relay.

Four years later, Kok enjoyed the biggest moment of her career when she captured the gold medal in the 200 butterfly at the 1968 Olympics in Mexico City. However, that triumph was not without some drama. Before besting the competition in the 200 butterfly, Kok was locked out of the medals in the 100 butterfly despite being the world-record holder. It was a setback that devastated Kok and sent her into the final of the 200 butterfly in a fragile mental state.

"For the 200 meter final, I was so stiff and rigid that I couldn't even see myself getting my tracksuit bottoms off," she said. "My fingers couldn't get the zipper undone. An official had to help me with it. I don't remember anything now of the first hundred meters. It's a black hole. After 150 meters, I was in the lead. Twenty meters from the finish, I saw someone catching up with me. I thought, 'Jesus, no, she is not getting past me.' Fortunately, I was able to keep in front."

Kok was a five-time medalist at the European Championships, including gold-medal performances in the 100 butterfly in 1962 and 1966. As proof of her versatility, she added a silver medal in the 400 freestyle in 1966. A 1976 inductee into the International Swimming Hall of Fame, Kok was the world-record holder in the 100 butterfly and 200 butterfly from 1965 to 1970. After her competitive career, Kok remained involved in the sport as a representative for Speedo.

90

Jim Montgomery

Country: United States
Birth date: January 24, 1955
Event: Freestyle
Olympic medals: Four
World Championship medals: Nine

The men before him had established a tradition of excellence in the sprint-freestyle events, names such as Duke Kahanamoku, Johnny Weissmuller, and Mark Spitz. All Jim Montgomery did was continue the momentum of the American swimmers and, thanks to a well-timed career, become a barrier breaker who will never be forgotten.

Throughout a majority of the 1970s, Montgomery was the best 100 freestyler in the world, a hefty distinction considering the event's reputation as the sport's blue-ribbon discipline. Another of Indiana University's stars, Montgomery was a regular on the podium in international competition, but nothing matched what he pulled off at the 1976 Olympic Games in Montreal, for on the night of July 25, Montgomery became the first man to break the 50-second barrier in the 100 freestyle.

En route to the gold medal in his primary event, Montgomery didn't easily surpass the barrier. In fact, he clipped it by the smallest of margins, just a hundredth of a second. And a few weeks later, his record was considerably lowered by South African Jonty Skinner, who was denied an Olympic invitation because of his country's apartheid practices and subsequent Olympic ban. Still, Montgomery made history and will always be connected with that special moment.

"Breaking this barrier was equivalent to Roger Bannister's four minute mile in track," states Montgomery's profile at the International Swimming Hall of Fame, to which he was inducted in 1986. "That Montgomery did it while winning an Olympic gold medal at Montreal is a double dose of immortality."

At those 1976 Games, Montgomery added gold medals in a pair of relays and demonstrated his ability to handle longer events through a bronze medal in the 200 freestyle. Three years earlier at the inaugural World Championships, Montgomery provided an inkling that a stellar career was set to unfold. A four-time world-record setter in the 100 freestyle, Montgomery highlighted the first World Championships by prevailing in five events: the 100 freestyle, the 200 freestyle, and three relays. His success prompted quick comparisons to Mark Spitz, who was fresh off his seven-gold-medal showing at the 1972 Olympics. Montgomery had a quick retort for reporters drawing parallels: "Come back and see me in three years with your Spitz comparisons."

Ultimately, Montgomery didn't match what Spitz achieved, but he added a bronze medal in the 100 freestyle at the 1975 World Championships and moved up to the silver medal in the event at the 1978 World Championships. Both meets also featured gold medals for Montgomery in the 400 freestyle relay.

91

Sarah Sjostrom

Country: Sweden
Birth date: August 17, 1993
Events: Freestyle and butterfly
Olympic medals: Three
World Championship medals: Twelve

Although hailing from a country that doesn't exactly boast a deep tradition in the sport, Sarah Sjostrom has become a national hero for her exploits in the pool. The Swede has come a long way from her breakthrough moment as a young teenager to become one of the dominant performers of her era.

As a 14-year-old during the 2008 season, Sjostrom captured the European title in the 100 butterfly and earned valuable experience at the Olympic Games in Beijing, where she was 27th in the 100 fly. But it was the next summer that thrust her into the global spotlight, as she walked away from the 2009 World Championships as the gold medalist in the 100 butterfly. In 2010, she defended her European crown in her prime event.

Faced with high expectations, Sjostrom had difficulty at her next two major competitions. At the 2011 World Championships, a trio of fourth-place finishes left her just off the podium and did not establish momentum heading into the 2012 Olympiad. However, the results were eye-opening for Sjostrom, especially for the way she approached her training.

"The World champs in Shanghai was a challenge," she said. "I learned a lot. One of the many things I learned was that I have to do better work in practice if I don't want to be fourth three times in one championship again. I can admit that this result was exactly what I needed to get more motivation to do better work in practice."

In London, Sjostrom again played the role of bridesmaid, placing fourth in the 100 butterfly. She was also eliminated from the semifinals of the 50, 100, and 200 freestyle events. Initially viewed as a superstar-in-development, Sjostrom was now followed by doubts concerning her ability to handle pressure situations. Those doubts, though, wouldn't last for long.

Between the 2013 and 2015 World Championships, Sjostrom made regular visits to the podium. In Barcelona in 2013, Sjostrom regained her world title in the 100 butterfly, and added a silver medal in the 100 freestyle. Two years later, she was even more impressive, setting a pair of world records on the way to gold in the 100 butterfly, and also winning gold in the 50 butterfly, silver in the 100 freestyle, and bronze in the 50 freestyle. Sjostrom was set to shine at the 2016 Olympic Games in Rio de Janeiro, and she did not disappoint.

At her third Olympiad, Sjostrom was one of the stars on the women's side, claiming gold in the 100 butterfly in world-record time, and collecting a silver medal in the 200 freestyle to go with a bronze medal in the 100 freestyle. The only event that did not work out was the 50 free, where Sjostrom surprisingly missed out on the final. Still, her victory in the 100 butterfly was satisfying.

"I knew I was the big favorite," she said. "I was under pressure, so I tried to focus on (having) no disasters. Before the start, I said to myself: 'It's just a pool. It's nothing. I know what to do.'"

Sjostrom followed her Olympic success by playing a starring role at the 2017 World Championships in Budapest. In addition to winning a third consecutive—and fourth overall—world crown in the 100 butterfly, Sjostrom repeated as champion of the 50 butterfly and stood atop the podium in the 50 freestyle. For good measure, she won the silver medal in the 100 freestyle, and set world records in the semifinals of the 50 freestyle and during her 100 freestyle leadoff leg of Sweden's 400 freestyle relay.

For her efforts, Sjostrom was named World Swimmer of the Year for 2017 and she ended the campaign with the 11-fastest performances in history in the 100 butterfly, a testament to her dominance of the event.

92

Laszlo Cseh

Country: Hungary
Birth date: December 3, 1985
Events: Multiple
Olympic medals: Six
World Championship medals: Thirteen

Had Laszlo Cseh been dropped in any
era other than his own, his name would
probably be found much higher on
this list. But athletes can't control their
competitive surroundings, and it just
happened that Cseh, part of a sterling
Hungarian tradition, continually ran
into a brick wall in his events, a barrier
by the name of Michael Phelps.

Since arriving on the international
scene as a 17-year-old at the 2003
World Championships, Cseh has been
repeatedly turned back by Phelps and
on other occasions by American Ryan
Lochte. Still, Cseh has put together an

impressive career, excelling not only in the individual medley events (his specialties)
but also in the butterfly and backstroke.

Cseh's first impactful performance on the global stage was a silver medal behind
Phelps in the 400 individual medley at the 2003 World Championships. A year later,
he captured a bronze medal in the 400 individual medley at the 2004 Olympics in

Athens. It was the first of six medals for Cseh in Olympic action, with Phelps prevailing in five of those races. His next three Olympic medals came in 2008 in Beijing, with Cseh placing behind Phelps in the 200 individual medley, 400 individual medley, and 200 butterfly. He added a bronze medal in the 200 individual medley at the 2012 Games in London, and he shared the silver medal in the 100 butterfly with Phelps and South African Chad Le Clos at the 2016 Games in Rio de Janeiro.

In addition to his Olympic success, Cseh owns 13 medals from the World Championships, including gold medals in 2005 and 2015. Racing in the 400 individual medley in Montreal in 2005, an event that Phelps bypassed, Cseh prevailed over Italian Luca Marin. Ten years later, at the 2015 World Champs in Kazan, Russia, Cseh bested the competition in the 200 butterfly.

Of the 17 silver or bronze medals Cseh has won between the Olympics and World Championships, the event was won by either Phelps or Lochte on 11 occasions. Three times, he finished behind Le Clos, who has become a rival in the latter portion of Cseh's career.

"I gave the maximum in Beijing," Cseh said. "I had perfect races, but nobody could beat Michael Phelps in Beijing. Come close? Yes. Beat? No."

Although Cseh has run into American blockades on the global stage, he's been nothing short of phenomenal in continental competition. He is a 14-time European champion, spanning the 200 individual medley, 400 individual medley, 100 butterfly, 200 butterfly, and 100 backstroke. He's also been a silver medalist in the 200 backstroke and 50 butterfly, bringing his total number of individual medal events at the European Championships to seven.

Despite his shortcomings against Phelps and Lochte, Cseh believes that their presence has carried him to greater heights, including European records in both medley events and the 200 butterfly—not bad for an athlete who has battled asthma since childhood.

"I think a lot about that," Cseh said of racing his rivals. "Maybe if there is no Phelps, no Lochte, I'm not as good. They make me better and the other swimmers better because of how fast they are swimming."

93

Jonty Skinner

Country: South Africa
Birth date: February 15, 1954
Event: Sprint freestyle

There are no Olympic medals displayed at Jonty Skinner's home. There are no Olympic medals safely stored away, either. That Skinner does not own a piece of hardware, which is a defining accomplishment in the sport, is no fault of the South African. Rather, Skinner is a victim—like countrywoman Karen Muir—of politics clashing with sports.

In the mid-1970s, Skinner was one of the best sprinters in the world, cruising through the water with his slender six-foot-five frame. He moved to the United States and became a standout on the collegiate scene at the University of Alabama, winning NCAA and U.S. national championships. But the big achievement was missing.

Because of South Africa's apartheid policies, athletes from that country were banned from the Olympics from 1964 to 1988. As a result, Skinner was denied the chance to race on the biggest stage and the opportunity to duel with American Jim Montgomery, his prime rival in the 100 freestyle. Skinner sought approval from Congress to allow him to compete at the 1976 U.S. Olympic Trials as an American citizen, but his pursuit of that injunction fell through.

With his Olympic dreams dashed, Skinner searched for a way to prove himself as the best sprinter in the world. That proving ground turned out to be the 1976 AAU Championships in Philadelphia. Held a few weeks after Montgomery won the Olympic gold medal and became the first man in history to break the 50-second barrier in the 100 freestyle with a 49.99 effort, the AAU Championships were Skinner's Olympics.

Skinner did not disappoint, as he registered a world-record time of 49.44 to win the 100 freestyle and anoint himself as the fastest sprinter in the world. Coming in faster than Montgomery at the Montreal Games only implied that the best man did not win the Olympic gold medal.

"Coach, I did it," Skinner said to Don Gambril, his coach at Alabama. "Since I couldn't swim against [Montgomery], my opponent had to be the clock. I just kept telling myself, 'This is your only chance. Don't blow it.'"

Inducted into the International Swimming Hall of Fame in 1985, Skinner followed his competitive career by working for USA Swimming in various coaching and technical analysis roles.

94

Norbert Rozsa

Country: Hungary
Birth date: February 9, 1972
Event: Breaststroke
Olympic medals: Three
World Championship medals: Seven

There is a long-standing tradition in Hungary of producing world-class breaststrokers and individual medley performers. It's not whether they will come along. It's a matter of when they will emerge. Norbert Rozsa made his appearance, falling into the category of elite breaststroker, throughout the 1990s.

Rozsa rose to prominence in 1991 when he became the world champion in the 100 breaststroke and earned the silver medal in the 200 breaststroke. That performance was supposed to be a springboard to at least one gold medal at the 1992 Olympics in Barcelona, but Rozsa ran into a pair of American buzzsaws, Nelson Diebel in the 100 distance and Mike Barrowman in the 200 distance. As a result, Rozsa settled for silver medals.

Young enough to remain a factor in the sport for years down the road, Rozsa continued to work toward that elusive Olympic gold medal, claiming victory in each breaststroke event at the 1994 World Championships, and the door opened in the 200 breaststroke when Barrowman opted for retirement. Rozsa finally attained his Olympic goal at the 1996 Games in Atlanta. Although his world-record-setting days were behind him and the 100 breaststroke was his slightly better event, Rozsa came through in the 200 breaststroke and completed his portfolio with a victory. Making the celebration even sweeter was the fact he was followed to the wall in the silver-medal position by countryman Karoly Guttler.

Inducted into the International Swimming Hall of Fame in 2005, Rozsa also competed at the 2000 Olympics in Sydney but failed to advance to a championship final. His career concluded with three Olympic medals, seven medals at the World Championships, and a gold medal in the 100 breaststroke at the 1991 European Championships, where he knocked off Great Britain's Adrian Moorhouse, who proved to be one of Rozsa's primary rivals. At the European Championships, Rozsa added a silver medal in the 200 breaststroke.

95

Rowdy Gaines

Country: United States
Birth date: February 17, 1959
Event: Freestyle
Olympic medals: Three
World Championship medals: Eight

Like several dozen fellow Americans, 1980 was a missed opportunity for Rowdy Gaines. The premier sprint freestyler in the world, Gaines was supposed to head to the Olympic Games in Moscow and return with a fistful of gold medals. Not only was he the world-record holder in the 200 freestyle, but Gaines was the favorite for victory in the 100 freestyle.

Gaines, however, never received his chance to perform during the peak time of his career. With the United States, under the direction of President Jimmy Carter, opting to boycott the Moscow Games, Gaines was forced to watch his competition vie for the most prestigious honors offered in the sport. It would be a long four years for Gaines's chance at Olympic success, but it was a worthwhile wait.

A world-record setter in the 50, 100, and 200 freestyle events at various points in his career, Gaines came through at the 1984 Olympics in Los Angeles. Motivated by his inability to compete four years earlier, when he was in the best condition of his life, Gaines won the 100 freestyle and powered the United States to a pair of relay gold medals. The victory in the 100 freestyle was a career-defining triumph and not without drama.

During a conversation with his coach Richard Quick prior to the start of the championship final of the 100 freestyle, Gaines was alerted to a tendency by the referee. Quick noticed that the official was a fast starter, not holding the athletes for long after placing them in the set position. As a result, Quick told Gaines to be prepared for a fast start and to react immediately. Indeed, when the race was held, there was a quick start, and Gaines got off the starting blocks faster than his competition, allowing him to surge into the lead. It was an edge that Gaines would not relinquish as he finished ahead of Australian Mark Stockwell, who won the silver medal. Stockwell was furious with the way the start unfolded, but the result stood, and Gaines had his Olympic glory.

"Part of me feels like it was yesterday," Gaines said. "I can remember specific details of the race. But another part of me feels like that was another person. I'm not sure how I did all that. It would not have been possible without Richard Quick. He had such a knack for picking up things to help his athletes, and that's what he did with the start. That was such an important time in the Olympic movement. We were coming off the boycott of 1980, and our country was starving for the Olympics. Patriotism was at an all-time high. There are definite memories."

The three Olympic medals won by Gaines accounted for just a portion of the accolades he earned during his career. In two appearances at the World Championships (1978 and 1982), Gaines won eight medals. He was also an eight-time medalist at the Pan American Games and a 1995 inductee into the International Swimming Hall of Fame.

Yet Gaines's exploits in the pool have been equally matched by his work as an analyst in the broadcast booth. The 2016 Olympics in Rio de Janeiro marked the seventh time Gaines worked as a commentator in Olympic competition (the past six for NBC), and his voice has become familiar to fans watching the NCAA Championships, the U.S. National Championships, and the World Championships, all events worked by Gaines. He is best known for his excitable nature while describing the action unfolding.

"The first and foremost thing I try to bring to my announcing is passion," Gaines said. "People can question some of my knowledge and my language or grammar, but they can't question my passion. I hope that's something that comes across because it's genuine and I love doing it. I have the best seat in the house."

96

Rick Carey

Country: United States
Birth date: March 13, 1963
Event: Backstroke
Olympic medals: Three
World Championship medals: Three

Intensity isn't hard to find along the pool deck, but intensity at the level once exhibited by Rick Carey is tough to come by. One of the most focused and demanding athletes the sport has seen, Carey was the premier backstroker in the world during the 1980s, sometimes satisfied with his sterling performances and other times dissatisfied with a showing that would have elated all others.

Carey broke onto the global scene in the early 1980s, showing potential that could change the backstroke record book. At the 1982 World Championships, that promise was revealed in a gold-medal effort in the 200 backstroke and a silver medal in the 100 backstroke. A year later, Carey won both backstroke events at the Pan American Games and set four of his five career world records. Carey's dominance made him the easy choice for World Swimmer of the Year.

Unlike the tall and lean John Naber, who preceded Carey as the last American to be regarded as the premier backstroker in the world, Carey was built more compactly, standing less than six feet. Yet his powerful arm strength propelled him through the water and enabled Carey to succeed, including breaking Naber's seven-year-old world records.

Competing in his first Olympics in 1984, Carey was coming off a world record in the 200 backstroke at the U.S. Olympic Trials and fully expected to sweep the backstroke events at the Los Angeles Games, and in world-record fashion. While Carey easily won a pair of individual gold medals, along with gold as a member of the American 400 medley relay, Carey was irked by his failure to lower his world marks. The disappointment was visible as Carey made his way to the medals podium for the 200 backstroke with a disgusted look. He was again disappointed in his effort in the 100 backstroke, but because of the criticism he took for his body language after the first event, Carey tried to mask his emotions.

"I've gone that fast in workouts," Carey said. "The Olympics are supposed to be more special. I still think I can go faster in both backstrokes. I don't know if I can rest knowing that."

Because of Carey's frustration, he remained in the sport and won both backstroke events at the 1985 Pan Pacific Championships, but never set another world record. A five-time NCAA champion at the University of Texas, Carey was inducted into the International Swimming Hall of Fame in 1993.

97

Bruce Furniss

Country: United States
Birth date: May 27, 1957
Events: Freestyle and individual medley
Olympic medals: Two
World Championship medals: Four

Half of one of the best sibling duos in the history of the sport along with his brother Steve, Bruce Furniss shone as a middle-distance freestyler and individual medley performer during the 1970s. Furniss was a member of the 1976 U.S. Olympic team, which won all but one gold medal in Montreal.

Furniss broke through at the international level at the 1975 World Championships, claiming the silver medal in the 200 freestyle and 400 freestyle behind Tim Shaw. Although his efforts were impressive, Furniss was motivated to higher heights by his inability to win. It was that deep desire to be the best that was a trademark of Furniss's career.

At the 1976 Olympics, Furniss won the gold medal in the 200 freestyle in a world-record time, fulfilling the potential he had shown. He was also a member of the American 800 freestyle relay, which prevailed in a rout over the Soviet Union. The world record by Furniss was his fourth in the event and lasted for almost three years.

"Bruce is too determined to play bridesmaid for long," said Dick Jochums, Furniss's coach at the Long Beach Swim Club. "He is intense, more intense than Shaw. He lives and dies swimming. . . . Bruce goes home and worries about his splits. He is the most talented swimmer I have ever coached. He is blessed with blazing speed."

Furniss would have contended for another gold medal at the 1976 Games, but the 200 individual medley was removed from the schedule. It was a move that also prevented a potential showdown between Bruce and his brother, who was a 1972 and 1976 Olympian. When Bruce Furniss broke the world record in the 200 individual medley in 1975, it was his brother's mark that he bettered.

A 1987 inductee into the International Swimming Hall of Fame, Furniss won 11 national championships spread between the 200 freestyle, 400 freestyle, 200 individual medley, and 400 individual medley, and was a six-time NCAA champion for the University of Southern California. He added a gold medal in the 800 freestyle relay at the 1978 World Championships.

98

Victor Davis

Country: Canada
Birth date: February 10, 1964
Death date: November 13, 1989
Event: Breaststroke
Olympic medals: Four
World Championship medals: Four

While some countries boast a number of individuals who can be considered the best of the best from their nation, Canada has a much shorter list. Almost always, Victor Davis's name is near the top. More than 20 years after his premature death at the age of 25, Davis remains renowned as one of the finest breaststrokers the sport has seen.

Davis was a force in the 100 and 200 breaststrokes throughout the 1980s, his best days arriving in the first half of the decade. From 1982 through 1984, Davis lowered the world record in the 200 breaststroke on three occasions, his time of 2:13.34 from the 1984 Olympic Games enduring as the world record for more than five years.

Fiery and unafraid to speak his mind, Davis established himself on the international scene in 1982 thanks to sterling performances at the World Championships and Commonwealth Games. Davis set his first world record en route to the gold medal in the 200 breaststroke at the World Championships, where he also won the silver medal in the 100 breaststroke. A little more than a month later, Davis repeated those performances at the Commonwealth Games, winning gold in the longer event and a silver medal in the 100 breaststroke.

Two years later, Davis enjoyed the finest performances of his career at the 1984 Olympic Games in Los Angeles. Aside from winning the 200 breaststroke by more than two seconds, Davis picked up silver medals in the 100 breaststroke and as a member of the Canadian 400 medley relay.

Despite being better known for his talent in the 200 breaststroke, Davis won the world title in 1986 in the 100 breaststroke while settling for the silver medal in the 200 distance. By the time the 1988 Olympics rolled around, Davis was not at the top of his career but still managed to finish fourth in the 100 breaststroke and help Canada to the silver medal in the 400 medley relay. A little more than a year later, he was gone.

After announcing his retirement a few months earlier, Davis was the victim of a hit-and-run accident outside a nightclub on November 11, 1989. He suffered a fractured skull and brain and spinal cord injuries and was pronounced clinically dead by doctors. Two days after the accident, Davis died after his parents made the decision to remove life support. According to Davis's wishes, several of his organs were donated for transplant, including his heart.

In 2009, the television movie *Victor* was released. The biography of Davis's life was directed by Jerry Ciccoritti and written by Mark Lutz, who also played the role of Davis.

99

Martin Zubero

Country: Spain
Birth date: April 23, 1969
Events: Backstroke and butterfly
Olympic medal: One
World Championship medals: Four

He could have been next in line among the great American backstrokers. Instead, he might be the best swimmer in Spain's history. Although born in Florida, Martin Zubero took advantage of his dual citizenship and father's Spanish roots and represented that nation admirably on the international stage during the late 1980s and first half of the 1990s.

A three-time Olympian with appearances in 1988, 1992, and 1996, Zubero enjoyed his greatest success from 1991 to 1994. Nothing, however, could measure up to what he accomplished in 1992. Competing at the 1992 Olympics in Barcelona, Zubero captured the gold medal in the 200 backstroke and gave the crowd the opportunity to celebrate a victory by an athlete from its homeland. He added a fourth-place finish in the 100 backstroke and also advanced to the final of the 100 butterfly, finishing seventh.

"I was born and raised in the United States," said Zubero, who embarked on a coaching career following his retirement. "But I'm very much Spanish. I was raised Spanish at home. I come over here, and I feel part of the country. It wasn't even a decision for me [on which country to represent]."

Sandwiching that Olympic triumph was success at the World Championships. At the 1991 World Championships, Zubero was the gold medalist in the 200 backstroke and earned the bronze medal in the 100 backstroke. Meanwhile, he was the champion in the 100 backstroke and silver medalist in the 200 backstroke at the 1994 World Championships.

An NCAA champion at the University of Florida, Zubero was a seven-time medalist at the European Championships, highlighted by four victories in the 100 backstroke and one in the 200 backstroke. He also earned a silver medal at the European Championships in the 100 butterfly, a testament to his range beyond the backstroke.

Zubero, whose brother David was the 100 butterfly bronze medalist at the 1980 Olympics in Moscow, was inducted into the International Swimming Hall of Fame in 2004. He set two world records in the 200 backstroke, the latter lasting from 1991 to 1999.

100

Brendan Hansen

Country: United States
Birth date: August 15, 1981
Event: Breaststroke
Olympic medals: Six
World Championship medals: Nine

Brendan Hansen is widely thought of as one of the best breaststrokers in history, a distinction made possible by his exploits at the international level and his longevity. Excelling at the top of the sport for more than a decade, Hansen earned a reputation for overcoming adversity.

As an 18-year-old upstart and recent high school graduate at the 2000 Olympic Trials, Hansen narrowly missed qualifying for the Sydney Games in the 100 breaststroke and 200 breaststroke, placing third in both events. Only the top-two finishers advanced to the Olympic Games. Rather than allow the outcome to derail him, Hansen returned to training and a year later won the world championship in the 200 breaststroke. It was the start of a splendid career.

The silver medalist in the 100 breaststroke and the bronze medalist in the 200 breaststroke at the 2003 World Championships, Hansen made his biggest impact to date at the 2004 U.S. Olympic Trials, where he set world records in each breaststroke event, the first of his career. However, he could not turn those records into individual Olympic gold, as he was the silver medalist in the 100 breaststroke and the bronze medalist in the 200 breaststroke at the Athens Games. Hansen, though, won a gold medal in the 400 medley relay.

Controversy surrounded Hansen's silver medal in the 100 breaststroke when video showed that Japan's Kosuke Kitajima, who won the gold medal, used an illegal dolphin kick at the start of the race and after the turn. At the time, the dolphin kick was an illegal maneuver in the breaststroke, but the violation was not cited by officials. Hansen's teammate, Aaron Peirsol, spoke out against Kitajima, but Hansen took the high road.

"It would be a big deal for an official to come out and to disqualify somebody," Hansen said. "I can only account for my actions, and I know exactly what I did in my race. Everything else, I hope the officials who are sitting right next to me will take care of that. They are not there to have a front-row seat and watch the Olympic Games. They're there to take care of the rules. I believe that's what they do."

An eight-time individual NCAA champion for the University of Texas, Hansen rebounded at the 2005 World Championships, defeating Kitajima in the 100 breaststroke and 200 breaststroke. A year later, he won both events at the Pan Pacific Championships and lowered his world record in the 200 breaststroke. He also won the 100 breaststroke at the 2007 World Championships, but Hansen again struggled at the Olympics, finishing fourth at the 2008 Games in the 100 breaststroke. He added another gold medal in the medley relay.

Following the Beijing Games, Hansen retired and had no intention of returning to the sport. However, after two years, he resumed training and eventually qualified for a third Olympiad. At the 2012 Games in London, Hansen won a third gold medal in the 400 medley relay and added a surprise bronze medal in the 100 breaststroke. Hansen saw his individual effort as one of the highlights of his career.

"I never counted myself out," Hansen said. "I think a lot of people counted me out after the semifinals. That was a gutsy swim. To miss in Beijing and then get on the podium here is a great feeling. This is the shiniest bronze medal ever. It's definitely the hardest one I ever won. When I came back, I wasn't thinking about winning a medal. I outperformed myself."

Overall, Hansen won six Olympic medals and nine medals at the World Championships. He set a pair of world records in the 100 breaststroke and three global standards in the 200 breaststroke.

Under Consideration

These athletes received consideration for inclusion in the list of the top-100 swimmers in history but ultimately missed the cut. However, their accomplishments are worth a glance. Athletes are listed in alphabetical order.

Rebecca Adlington: The British standout was the gold medalist in the 400 freestyle and 800 freestyle at the 2008 Olympics, where she also broke the long-standing world record of Janet Evans in the 800 freestyle. Her win in the 400 freestyle ended a 48-year gold-medal drought by British women in swimming. Adlington won bronze medals in the 400 freestyle and 800 freestyle at the 2012 Olympics and is a two-time world champion.

Nathan Adrian: A force on the sprint scene for a decade, the American captured the gold medal in the 100 freestyle at the 2012 Olympics, and left the 2016 Games with bronze medals in the 50 freestyle and 100 freestyle. Adrian is also known for being one of the most reliable relay performers in history, particularly on the anchor leg. He owns four Olympic gold medals in relay action and a silver medal. Adrian is a three-time individual medalist in sprint-freestyle events at the World Championships, where he has earned 10 relay medals, including eight gold.

Gertrude Ederle: The American is best known for becoming the first woman to cross the English Channel, a feat she accomplished in 1926. Prior to that open-water exploit, Ederle was a world-record holder in the 100 freestyle, 200 freestyle, 400 freestyle, and 800 freestyle. At the 1924 Olympics, Ederle was the bronze medalist in the 100 freestyle and 400 freestyle and helped the United States to the gold medal in the 400 freestyle relay.

Missy Franklin: A two-time Olympian for the United States, Franklin broke onto the international scene with a gold medal in the 200 backstroke at the 2011 World Championships, and followed with two of the finest years put together by a female swimmer. After winning five medals at the 2012 Olympics, including gold in the

100 backstroke and 200 backstroke, Franklin won six gold medals at the 2013 World Championships, headlined by solo triumphs in the 200 freestyle and the 100 and 200 backstroke events. Franklin added five medals at the 2015 World Championships, but back and shoulder injuries took their toll and she narrowly qualified for the 2016 Olympic Games in Rio de Janeiro, where she was limited to a gold medal in the 800 freestyle relay, a medal earned due to her participation in the preliminary heats.

Ute Geweniger: The 1980 Olympic champion in the 100 breaststroke and as a member of East Germany's 400 medley relay, Geweniger's career is tarnished by her involvement in her homeland's systematic doping program that had a major impact on the sport in the 1970s and 1980s. Geweniger set world records in the 100 breaststroke and 200 individual medley, and she won gold in the 100 breaststroke and silver in the 200 breaststroke and 200 individual medley at the 1982 World Championships. Geweniger won European titles in the 100 breaststroke, 200 breaststroke, 100 butterfly, and 200 medley, and was also a European medalist in the 400 individual medley. While several East German swimmers have requested their achievements be stricken from the record due to their doping history, Geweniger has argued that her efforts should remain a part of history, citing the time and work she dedicated to her training, but ignoring the helpful effects of the performance-enhancing drugs.

Stephen Holland: An Australian distance legend, Holland made his mark by setting seven world records in the 800 freestyle and four in the 1500 freestyle during the 1970s. However, he never won Olympic gold, with his best finish at the Games a bronze medal in the 1500 freestyle in 1976. He also placed fifth in the 400 freestyle. Holland's best international performance was a gold medal in the 1500 freestyle at the 1973 World Championships.

Eleanor Holm: A star of American swimming during the first half of the 20th century, Holm captured the gold medal in the 100 backstroke at the 1932 Olympics. She was the favorite to defend her championship at the 1936 Games but was suspended by U.S. officials after drinking alcohol at a party.

Tom Jager: A six-time world-record setter in the 50 freestyle, Jager ranks as one of the elite pure sprinters in history. Although he could extend to the 100 freestyle, in which he was the bronze medalist at the 1986 World Championships, Jager etched his legacy in the one-lap sprint. The world champion in the event in 1986 and 1991, Jager saw his last world mark endure from 1990 to 2000. A five-time Olympic gold medalist in relay duty for the United States, Jager couldn't secure an individual Olympic title, winning silver behind American teammate and rival Matt Biondi at the 1988 Games and bronze at the 1992 Olympics behind Russian Alexander Popov and Biondi. An 11-time national champion and three-time titlist in the 50 freestyle at the Pan Pacific Championships, Jager was inducted into the International Swimming Hall of Fame in 2001.

Barbara Krause: The East German excelled as a freestyler in the late 1970s and early 1980s, highlighting her career by winning the gold medal in the 100 freestyle and 200 freestyle at the 1980 Olympics in Moscow. At the 1978 World Championships, Krause was the champion of the 100 freestyle and silver medalist in the

200 freestyle. A world-record holder in the 100 freestyle and 200 freestyle, Krause's accomplishments are tarnished by her involvement in East Germany's systematic doping program.

Chad Le Clos: The South African made his biggest mark in the sport when he won the gold medal in the 200 butterfly at the 2012 Olympics, upsetting Michael Phelps and denying the Olympic legend a third straight title. Le Clos also won a silver medal in the 100 butterfly at the 2012 Games, and added another silver in that event at the 2016 Olympics, sharing second place with Phelps and Hungarian Laszlo Cseh. Le Clos added a surprise silver medal in the 200 freestyle at the 2016 Olympics, and is a two-time world champion in both the 100 butterfly and 200 butterfly.

Federica Pellegrini: The Italian has not fully met expectations at the Olympics but still warrants inclusion on this honorable-mention list. Pellegrini was the Olympic champion in the 200 freestyle in 2008, four years after winning the silver medal in the event. However, she failed to win gold in the 400 freestyle as the heavy favorite in 2008. Pellegrini is a three-time world champion in the 200 freestyle, a two-time titlist in the 400 freestyle, and has set multiple world records in each event. One of her more impressive achievements is medaling in the 200 freestyle at seven consecutive editions of the World Championships, spanning 2005–2017.

Rica Reinisch: The East German won the gold medal in the 100 backstroke and 200 backstroke at the 1980 Olympics, along with gold in the 400 medley relay. However, her accomplishments are tainted by her involvement in the systematic doping program overseen by East German coaches in the 1970s and 1980s. With the help of those performance-enhancing drugs, Reinisch set three world records in the 100 backstroke and one world record in the 200 backstroke.

Ulrike Richter: One of several East German athletes to either make the top 100 or the under-consideration list, Richter was a star in the 1970s, when her country's systematic doping program was at its height, and from which she benefited. From 1973 to 1975, Richter enjoyed significant success that set the table for her peak performance at the 1976 Olympic Games. Between the 1973 and 1975 World Championships, Richter won a pair of gold medals in the 100 backstroke and a bronze medal in the 200 backstroke in 1975. She added European titles in both backstroke events in 1974 and flourished at the 1976 Olympics, winning gold in the 100 backstroke, 200 backstroke, and as a member of the East German 400 medley relay. During her career, which earned her induction into the International Swimming Hall of Fame in 1983, Richter set eight world records in the 100 backstroke and two world records in the 200 backstroke.

Eva Szekely: A three-time Olympian for Hungary, Szekely was a standout in the breaststroke and individual medley, setting several world records. After just missing a medal with a fourth-place finish in the 200 breaststroke at the 1948 Olympics, Szekely rebounded to win gold in the event at the 1952 Games and the silver medal at the 1956 Games. She was inducted into the International Swimming Hall of Fame in 1976.

Nobutaka Taguchi: A leader in Japan's rich history of breaststroke success, Taguchi was a three-time Olympian who authored the finest chapter of his career at the 1972 Olympic Games in Munich. While American John Hencken and Great Britain's David Wilkie were the premier names in breaststroke, Taguchi managed to upset both to capture the gold medal in the 100 breaststroke in world-record time. Taguchi added a bronze medal in the 200 breaststroke in Munich, and was a three-time medalist in breaststroke events at the World Championships. Inducted into the International Swimming Hall of Fame in 1987, Taguchi was a six-time gold medalist at the Asian Games.

Satoko Tanaka: An argument can be made that Tanaka, a Japanese star in the late 1950s and first half of the 1960s, is one of the most underappreciated stars in history. While Tanaka won the bronze medal in the 100 backstroke at the 1960 Olympics in Rome and was the fourth-place finisher in the 100 backstroke at the 1964 Games, the absence of the 200 backstroke from the Olympic program denied her greater achievements. Between 1959 and 1963, Tanaka set 10 world records in the 200 backstroke, slicing more than nine seconds off the standard, and held the record for all but eight days, when American Lynn Burke became the record holder. Tanaka was inducted into the International Swimming Hall of Fame in 1991.

Ulrike Tauber: During the middle of the 1970s, Tauber was rated as one of the world's dominant performers, *Swimming World Magazine* naming her World Swimmer of the Year in 1974 and 1977. Those honors have since been rescinded, due to Tauber's connection with East Germany's systematic doping program, but her accomplishments in major competition remain on the books. At the 1976 Olympic Games in Montreal, Tauber set a world record and prevailed by more than five seconds in the 400 individual medley, and added a silver medal in the 200 butterfly. A member of the International Swimming Hall of Fame, Tauber was a four-time medalist at the World Championships and a six-time medalist at the European Championships, those podium finishes spread over four events. She set nine individual world records, lowering the 200 medley standard on six occasions and bettering the 400 medley record on three occasions, that standard dropped by 14 seconds between 1974 and 1976.

David Theile: In a country known best for its production of distance-freestyle greats, the Australian emerged as the premier backstroker during the 1950s and early 1960s. Theile was the Olympic champion in the 100 backstroke at the 1956 Games, and after returning from a brief retirement, Theile repeated as Olympic titlist at the 1960 Games. A world-record holder in the 100 backstroke, Theile added a silver medal in the 400 medley relay at the 1960 Olympics.

Franziska van Almsick: The German collected 10 medals—four silver and six bronze—between four Olympic appearances, spanning 1992–2004. She won three individual medals during that time and seven relay medals, but the lack of a gold medal is the glaring omission in an otherwise spectacular career. A six-time medalist at the World Championships, Van Almsick won the world title in the 200 freestyle in Rome in 1994, thanks to a world record that endured for nearly 13 years (September 1994–March 2007). She was also an 18-time gold medalist at the European Championships, with her individual victories covering the 50 freestyle, 100 freestyle, 200 freestyle, and 400 freestyle.

Amy Van Dyken: The American was one of the premier sprinters in the 1990s and flourished at the 1996 Olympics in Atlanta. In addition to winning gold medals in the 50 freestyle and 100 butterfly, Van Dyken helped two relays to gold medals. She was the gold medalist in the 50 freestyle at the 1998 World Championships and earned the bronze medal in the event at the 1994 World Championships. Overall, Van Dyken won six Olympic gold medals—four in relays—and six medals at the World Championships.

Michael Wenden: The freestyler represented Australia at the 1968 and 1972 Olympics, with his first appearance his best. At the 1968 Games, Wenden won the gold medal in the 100 freestyle and 200 freestyle, setting a world record in the shorter event, and helped Australia to medals in a pair of relays. Although Wenden was shut out of the medals at the 1972 Olympics, he won a bronze medal in the 100 freestyle at the 1973 World Championships.

Coaching Greats

A new addition to *The 100 Greatest Swimmers in History* is this look at the greatest coaches in history. As is the case with the athletes who comprise the top-100 list, there will be debate over the names included in this coaching list, but be assured, each of these coaches was a mentor to greatness. The coaches are listed in alphabetical order.

Bob Bowman: How can the architect of the greatest career in swimming history be excluded from a list of legendary coaches? Simple: He can't. While Michael Phelps was blessed with an immense amount of God-given talent, someone had to mold that skill, serve as a motivator, and manage Phelps through the grueling schedules he attacked at the Olympic Games and World Championships.

Bowman is the one-and-only coach of Phelps, a stunning reality considering the length of Phelps's career and the inclination for swimmers to seek a change in input somewhere along the way. But Bowman and Phelps joined forces at the North Baltimore Aquatic Club when Phelps was 11 years old, and their partnership produced dividends for two decades, Bowman predicting Olympic success when his protégé was just 12 years old.

With Bowman guiding the way, Phelps won twenty-eight Olympic medals, including twenty-three of the gold variety. Bowman also mentored Phelps to thirty-nine world records and thirty-three medals at the World Championships, with twenty-six being gold. It's difficult to foresee a coach–swimmer relationship ever surpassing the achievements of Bowman and Phelps.

The head coach of the 2016 United States men's Olympic Team, Bowman served as a Team USA assistant during the 2004, 2008, and 2012 Games, and was the head coach for the U.S. at the 2007, 2009, and 2013 World Championships. The former

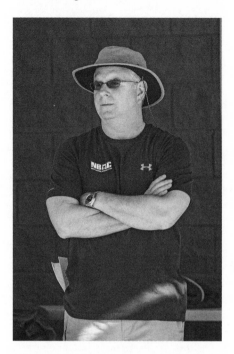

Bob Bowman

men's coach at the University of Michigan (2005–2008), Bowman took the reins of the men's and women's programs at Arizona State University in 2015.

Bowman coached Allison Schmitt to five medals, including three gold, at the 2012 Olympics in London, and has coached several other Olympians, including Chase Kalisz, Conor Dwyer, and Peter Vanderkaay. Bowman has been named USA Swimming's Coach of the Year on six occasions.

"He's a father figure to me," Phelps said of Bowman. "He knew how to get the most out of me in the water, but he's helped me through some of the worst times in my life. He's been there every step of the way and I'm forever thankful."

Forbes Carlile: Forward-thinking and not afraid to implement a training approach that went against the norm, Carlile was acclaimed in his native Australia and around the world. During his career, Carlile emphasized technical advances such as interval training, the pace clock, heart-rate monitoring, and tapering, otherwise known as the reduction in training workload ahead of a major competition.

An Olympic coach for Australia in 1948 and 1956, Carlile was an athlete for his homeland at the 1952 Olympic Games in Helsinki, where he competed in the modern pentathlon. He also served as the Netherlands' Olympic coach in 1964, and is credited for pushing the two-beat kick to prominence (as opposed to the six-beat kick) as a method of preserving his athletes' energy.

Carlile's most-prized pupil was Shane Gould, who captured five individual medals at the 1972 Olympic Games in Munich, where she shared a starring role with

American Mark Spitz, who went on to win seven gold medals during that Olympiad. Under Carlile's watch, Gould once held every freestyle world record, spanning 100 meters through 1500 meters, and was also the world-record holder in the 200 individual medley.

A 1976 inductee into the International Swimming Hall of Fame, Carlile coached alongside his wife, Ursula, for the majority of his career, and enjoyed broadcasting stints as a swimming analyst for the Australian Broadcasting Commission. In 1963, he authored the book *Forbes Carlile on Swimming*, which was revered for its technical expertise and coaching insights.

"A swimmer has got to have attributes—body build, the right type of muscles," Carlile said. "You use psychological techniques, yes, but they are mostly intuitive. They're not programmed. Physiological and anatomic makeup are primary in a young swimmer. Psychology is secondary. Swimming is an endurance-type sport. If you don't have it physically, psychology doesn't matter."

James "Doc" Counsilman: Innovative in his techniques and motivational through his approach with his athletes, Counsilman is arguably the greatest coach the sport has seen. Known as "Doc" on the deck, Counsilman established himself as an elite leader on both the collegiate and international levels, compiling a lengthy list of achievements.

An NCAA champion swimmer at Ohio State University in the late 1940s, Counsilman moved into coaching after his competitive career, serving as an assistant coach at the University of Illinois and University of Iowa before becoming the head coach at Cortland State University from 1952 to 1957. In 1958, Counsilman took the reins at Indiana University and built the Hoosiers program into a powerhouse.

At Indiana, Counsilman won six consecutive NCAA Championships from 1968 to 1973 and led his teams to twenty-three Big Ten Conference crowns, including twenty straight from 1961 to 1980. During this time, Counsilman mentored some of the biggest names in swimming, none bigger than Mark Spitz. It was Counsilman who prepared Spitz to win seven gold medals—all in world-record time—at the 1972 Olympic Games in Munich. He also coached Jim Montgomery, Gary Hall Sr., Chet Jastremski, Charles Hickcox, and Mike Troy. During his tenure at Indiana, Counsilman developed more than sixty Olympians.

After coaching the American men to seven gold medals and fourteen overall medals at the 1964 Olympics in Tokyo, Counsilman returned to lead Team USA at the 1976 Olympics in Montreal. That American squad captured gold medals in twelve of the thirteen events contested and is considered the greatest swim team in history. Under Counsilman's watch, the United States men added ten silver medals and five bronze medals, and swept the podium in five events.

Counsilman earned enshrinement into the International Swimming Hall of Fame in 1976 and is known for his innovative coaching tactics, including film analysis of technique, strength training, altitude training, and hypoxic training. Counsilman authored *The Science of Swimming*, a book viewed as the bible of the sport.

"He was the most instrumental person in my career," Spitz said of Counsilman. "Especially because he was the one who gave me the self-confidence and belief in myself. He was a pillar of strength in regard to self-motivation. He was somebody capable of making somebody rise to the occasion and get the most out of that person. He seemed to do that the best out of all the coaches I had, and it was at the most critical time of my life, when I was in college."

Peter Daland: Born in New York City, Peter Daland spent his formative coaching years in the Philadelphia area, and it was his demanding East Coast persona that defined him when he ventured west and took the reins as the head coach of the University of Southern California swim team in 1958. At the USC helm until 1992, Daland led the Trojans to nine NCAA championships and eleven second-place finishes, the traits of hard work, respect, and determination ingrained in his athletes.

Daland mentored some of the best swimmers in history, including John Naber, Murray Rose, and Bruce Furniss. Daland compiled a career record of 318-31-1, with his swimmers capturing ninety-three individual NCAA championships. Additionally, he guided Southern Cal to twenty undefeated seasons.

Inducted into the International Swimming Hall of Fame in 1977, Daland twice served as a head coach in Olympic action, guiding the American women at the 1964 Games and the American men at the 1972 Games, where Mark Spitz claimed seven gold medals, all in world-record time.

"He was a rarity in college coaching because he was equally concerned with his team's academic and social growth as he was with his swimmers' athletic accomplishments," Naber said of Daland. "When Coach Daland was on deck, the pool at USC held no stars, only squad members. He made it a point to address each swimmer by name at least once per workout. He wanted his swimmers to be self-reliant, responsible, and as good as they could possibly be in all aspects of life. He challenged his teams to live up to the standards set by prior teams. He brought a wealth of knowledge and understanding on how to get the most out of his teams, and his swimmers repaid him with great admiration, loyalty, and respect."

George Haines: Like many coaches, George Haines made multiple stops during his career, but he'll always be first and foremost linked to what he achieved as the head man at the Santa Clara Swim Club. Haines started the club with a modest group of about ten athletes, and built Santa Clara into a global powerhouse, spending twenty-five years at the helm of the esteemed club.

Haines led Santa Clara to thirty-five Amateur Athletic Union team championships, a total split between the women's and men's squads, and used his expertise in the field to develop some of the great names in the sport. Under Haines's watch, Don Schollander, Claudia Kolb, Donna de Varona, and Chris von Saltza were turned into Olympic champions and world-record holders. Haines also worked with Mark Spitz at one point during the career of the eleven-time Olympic medalist.

Inducted into the International Swimming Hall of Fame in 1977, Haines was a coach for numerous United States international teams, including Olympic head-coaching stints of the 1960 women and 1968 men. He was also named a head coach for the 1980 Olympics, but the boycott of the Moscow Games by the United States negated that duty.

In addition to coaching the Santa Clara Swim Club, Haines served as the men's coach at UCLA and the women's coach at Stanford University. While Haines molded numerous individual champions, he preferred to emphasize the team aspect of the sport.

"We talked about team all the time," Haines said. "When we went to a meet, and I did this as an Olympic coach, too, I made every kid on the team aware of the first event. That first event is the most important event in the meet. The team would be there to encourage those guys in the first event. And if they swam really well, then I could turn around to the others and say, 'See that? Man, those guys swam good. And if they can swim like that, look how ready you are.' And it worked."

Robert Kiphuth: One of the first coaches to emerge as a legendary mentor in the sport, Kiphuth was the architect of Yale University's dominant program. While leading the Bulldogs to four NCAA championships and eight second-place finishes during a tenure that spanned 1918 to 1959, Kiphuth compiled a career record of 528-12.

Inducted into the International Swimming Hall of Fame in 1965, Kiphuth is viewed as one of the great innovators in the sport. In addition to implementing dry-land training and weightlifting into the workout schedule, Kiphuth placed a greater emphasis on interval training. He was widely respected by experts in the physical education community.

Kiphuth served as a United States Olympic coach on five occasions, guiding the American women at the 1928 Games in Amsterdam. He was the men's coach in 1932 (Los Angeles), 1936 (Berlin), 1948 (London), and 1952 (Helsinki). Among his top athletes were Jeff Farrell and Alan Ford.

Since 1968, the high-point award at the United States National Championships has been named for Kiphuth, and he was the founder of *Swimming World Magazine* in the early 1950s.

Richard Quick: During a four-decade coaching career, Richard Quick established himself as one of the great collegiate coaches in history, but also as one of the leading coaching minds on the international stage. For his sport, his surname was a perfect fit, for Quick routinely elicited swift performances from his athletes.

Between his primary college stints at the University of Texas, Stanford University, and Auburn University, Quick led his teams to thirteen NCAA championships. After guiding the women's program at Texas to five straight national crowns between 1984 and 1988, Quick shifted his coaching base to Stanford, where he led the women's program to seven NCAA titles. For one final hurrah, he put together a blueprint that produced a national championship for the Auburn University men in 2009.

The success Quick managed in the collegiate ranks enabled him to serve as a Team USA coach at all of the world's major competitions, including three nods as a head coach for the United States Olympic Team (1988, 1996, 2000). Quick was also a three-time assistant coach at the Olympic Games, with other duties including work at the World Championships and Pan Pacific Championships.

Athletes who benefited from Quick's tutelage include some of the biggest names the sport has seen, including Rowdy Gaines, Jenny Thompson, Dara Torres, and Janet Evans, all members of this book's top-100 list. Quick's swimmers were pushed to the limit, grueling practices a trademark of his approach, along with a willingness to implement new diets and training tools.

"Richard was in a league of his own when it came to making people believe they can do the impossible," said Summer Sanders, whom Quick guided to the 1992 Olympic title in the 200 butterfly. "I had goal times that were ridiculous. I don't know if people have gone that fast yet."

Quick was inducted into the International Swimming Hall of Fame in 2000.

Eddie Reese: Widely considered the greatest college coach in history, Reese has packaged a four-decade career among the best the sport has seen on an overall basis, too. After spending six years as the head man at Auburn University, Reese moved to the University of Texas for the 1979 season and has produced excellence from his Austin base ever since.

After guiding the Longhorns to a twenty-first-place finish at the NCAA Championships in his first season in charge of the Longhorns, Reese has led Texas to thirty-nine consecutive top-ten NCAA finishes, including a record fourteen titles, eleven runner-up showings, and thirty-two top-three placements. His teams have also won thirty-nine consecutive conference championships, with his athletes producing more than 100 NCAA event crowns between individual and relay action.

But Reese's success has hardly been limited to the collegiate ranks, as he's been one of the most influential coaches in American swimming on the international stage. The head coach of the United States men's team at the 1992, 2004, and 2008 Olympic Games, Reese also served as a Team USA assistant coach for the Olympics of 1988, 1996, 2000, and 2012. Meanwhile, he has mentored twenty-nine Olympians, with those athletes combining to win thirty-nine gold medals, sixteen silver medals, and eight bronze medals. In 2016, Reese served as an assistant coach for the Singapore Olympic Team, and guided his University of Texas pupil Joseph Schooling to a gold medal in the 100 butterfly.

Inducted into the International Swimming Hall of Fame in 2002, Reese has molded the careers of Aaron Peirsol, Rick Carey, and Brendan Hansen, all ranked among the top-100 swimmers in history in this book. Reese also coached Ian Crocker, one of the great butterfly swimmers of all time. The number of medals won by Reese's athletes at the World Championships easily surpasses fifty.

Eddie Reese

"I've always worried about the individual first," Reese said. "We don't talk about winning the NCAA Championship. We talk about what it takes for each individual to get better. What satisfies me as a coach is seeing people go faster than they ever have before. With that focus, we are in a battle for the championship every year. I like that, too.

"A lot of people look for the easy way to do anything. In swimming, there is no easy way. To succeed in any sport there are two keys—after the obvious needs of a certain amount of ability and hard work—and these keys are self-image and enjoyment. It's something you have to work on every day, day-in and day-out. Everybody knows how to work people hard. The key is to work them hard and protect the mind."

Mark Schubert: One of the most demanding coaches in the history of the sport, Schubert's coaching imprint started with the Mission Viejo Nadadores, which he turned into the top club program in the United States. In charge at Mission Viejo from 1972 to 1985, Schubert guided the club to forty-four national championships and routinely produced some of the world's best swimmers.

Utilizing a training program that relied on a heavy workload, Schubert also brought extreme intensity to the pool deck, an approach that elicited the most from many of his athletes, but also led to criticism and early burnout in other swimmers. But the results far outweighed the negative commentary, and starting with the 1980 Olympiad, Schubert was a member of seven consecutive United States Olympic coaching staffs.

After leaving Mission Viejo, Schubert proved himself on the collegiate scene, leading the University of Texas women to a pair of NCAA titles, and the University of Southern California women to an NCAA crown. Eventually, Schubert left the college ranks when USA Swimming tabbed him as its first National Team Director in 2006, a position he held until 2010.

Among the Hall of Fame swimmers molded by Schubert are Brian Goodell, Janet Evans, Shirley Babashoff, Dara Torres, and Mary T. Meagher, all Olympic champions and all occupying places in this book as top-100 performers. For his success, Schubert was enshrined in the International Swimming Hall of Fame as part of the 1997 class.

"When Mark came here, nobody in the club liked him," Goodell said of Schubert's early days at Mission Viejo. "He was always yelling, but he kind of grows on you. Besides, he got the best out of us. Mark runs the toughest program in the country, and sometimes I ask myself if it's worth it. But I like to win, and that's what it takes."

Don Talbot: A disciplinarian and taskmaster, the Australian established himself as one of the world's premier coaches initially in his homeland, and then at stops in Canada and the United States. Talbot first displayed his coaching touch when he mentored the brother-sister combination of John and Ilsa Konrads to international success, with John Konrads winning the Olympic title in the 1500 freestyle and a bronze medal in the 400 freestyle at the 1960 Games in Rome.

Talbot remained a coaching staple for the Australian National Team and continued to produce top-flight results, including guiding Kevin Berry to the gold medal in the 200 butterfly at the 1964 Olympics in Tokyo. His influence also carried Gail Neall and Beverley Whitfield to the podium at the 1972 Olympics in Munich, with Neall prevailing in the 400 individual medley.

A 1979 International Swimming Hall of Fame inductee, Talbot shifted his focus to Canada in the mid-1970s and then spent a stint in the United States ahead of the 1980 Olympics before returning to Australia for a brief time. Canada lured Talbot back as National Team Coach for a stint that saw him lead Canada to its greatest success between the 1984 and 1988 Olympics. Although Talbot was let go just before the 1988 Games, the work he had done with the country's athletes was already in place and carried into Seoul.

In 1989, Talbot took control as Australia's National Team Head Coach and began delivering strong results. At its home Olympics in 2000 in Sydney, Australia won eighteen medals, including five gold. A year later, Australia won the most gold medals of any country at the World Championships, Talbot's demanding style paying off.

Appendix A

The Men's Rankings

1. Michael Phelps
2. Mark Spitz
3. Johnny Weissmuller
4. Ian Thorpe
5. Matt Biondi
6. Don Schollander
7. Tamas Darnyi
8. Ryan Lochte
9. Alexander Popov
10. Roland Matthes
11. Vladimir Salnikov
12. Grant Hackett
13. Murray Rose
14. Aaron Peirsol
15. Michael Gross
16. Kosuke Kitajima
17. Duke Kahanamoku
18. Kieren Perkins
19. Pieter van den Hoogenband
20. John Naber
21. Sun Yang
22. Adolph Kiefer
23. Gary Hall Jr.
24. Tom Dolan
25. Mike Burton
26. Arne Borg
27. Charles Daniels
28. Mike Barrowman
29. John Hencken
30. David Wilkie
31. Tim Shaw
32. Yoshiyuki Tsuruta
33. Charles Hickcox
34. John Konrads
35. Alex Baumann
36. Brian Goodell
37. Lenny Krayzelburg
38. Gunnar Larsson
39. Anthony Ervin
40. Denis Pankratov
41. Norman Ross
42. Andrew Charlton
43. Gary Hall Sr.
44. Zoltan Halmay
45. Henry Taylor
46. Adam Peaty
47. Jim Montgomery
48. Laszlo Cseh
49. Jonty Skinner
50. Norbert Rozsa

51. Rowdy Gaines
52. Rick Carey
53. Bruce Furniss

54. Victor Davis
55. Martin Zubero
56. Brendan Hansen

Appendix B

The Women's Rankings

1. Katie Ledecky
2. Tracy Caulkins
3. Krisztina Egerszegi
4. Janet Evans
5. Dawn Fraser
6. Shane Gould
7. Mary T. Meagher
8. Kornelia Ender
9. Debbie Meyer
10. Kristin Otto
11. Inge de Bruijn
12. Natalie Coughlin
13. Shirley Babashoff
14. Leisel Jones
15. Yana Klochkova
16. Claudia Kolb
17. Ragnhild Hveger
18. Jenny Thompson
19. Kirsty Coventry
20. Helene Madison
21. Penny Heyns
22. Rebecca Soni
23. Lorraine Crapp
24. Ethelda Bleibtrey
25. Donna de Varona
26. Dara Torres
27. Sybil Bauer
28. Petra Schneider
29. Tracey Wickham
30. Hendrika Mastenbroek
31. Galina Prozumenshchikova
32. Ann Curtis
33. Karen Muir
34. Fanny Durack
35. Susie O'Neill
36. Martha Norelius
37. Katinka Hosszu
38. Brooke Bennett
39. Petria Thomas
40. Amanda Beard
41. Cynthia Woodhead
42. Libby Trickett
43. Ada Kok
44. Sarah Sjostrom

Appendix C

The Top 100 by Country

United States	48
Australia	15
Hungary	6
East Germany	4
Netherlands	4
Great Britain	3
South Africa	3
Sweden	3
Canada	2
Japan	2
Russia	2
Soviet Union	2
China	1
Denmark	1
Spain	1
Ukraine	1
West Germany	1
Zimbabwe	1

Appendix D

Olympic Medals by Country

A look at the countries that have won at least 14 medals in Olympic competition.

Country	Total Medals	Gold	Silver	Bronze
United States	553	246	172	135
Australia	188	60	64	64
East Germany	92	38	32	22
Japan	80	22	26	32
Great Britain	74	16	28	30
Hungary	73	28	25	20
Germany	61	13	19	29
Netherlands	59	22	18	19
Soviet Union	59	12	21	26
Canada	49	8	15	26
China	43	13	19	11
France	43	8	15	20
Sweden	38	9	15	14
Russia	23	5	9	9
Italy	22	5	5	12
West Germany	22	3	5	14
South Africa	18	6	6	6
Denmark	14	3	5	6
Brazil	14	1	4	9

Appendix E

Olympic Medals by Individuals

A look at the athletes who have won at least seven medals in Olympic competition.

Name	Country	Total Medals	Gold	Silver	Bronze
Michael Phelps	United States	28	23	3	2
Jenny Thompson	United States	12	8	3	1
Ryan Lochte	United States	12	6	3	3
Dara Torres	United States	12	4	4	4
Natalie Coughlin	United States	12	3	4	5
Mark Spitz	United States	11	9	1	1
Matt Biondi	United States	11	8	2	1
Gary Hall Jr.	United States	10	5	3	2
Franziska van Almsick	Germany	10	0	4	6
Ian Thorpe	Australia	9	5	3	1
Alexander Popov	Russia	9	4	5	0
Leisel Jones	Australia	9	3	5	1
Nathan Adrian	United States	8	5	1	2
Dawn Fraser	Australia	8	4	4	0
Kornelia Ender	East Germany	8	4	4	0
Roland Matthes	East Germany	8	4	2	2
Inge de Bruijn	Netherlands	8	4	2	2
Jason Lezak	United States	8	4	2	2
Allison Schmitt	United States	8	4	2	2
Petria Thomas	Australia	8	3	4	1
Shirley Babashoff	United States	8	2	6	0
Susie O'Neill	Australia	8	2	4	2

Name	Country	Total Medals	Gold	Silver	Bronze
Aaron Peirsol	United States	7	5	2	0
Krisztina Egerszegi	Hungary	7	5	1	1
Tom Jager	United States	7	5	1	1
Charles Daniels	United States	7	4	1	2
Kosuke Kitajima	Japan	7	4	1	2
Libby Trickett	Australia	7	4	1	2
Pieter van den Hoogenband	Netherlands	7	3	2	2
Amanda Beard	United States	7	2	4	1
Kirsty Coventry	Zimbabwe	7	2	4	1

Appendix F

Olympic Medals, Men

A look at the male athletes who have won at least seven medals in Olympic competition.

Name	Country	Total Medals	Gold	Silver	Bronze
Michael Phelps	United States	28	23	3	2
Ryan Lochte	United States	12	6	3	3
Mark Spitz	United States	11	9	1	1
Matt Biondi	United States	11	8	2	1
Gary Hall Jr.	United States	10	5	3	2
Ian Thorpe	Australia	9	5	3	1
Alexander Popov	Russia	9	4	5	0
Nathan Adrian	United States	8	5	1	2
Roland Matthes	East Germany	8	4	2	2
Jason Lezak	United States	8	4	2	2
Aaron Peirsol	United States	7	5	2	0
Tom Jager	United States	7	5	1	1
Charles Daniels	United States	7	4	1	2
Kosuke Kitajima	Japan	7	4	1	2
Pieter van den Hoogenband	Netherlands	7	3	2	2

Appendix G

Olympic Medals, Women

A look at the female athletes who have won at least seven medals in Olympic competition.

Name	Country	Total Medals	Gold	Silver	Bronze
Jenny Thompson	United States	12	8	3	1
Dara Torres	United States	12	4	4	4
Natalie Coughlin	United States	12	3	4	5
Franziska van Almsick	Germany	10	0	4	6
Leisel Jones	Australia	9	3	5	1
Dawn Fraser	Australia	8	4	4	0
Kornelia Ender	East Germany	8	4	4	0
Inge de Bruijn	Netherlands	8	4	2	2
Allison Schmitt	United States	8	4	2	2
Petria Thomas	Australia	8	3	4	1
Shirley Babashoff	United States	8	2	6	0
Susie O'Neill	Australia	8	2	4	2
Krisztina Egerszegi	Hungary	7	5	1	1
Libby Trickett	Australia	7	4	1	2
Amanda Beard	United States	7	2	4	1
Kirsty Coventry	Zimbabwe	7	2	4	1

Appendix H

World Championship Medals by Individuals

A look at the athletes who have won at least eleven medals in World Championship competition.

Name	Country	Total	Gold	Silver	Bronze
Michael Phelps	United States	33	26	6	1
Ryan Lochte	United States	27	18	5	4
Natalie Coughlin	United States	20	8	7	5
Grant Hackett	Australia	19	10	6	3
Missy Franklin	United States	16	11	2	3
Ranomi Kromowidjojo	Netherlands	16	3	7	6
Katie Ledecky	United States	15	14	1	0
Libby Trickett	Australia	15	8	3	4
Sun Yang	China	14	9	2	3
Jenny Thompson	United States	14	7	5	2
Leisel Jones	Australia	14	7	4	3
Yuliya Efimova	Russia	14	5	6	3
Ian Thorpe	Australia	13	11	1	1
Nathan Adrian	United States	13	8	3	2
Katinka Hosszu	Hungary	13	7	1	5
Michael Gross	Germany	13	5	5	3
Laszlo Cseh	Hungary	13	2	6	5
Aaron Peirsol	United States	12	10	2	0
Sarah Sjostrom	Sweden	12	7	4	1
Kosuke Kitajima	Japan	12	3	4	5
Michael Klim	Australia	11	7	2	2
Alexander Popov	Russia	11	6	4	1
Matt Biondi	United States	11	6	2	3

Appendix I

World Championship Medals, Men

A look at the male athletes who have won at least eleven medals in World Championship competition.

Name	Country	Total	Gold	Silver	Bronze
Michael Phelps	United States	33	26	6	1
Ryan Lochte	United States	27	18	5	4
Grant Hackett	Australia	19	10	6	3
Sun Yang	China	14	9	2	3
Ian Thorpe	Australia	13	11	1	1
Nathan Adrian	United States	13	8	3	2
Michael Gross	Germany	13	5	5	3
Laszlo Cseh	Hungary	13	2	6	5
Aaron Peirsol	United States	12	10	2	0
Kosuke Kitajima	Japan	12	3	4	5
Michael Klim	Australia	11	7	2	2
Alexander Popov	Australia	11	6	4	1
Matt Biondi	United States	11	6	2	3

Appendix J

World Championship Medals, Women

A look at the female athletes who have won at least twelve medals in World Championship competition.

Name	Country	Total	Gold	Silver	Bronze
Natalie Coughlin	United States	20	8	7	5
Missy Franklin	United States	16	11	2	3
Ranomi Kromowidjojo	Netherlands	16	3	7	6
Katie Ledecky	United States	15	14	1	0
Libby Trickett	Australia	15	8	3	4
Jenny Thompson	United States	14	7	5	2
Leisel Jones	Australia	14	7	4	3
Yuliya Efimova	Russia	14	5	6	3
Katinka Hosszu	Hungary	13	7	1	5
Sarah Sjostrom	Sweden	12	7	4	1

Bibliography

BOOKS AND ARTICLES

Abrams, Jonathan. "Ukraine's Klochkova Is Back from Break." *Los Angeles Times* (19 June 2005). http://articles.latimes.com/2005/jun/19/sports/sp-swim19.

Almond, Elliott. "Swimmer Victor Davis, 25, Dies of Injuries." *Los Angeles Times* (14 November 1989). http://articles.latimes.com/1989-11-14/sports/sp-1756_1_victor-davis.

"American Torres Wins Bronze." ESPN (23 September 2000). http://static.espn.go.com/oly/summer00/news/2000/0922/769314.html.

Anderson, Bruce. "On Top of the World." *Sports Illustrated* (14 August 1989): 40–41.

Anderson, Kelli. "The Next Golden Girl." *Sports Illustrated* (28 July 2003). http://sportsillustrated.cnn.com/vault/article/magazine/MAG1029211/2/index.htm.

———. "Headline Writers' Headache." *Sports Illustrated* (19 August 2004). http://sportsillustrated.cnn.com/2004/olympics/2004/writers/08/19/hoogenband.swim/index.html.

Antoniades, Christina Breda. "Memory Games." *Washington Post* (27 July 2008). http://www.washingtonpost.com/wp-srv/artsandliving/features/2008/memory-games-072708/dolan.html.

Attard, Monica. "Dawn Fraser: Still Kicking." Australian Broadcasting Company (15 April 2007). http://www.abc.net.au/sundayprofile/stories/s1897086.htm.

Biondi, Matt. "Diary of a Champion." *Sports Illustrated* (3 October 1988). http://sportsillustrated.cnn.com/vault/article/magazine/MAG1067810/3/index.htm.

Blanchette, John. "Olympics Recall Fond Memories for Claudia Thomas." *Spokane Chronicle* (22 September 1988): S1.

Bondy, Filip. "It's a First! Lopez-Zubero Strikes Gold for Spain." *New York Times* (29 July 1992). http://www.nytimes.com/1992/07/29/sports/barcelona-swimming-it-s-a-first-lopez-zubero-strikes-gold-for-spain.html.

———. "Evans Shows Her Teeth." *New York Daily News* (6 March 1996). http://articles.nydailynews.com/1996-03-06/sports/17997552_1_janet-evans-jessica-foschi-brooke-bennett.

Brennan, Christine. "Babashoff Had Mettle to Speak Out about Steroids." *USA Today* (15 July 2004). http://www.usatoday.com/sports/columnist/brennan/2004-07-15-brennan_x.htm.

———. "With Five Medals in Rio, Katie Ledecky Talks About What's Next." *USA Today* (13 August 2016). https://www.usatoday.com/story/sports/columnist/brennan/2016/08/13/five-medals-rio-katie-ledecky-talks-whats-next/88683606/.

Brown, Gwilym. "A Dominant Swimmer for a Dominant Country." *Sports Illustrated* (26 October 1964): 30–31.

Callahan, Gerry. "A Breath of Fresh Air." *Sports Illustrated* (3 April 1995): 62–64.

Campbell, Charlie. "Is It Really Fair to Call Chinese Swimmer Sun Yang a Drug Cheat?" *Time* (10 August 2016). http://time.com/4446058/rio-2016-swimming-sun-yang-drug-cheat-china/.

Cazeneuve, Brian. "Catching Up with . . . Tim Shaw." *Sports Illustrated* (8 December 2003): 16.

"China's Sun Served Three-Month Ban For Doping Test." Reuters (24 November 2014). https://www.reuters.com/article/us-swimming-sun-doping/chinas-sun-served-three-month-ban-for-doping-test-idUSKCN0J80F120141124.

Clarey, Christopher. "A Dolphin Swimming with the Sharks." *New York Times* (14 July 1996): 5.

———. "Testing the Waters Down Under." *New York Times* (6 January 1997): 4.

Colwin, Cecil. "An Interview with Penny Heyns." *Swim News* (January 1997). http://www.swimnews.com/Magazine/1997/janmag97/heynsinterview.shtml.

"Controversial DQ Was Reversed." ESPN (20 August 2004). http://sports.espn.go.com/oly/summer04/swimming/news/story?id=1864165.

Cowley, Michael. "Klim Relives the Night We Smashed Them Like Guitars." *Sydney Morning Herald* (8 September 2010). http://www.smh.com.au/sport/swimming/klim-relives-the-night-we-smashed-them-like-guitars-20100907-14zms.html.

———. "Inspired a Generation: Murray Rose Dies at 73." *Sydney Morning Herald* (16 April 2012). http://www.smh.com.au/sport/swimming/inspired-a-generation-murray-rose-dies-at-73-20120415-1x1q5.html.

Crouse, Karen. "Laszlo Cseh Uses Silver as a Steppingstone." *New York Times* (17 December 2011). http://www.nytimes.com/2011/12/18/sports/laszlo-cseh-uses-silver-as-a-stepping stone-swimming.html.

———. "Michael Phelps: A Golden Shoulder to Lean On." *New York Times* (21 September 2017). https://www.nytimes.com/2017/09/21/sports/michael-phelps-grant-hackett-tiger-woods.html.

Deford, Frank. "The Swimming Legend You Never Heard Of." National Public Radio (13 August 2008). http://www.npr.org/templates/story/story.php?storyId=93539864.

Dillman, Lisa. "Peirsol Calls Winner a Cheat." *Los Angeles Times* (16 August 2004). http://articles.latimes.com/2004/aug/16/sports/sp-olyswimside16.

Dodds, Tracy. "Stroked for Success: Janet Evans, Only 16, May Have That Golden Touch." *Los Angeles Times* (5 July 1988). http://articles.latimes.com/1988-07-05/sports/sp-5348_1_janet-evans/4.

Drehs, Wayne. "Woodhead Was Devastated by Boycott." *ESPN.com* (19 September 2000). http://assets.espn.go.com/oly/summer00/s/boycott/woodhead.html.

Dunai, Marton. "Laszlo Cseh." *New York Times* (29 July 2012). http://london2012.nytimes.com/athletes/laszlo-cseh.

———. "Hungary's Hosszu Denies Taking Performance-Enhancing Drugs." Reuters (26 May 2015). https://uk.reuters.com/article/uk-swimming-doping-hungary-hosszu/hungarys-hosszu-denies-taking-performance-enhancing-drugs-idUKKBN0OB2DC20150526.

"Dutch Defense after Drug Talk." BBC Sport (21 September 2000). http://news.bbc.co.uk/sport2/hi/olympics2000/swimming/935467.stm.

Eskenazi, David. "Wayback Machine: Queen Helene Madison." *SportsPress Northwest* (19 April 2011). http://sportspressnw.com/2011/04/wayback-machine-queen-helene-madison.

"Fanny Durack: World Champion's Career." *Sydney Morning Herald* (25 March 1914). http://trove.nla.gov.au/ndp/del/article/15467185.

Farber, Michael. "The Last Lap." *Sports Illustrated* (13 August 2012). http://sportsillustrated.cnn.com/vault/article/magazine/MAG1204386/index.htm.

Forde, Pat. "Veterans Coughlin, Peirsol Help U.S. Swim Team Save Face in Beijing." ESPN (12 August 2008). http://sports.espn.go.com/oly/summer08/columns/story?columnist=forde_pat&id=3530905.

Glauber, Bill. "Swimming Healed Australia's Perkins; Now He's in It for Long Haul." *Baltimore Sun* (25 July 1992). http://articles.baltimoresun.com/1992-07-25/sports/1992207075_1_perkins-swimming-kieren.

Glock, Allison. "Do You Really Still Hate Ryan Lochte?" *ESPN The Magazine* (6 June 2017). http://www.espn.com/espn/feature/story/_/id/19506033/will-hate-ryan-lochte-end-story.

Harris, Beth. "Swimmer Adolph Kiefer, Who Was the Oldest Living U.S. Olympic Gold Medalist, Dies at 98." *Chicago Tribune* (5 May 2017). http://www.chicagotribune.com/sports/breaking/ct-swimmer-adolph-kiefer-dead-20170505-story.html.

Hattman, Patrick. "Charles Daniels: America's First Great Swimmer." *Yahoo! Sports* (25 April 2012). http://sports.yahoo.com/news/olympic-flashback-charles-daniels-americas-first-great-swimmer-034500132.html.

Healy, Michelle D. "Breaststroker Designs Future." *Harvard Crimson* (8 April 1981). http://www.thecrimson.com/article/1981/4/8/breaststroker-designs-future-pbreaststrokers-beware-the.

Helmstaedt, Karin. "Pankratov: The Return." *Swim News* (June 1998). http://www.swim-news.com/Magazine/1998/junmag98/pankratov.shtml.

"Hopeless Thomas Reveals Drug Overdose." *Sydney Morning Herald* (29 June 2005). http://www.smh.com.au/news/sport/hopeless-thomas-reveals-drug-overdose/2005/06/29/1119724670090.html.

Hovey, Sue. "Jenny Gold." *ESPN The Magazine* (18 September 2000). http://espn.go.com/magazine/0925hoveyolympicpostcard.html.

Janofsky, Michael. "Coaches Concede That Steroids Fueled East Germany's Success in Swimming." *New York Times* (3 December 1991). http://www.nytimes.com/1991/12/03/sports/olympics-coaches-concede-that-steroids-fueled-east-germany-s-success-in-swimming.html.

Jeffery, Nicole. "Madame Butterfly Still Haunted." *Australian* (13 September 2010). http://www.theaustralian.com.au/sport/madame-butterfly-still-haunted/story-e6frg7mf-1225919890941.

Kelly, Fran. "Petria Thomas Beats Inge de Bruijn for Gold in the 100 Butterfly." Australian Broadcasting Company (16 August 2004). http://www.abc.net.au/am/content/2004/s1177176.htm.

Kirshenbaum, Jerry. "Big Splash by the Mighty Madchen." *Sports Illustrated* (17 September 1973): 44–49.

———. "In the Back, He's Way Out Front." *Sports Illustrated* (10 May 1976): 38–48.

———. "A Feat of Olympian Proportions." *Sports Illustrated* (23 August 1976): 14–15.

Kiss, Laszlo. "Krisztina Egerszegi: The Development of a World Champion Backstroker." *Swimming Technique* (July 1997): 11–13.

Krump, Jason. "Let Him Swim: The Tom Jager Story." *Washington State Magazine* (Spring 2012). http://wsm.wsu.edu/s/index.php?id=933.

Ladin, Rob. "Leisel Jones Wins 100-Meter Breaststroke Gold." *Olympic Times* (12 August 2008). http://www.robladin.com/sports/2008/08/12/leisel-jones-wins-100m-breaststroke-gold.html.

Layden, Tim. "Naber's Glory Dies Out, but Success Flourishes." *Schenectady Gazette* (18 July 1981): 18.

———. "Hold Your Breath." *Sports Illustrated* (2 August 2004). http://sportsillustrated.cnn.com/vault/article/magazine/MAG1032577/2/index.htm.

———. "After Rehabillitation, the Best of Michael Phelps May Lie Ahead." *Sports Illustrated* (9 November 2015). https://www.si.com/olympics/2015/11/09/michael-phelps-rehabilitation-rio-2016.

Levin, Dan. "She's Set Her Sights on L.A." *Sports Illustrated* (18 June 1984): 40–48.

Lidz, Franz. "A Hungarian Who's Still Hungary." *Sports Illustrated* (30 July 1990): 6–7.

Litsky, Frank. "From Teddy Bear to Precious Medals, Beard Matures." *New York Times* (28 July 2004). http://www.nytimes.com/2004/07/28/sports/olympics-from-teddy-bear-to-precious-medals-beard-matures.html.

———. "Ann Curtis, Barrier-Breaking Star Swimmer, Dies at 86." *New York Times* (24 July 2012). http://www.nytimes.com/2012/07/25/sports/ann-curtis-barrier-breaking-star-swimmer-dies-at-86.html?_r=0.

———. "Forbes Carlile, Innovative Coach Who Studied Science of Swimming, Dies at 95." *New York Times* (2 August 2016). https://www.nytimes.com/2016/08/03/sports/olympics/forbes-carlile-olympic-swimming-coach-for-australia-dies-at-95.html.

Lohn, John. "Encore to Athens." *Swimming World Magazine* (September 2005): 12–17.

———. "Just Call Him Rowdy." *Swimming World Magazine* (5 August 2009). http://www.swimmingworldmagazine.com/lane9/news/21988.asp.

———. "Swimming under the Radar." *Swimming World Magazine* (January 2011): 18–19.

———. "Bronze Finish Makes Hansen's Comeback Even Sweeter." *Delaware County Daily Times* (30 July 2012). http://www.delcotimes.com/articles/2012/07/30/sports/doc50160781e44c9923657945.txt.

———. "Sixteen Years Later, Anthony Ervin Writes Another Golden Chapter in 50 Freestyle." *SwimVortex* (12 August 2016). http://www.swimvortex.com/sixteen-years-later-anthony-ervin-writes-another-golden-chapter-in-50-freestyle/.

Longman, Jere. "Popov Defeats Hall in 100 by Eyelash." *New York Times* (23 July 1996). http://www.nytimes.com/specials/olympics/0723/oly-swm-popov-hall.html.

———. "Thompson Hopes to Touch Gold at End of the Pool." *New York Times* (7 August 2000). http://partners.nytimes.com/library/sports/olympics/080700oly-thompson-profile.html.

———. "Thorpe Comes Up a Big Hand Short to a Flying Dutchman." *New York Times* (19 September 2000).

Lord, Craig. "Ignorance Is Bliss." *Swim News* (7 December 1991). http://www.swimnews.com/news/view/6496.

———. "Happy Half Century Vladimir Salnikov." *Swim News* (21 May 2010). http://www. swimnews.com/news/view/7732.

———. "Growing Pains of the War on Doping." *Swim News* (6 July 2011). http://www.swimnews.com/news/view/8742.

———. "Roland Matthes." *Swim News* (August 2012). http://olympics.swimnewslibrary.com/ legends-overview/roland-matthes-gdr.

———. "Adam Peaty: I'm Not Happy Being the Best. I want to Be Best." *Times* (22 July 2017). https://www.thetimes.co.uk/article/adam-peaty-im-not-happy-being-the-best-i-want-to-be-best-mkg7fh0wf.

Manning, Anita. "Hall Won't Let Diabetes Sink Successful Swimming Career." *USA Today* (29 July 2004). http://www.usatoday.com/sports/olympics/athens/swimming/2004-07-29-hall-jr-diabetes_x.htm.

Marsteller, Jason. "Adolph Kiefer Receives Highest Award; Surprised with Replica of His 1936 Stolen Olympic Medal." *Swimming World Magazine* (3 October 2007). http://www.swim mingworldmagazine.com/lane9/news/15676.asp.

McMullen, Paul. "Eyes Focus on Phelps and His Future." *Baltimore Sun* (20 September 2000). http://www.baltimoresun.com/sports/olympics/bal-te.sp.phelps20sep20,0,1069581.story.

———. *Amazing Pace: The Story of Olympic Champion Michael Phelps from Sydney to Athens to Beijing*. New York: Rodale, 2006.

Morgan, Piers. "Interview with Mark Spitz." *Piers Morgan Tonight* (14 July 2012). http://edi tion.cnn.com/TRANSCRIPTS/1207/14/pmt.01.html.

Mullen, P. H. *Gold in the Water*. New York: Thomas Dunne Books, 2001.

Murphy, Damien. "From Golden Girl to Olympic Villain: The Crucifixion of Tracey Wickham." *Sydney Morning Herald* (1 January 2011). http://www.smh.com.au/national/from-golden-girl-to-olympic-villain-the-crucifixion-of-tracey-wickham-20101231-19bzq.html.

Nakamura, David. "Suddenly, in the Distance, It's Dolan." *Washington Post* (7 April 1994). http://www.washingtonpost.com/wp-srv/sports/olympics/longterm/locals/dolan1.htm.

Neff, Craig. "The Albatross Will Fly." *Sports Illustrated* (18 July 1984).

———. "Four Finals, Two Records and Five Gold Medalists." *Sports Illustrated* (6 August 1984): 34–46.

———. "The U.S. Is Back . . . and How!" *Sports Illustrated* (13 August 1984): 18–36.

———. "Swim Six, Win Six." *Sports Illustrated* (3 October 1988): 54–55.

"Obituary: Ragnhild Hveger." *Telegraph* (22 December 2011). http://www.telegraph.co.uk/ news/obituaries/sport-obituaries/8973925/Ragnhild-Hveger.html.

"Oldham's Triple Gold Olympian." BBC (August 2008). http://www.bbc.co.uk/manchester/ content/articles/2008/08/20/200808_henry_taylor_feature.shtml.

"An Olympian Wave of Records." *Time* (11 September 1972): 68–76.

"Olympic Medalist Accused of Doping by German Teammates." Associated Press (1 June 2007).

O'Toole, Mark. "Kirsty Coventry: The Olympian Who Unifies Zimbabwe." *JOE* (28 July 2012). http://www.joe.ie/london-2012/olympic-features/interview-kirsty-coventry-the-olympian-who-unifies-zimbabwe-0027262-1.

Parker, Stan. "Golden Memories: Mike Burton Takes a Look Back at His Olympic History." *KTVQ.com* (27 July 2012). http://www.ktvq.com/videos/golden-memories-mike-burton-takes-a-look-back-at-his-olympic-history.

Pearce, Nick. "Ian Thorpe Vows to Continue after Australian Olympic Trials Even If He Fails to Make London 2012 Olympics." *Daily Telegraph* (16 March 2012). http://www.telegraph.

co.uk/sport/olympics/swimming/9149272/Ian-Thorpe-vows-to-continue-after-Australian-Olympic-trials-even-if-he-fails-to-make-London-2012-Olympics.html.

Perkins, Kieren. "Kieren Perkins Reveals Why, at One Point, He Didn't Want to Make the 1500-Meter Final at the 1996 Atlanta Olympic Games." *Herald Sun* (26 July 2012). http://www.heraldsun.com.au/sport/winners-circle/story-fnewbvoh-1226432929746.

"Phelps Claims Olympic-Record Eighth Gold Medal with Relay Win." *Sports Illustrated* (16 August 2008). http://sportsillustrated.cnn.com/2008/olympics/2008/08/16/bc.oly.swm.phelps.medley.relay.ap/index.html.

Reed, Ron. "Grant Hackett: Kieren Perkins and I Were Never Close Mates." *Perth Now* (18 October 2010). http://www.perthnow.com.au/sport/kieren-perkins-and-i-were-never-close-mates-grant-hackett/story-e6frg1wu-1225940103103.

Reed, William. "It's the Hoosier Title Wave." *Sports Illustrated* (22 March 1971): 28–33.

———. "What the Fans Came to See Is What They Got." *Sports Illustrated* (5 April 1971): 77–79.

Reid, Scott. "1980 Olympic Profile: Brian Goodell." *Orange County Register* (16 July 2010). http://www.ocregister.com/articles/goodell-258087-olympic-carter.html.

Rieder, David. "Sixteen Years After Her First, Kirsty Coventry Enjoying One Last Olympic Run." *Swimming World Magazine* (28 July 2016). https://www.swimmingworldmagazine.com/news/16-years-after-her-first-kirsty-coventry-enjoying-one-last-olympic-run/.

———. "Katie Ledecky Ready to Chase Ambitious New Goals." *Swimming World Magazine* (5 June 2017). https://www.swimmingworldmagazine.com/news/katie-ledecky-ready-to-chase-ambitious-new-goals/.

Robb, Sharon. "Biondi Stepping In as the Next Spitz." *Sun Sentinel* (26 July 1987). http://articles.sun-sentinel.com/1987-07-26/sports/8703020563_1_olympic-trials-meter-matt-biondi.

Romei, Michael. "Troubled Waters." *Reportage* (24 September 2009). http://www.reportageonline.com/2009/09/troubled-waters.

Ross, Albion. "Japanese Men Second: Trail, 83–77, as Victors Amass Diving Points, Wayne, Root Scoring." *New York Times* (16 August 1936): S1.

Rutemiller, Brent. "Shirley Babashoff Breaks 30-Year Silence on East Germany's Systematic Doping of Olympians." *Swimming World Magazine* (11 January 2007). http://www.swimmingworldmagazine.com/lane9/news/13191.asp.

Shipley, Amy. "Katie Ledecky, 15, Makes Big Splash with Olympic Gold Medal in 800 Meters." *Washington Post* (3 August 2012). https://www.washingtonpost.com/sports/olympics/katie-ledecky-15-makes-big-splash-with-olympic-gold-medal-in-800-meters/2012/08/03/88bd4c2c-ddc1-11e1-af1d-753c613ff6d8_story.html?utm_term=.e3e981354762.

Steele, David. "Back in the Swim: Dara Torres' Remarkable Revival in the Pool Is Making Those Tae-Bo Commercials Ancient History." *San Francisco Chronicle* (9 August 2000). http://www.sfgate.com/sports/article/Back-in-the-Swim-Dara-Torres-remarkable-3303356.php.

———. "Thompson Left Out of Swimming Gold." *San Francisco Chronicle* (18 September 2000). http://www.sfgate.com/sports/article/Thompson-Left-Out-Of-Swimming-Gold-3237535.php.

Svrluga, Barry. "Katinka Hosszu, Swimming's Iron Lady, Is Raising All Kinds of Eyebrows." *Washington Post* (7 August 2016). https://www.washingtonpost.com/sports/olympics/katinka-hosszu-swimmings-iron-lady-is-raising-all-kinds-of-eyebrows/2016/08/07/3221c0be-5ccf-11e6-9d2f-b1a3564181a1_story.html?utm_term=.3e5db6c8cff6.

"Sweat Dreams: July 1976—David Wilkie's Golden Swim." *Dear Scotland* (21 July 2009). http://dearscotland.com/2009/07/21/sweet-dreams-july-24-1976-david-wilkies-golden-swim.

Swift, E. M. "Detour on the High Road." *Sports Illustrated* (21 July 1980): 35–37.

Thompson, Peter. "Talking Heads: Forbes Carlile." Australian Broadcasting Company (8 April 2008). http://www.abc.net.au/tv/talkingheads/txt/s2316987.htm.

Tower, Whitney. "Dawn Keeps Churning Along." *Sports Illustrated* (17 February 1964): 26–31.

Tresolini, Kevin. "Thorpe Strikes Gold Again." *USA Today* (17 August 2004): 7B.

Trevelyan, Mark. "Swimming: Sjostrom Avoids 'Disasters' to Win 100 Butterfly." Reuters (7 August 2016). https://www.reuters.com/article/us-olympics-rio-swimming-w-100mbutter fly/swimming-sjostrom-avoids-disasters-to-win-100m-butterfly-idUSKCN10J038.

"12-Year-Old Sets Mark in 110-Yard Backstroke." *Sarasota Journal* (11 August 1965): 14.

Ulman, Howard. "Bennett Steps Up; Evans Steps Down." *Post and Courier* (26 July 1996): 1C.

Verschoth, Anita. "Furniss Was Really Stoked Up." *Sports Illustrated* (1 September 1975). 18–19.

Vinton, Nathaniel. "Doubters Questioning Dara Torres' Splashing Success." *New York Daily News* (12 July 2008). http://articles.nydailynews.com/2008-07-12/sports/17902694_1_dara-torres-urine-blood-parameters.

Virgen, Steve. "Peirsol Talks about His Retirement." *Daily Pilot* (2 February 2011). http://articles.dailypilot.com/2011-02-02/sports/tn-dpt-0202-spaaron-peirsol-explains-20110202_1_irvine-aquazots-backstroke-swimmer-aaron-peirsol.

Vorel, Mike. "Q&A: Donna de Varona." *Omaha World Herald* (2 July 2012). http://www.omaha.com/article/20120702/SWIMTRIALS/707029889/-1.

Wade, Lamar. "The California Gold Rush of '84." *Saturday Evening Post* (July 1983): 64–98.

Williams, Dan. "Oz's Teen Sensation, a Nice Dry Guy, Is a Terror in the Pool." *Time* (11 September 2000).

Williams, Rebecca. "Golden Girl Libby Trickett Beats Her Nerves." *Australian* (12 August 2008). http://www.theaustralian.com.au/golden-girl-libby-trickett-beats-her-nerves/story-e6freyqi-1111117165848.

Wright, Sylas. "Golden Moments: Debbie Meyer Talks Olympic Swimming." *Sierra Sun* (15 August 2008). http://www.sierrasun.com/article/20080815/sports/463869672.

WEBSITES

www.fina.org: The official website of the Federation Internationale de Natation, the international governing body for the five aquatic sports: swimming, diving, open-water swimming, water polo, and synchronized swimming.

www.imdb.com: The Internet Movie Database contains information related to the film industry, including biographical information and quotations related to actors and industry personnel, such as directors and screenwriters.

www.ishof.org: The official website of the International Swimming Hall of Fame. Includes biographies of individuals inducted into the Hall of Fame.

www.olympic.org: The official website of the International Olympic Committee. The website includes lists of all Olympic medal winners, biographical information on numerous athletes, and details of the Olympic movement.

www.sports-reference.com: Website with comprehensive historical information on a variety of sports, including a section on Olympic sports.

www.swimming.org.au: The official website of Swimming Australia, the governing body of the sport in that country. The website includes archived results of national and international competition and biographical information on Australian athletes.

www.swimmingworldmagazine.com: Website of *Swimming World Magazine*. The website includes archived articles from magazine issues from 1960 to the present.

www.swimvortex.com: The website of Europe-based *Swim Vortex*. The website includes up-to-date world rankings and results, news articles, and columns.

www.usaswimming.org: The official website of USA Swimming, the governing body of the sport in that country. The website includes archived results of national and international competition and biographical information on U.S. athletes.

Index

About the Author

John Lohn has served as the senior writer for *Swimming World Magazine*, supplying content for the organization's print and online products, and has served as the United States correspondent for *SwimVortex*, a European-based website providing meet coverage, analysis, and commentary. He has been covering the sport of swimming at the international level for nearly two decades. The former deputy sports editor for the *Delaware County Daily Times*, his passion for the sport was ignited in 1998 when he began covering Brendan Hansen, a future six-time Olympic medalist. From that point forward, his coverage expanded from the local level to national and international circles. During his career, he has covered the 2008, 2012, and 2016 Olympic Games, during which time he chronicled the record-breaking accomplishments of Michael Phelps. He has covered every U.S. Olympic Trials since 2000 and has regularly provided coverage of other major meets, such as the World Championships, the Pan Pacific Championships, the U.S. Nationals, and the NCAA Championships. Through the years, he has been a guest analyst on several networks, including ESPN and the BBC, and has been cited by numerous national and international newspapers, websites and magazines, including *USA Today*, CNN, and the *Christian Science Monitor*, along with outlets in Australia, Japan, China, Brazil, and Europe. He previously authored *The Historical Dictionary of Competitive Swimming* and *The Most Memorable Moments in Olympic Swimming*, also published by Rowman & Littlefield, and contributed multiple chapters to *Swimmers: Courage and Triumph*. His work has been award winning, most notably a 2009 piece on a blind swimmer who competed at the high school level despite his handicap. The article won several newspaper awards and received honorable-mention status in the 2010 edition of *The Best American Sports Writing*. A Pennsylvania native and graduate of La Salle University, he resides in New Jersey with his wife, Dana, and daughters, twins Taylor and Tiernan, and Tenley. He currently works as a media specialist, and enjoys vacationing and fitness training.